FORTRAN OPTIMIZATION

Revised Edition

This is volume 25 in A.P.I.C. Studies in Data Processing
General Editors: Fraser Duncan *and* M. J. R. Shave
A complete list of titles in this series appears at the end of this volume

FORTRAN
OPTIMIZATION

Revised Edition

Michael Metcalf

CERN
Geneva, Switzerland

1985

ACADEMIC PRESS

A Subsidiary of Harcourt Brace Jovanovich, Publishers

London   Orlando   San Diego   New York
Toronto   Montreal   Sydney   Tokyo

ACADEMIC PRESS INC. (LONDON) LTD.
24–28 Oval Road
LONDON NW1 7DX

United States Edition published by
ACADEMIC PRESS, INC.
Orlando, Florida 32887

LIBRARY OF CONGRESS CATALOGING IN PUBLICATION DATA

Metcalf, Michael.
    FORTRAN optimization.

    Bibliography: p.
    Includes index.
    1. FORTRAN (Computer program language)   I. Title.
QA76.73.F25M48   1985   001.64′24   85-47771
ISBN 0-12-492482-4 (alk. paper)

PRINTED IN THE UNITED STATES OF AMERICA

85 86 87 88   9 8 7 6 5 4 3 2 1

PREFACE

Throughout its more than two decades of history, one of Fortran's main strengths as a programming language has been its adherence to its original design aim of providing efficient program execution. However, advice on how to obtain the best possible performance has hitherto been scattered, being contained either in reports on specific computers and compilers *(e.g.* Smith *et al.,* 1977), or in parts of various books of rather too general a nature. This book brings together for the first time a detailed survey of the means by which Fortran source code may be optimized, and includes other background information which should enable the reader to understand better how a Fortran program is processed by a compiler, and subsequently executed. As such, it is intended to help all those who write or run Fortran programs to make efficient use of computer resources without making unjustifiably great demands on their own time. The reasons why one might want or have to undertake such a study are examined in Chapter 1.

It is obviously useful, and sometimes essential, to have some background knowledge of specific computers and compilers, and this is provided in the case of some popular computers by describing, in Chapter 2, the relevant parts of the architecture of two of those most widely used in scientific work. Chapter 3 discusses the techniques used by compilers to produce the best possible object code from the source code written by the programmer.

Chapter 4 deals with the need to exercise great care in the choice of the algorithms used to solve scientific and numerical problems, before beginning to optimize only those parts of the resulting program which will demonstrably have any appreciable effect on the program's overall performance. The sometimes negative effects of optimization, on clarity and portability, are also considered, and space optimization is described.

A major difficulty with such a book is the inevitable dependence of source code optimization techniques on a particular computer model and a particular version of a compiler. This problem is tackled by breaking down the optimizing task into basic components, and considering each in turn. General techniques, applicable with most compilers, are described in Chapter 5. Chapter 6 contains advice relating to non-optimizing compilers, and Chapter 7 deals with the very different requirements imposed by the use of an optimizing compiler instead. Chapters 8 and 9 are devoted to a number of particular computers and compilers, and should serve as a reminder of points to be considered when using the numerous computer models and compiler versions which cannot be discussed here. These five chapters form the kernel of the book.

Some general remarks on program portability follow in Chapter 10, and Chapter 11 deals with recent aspects of optimization: the advent and impact of vector processors and their associated compilers. The longer term future of the Fortran language and its implementation form the subjects of Chapter 12.

This book should be useful as a reference work for anyone engaged in Fortran programming on any scale greater than simple, single-shot, short jobs, and as a supplementary text in any course on Fortran programming beyond the preliminary stages.

One of the persistent problems associated with good Fortran programming practice of any sort is that many programmers acquire their knowledge of the language in courses which are too skimpy, or have simply picked it up from their colleagues by example. The more refined aspects of the craft are thus never properly learned. The rush to produce a working program as quickly as possible is often an additional hindrance to producing good code. By presenting the material here in a systematic fashion, some of the deficiencies in past Fortran training can perhaps be overcome (see also Metcalf, 1985).

To make the book a self-contained document, an Appendix has been included in which ANSI Fortran 77 is briefly described, with the differences from Fortran 66 indicated. For those who have never received a proper introduction to the features of the present standard, a study of this appendix should be rewarding. It will also serve to indicate, by their absence, those features of current compilers which are extensions of the standard, and which represent significant obstacles to the coding of portable programs. A second Appendix is an example of a layout program written in ANSI Fortran 77.

ACKNOWLEDGEMENTS

A book such as this one is to a large extent a collection of points gathered together from numerous sources. In all cases where significant material has been taken from published documents, this is acknowledged by appropriate references in the text. I thank here all those who have provided me, knowingly or unknowingly, with smaller items which are published here for the first time in the open literature.

The many details and examples have required careful checking, and I am grateful to Joanne Brixius (X3J3), N. Buss (CDC), C. Heritier, R. Teed and G. Waldbaum (IBM), M. Hirai (Hitachi), A. Mills (Cray Research), D. Muxworthy (University of Edinburgh) and D. Vallance (University of Salford) for their help and advice in this respect. Many friends and colleagues at CERN have also assisted and encouraged me with the task; it is a pleasure to thank T. Bloch, H. Grote, F. James, R. Matthews, J. Panman, R. Russel, V. Zacharov and P. Zanella for their valuable contributions, and I am particularly grateful to J. Allaby and D. O. Williams who both carefully read the complete text.

I am indebted to CERN, and especially to P. Zanella, for giving me every encouragement to undertake this project, and for providing me with the necessary resources.

The greater part of the typing has been carried out by Miss C. Buttay, Miss F. Nicholson and Miss J. Turner, and the layout for the CERN computer photo-composition system has been prepared with great dedication by F. de Bilio. I warmly thank them, and all those who have helped in other ways to bring the production of the final camera-ready copy to a successful conclusion.

CONTENTS

APPENDICES

To Abigail and Nicole

1 WHY OPTIMIZE ?

When the first computers were introduced in the 1940's, it was considered by some that a dozen such machines would be sufficient to perform all of the numerical calculations which could be envisaged at that time. The dramatic growth of computing which has taken place since those misguided predictions were made, its spread into many and varied parts of our lives, and the increasing sophistication of computer hardware and software, all serve to demonstrate the innate difficulty of making predictions about newly evolving technologies. What can be said, in retrospect, is that a large number of past and present computer installations have been plagued by an almost permanent failure to provide sufficient capacity to cope with the ever increasing number of problems which are being found for them. For whatever reasons − insufficient funding, lack of planning for expansion, or unexpected growth in workloads as new users realise the advantages of these sophisticated tools − there has been an almost universal failure of supply to keep up with demand. This has occurred notwithstanding the spectacular drop in the costs of computing − the matrix inversion which occupied the whole of an expensive machine for minutes in the pioneering days is now performed in microseconds on today's large mainframes, which are physically smaller, far cheaper per unit of computation, and immensely more powerful and versatile.

The developments in computer hardware have been accompanied by equally impressive advances in computer software, both in the complex suites of programs required to control the machines − the operating systems − and in the associated methods by which an individual user accesses a computer − the application languages and the various interfaces to the operating system. Of the high-level languages used today in large-scale computing two dominate all others

– Cobol for mainly commercial applications, and Fortran for mainly scientific and numerical computing.

This book is an attempt to aid anyone concerned with Fortran programming, on any but the most trivial scale, to write programs which make the most efficient use of the computers on which they are run and, indirectly, of his own time. In spite of the ever decreasing cost of hardware, there are always various and compelling reasons why efficient programs are desirable and these, together with some counter examples, will be examined in the remainder of this chapter.

1. The Individual User's View

Let us imagine that a certain user has designed, coded and tested a program to solve a particular application problem, of whatever nature. If the program is to be run regularly on a given computer installation, there are a number of performance difficulties with which the implementor might be faced. In the first place, most installations have some sort of priority mechanism which schedules the workload according to the characteristics of the jobs in the input queues. This mechanism will often classify a job as a function of the run-time requested, together with other parameters such as its storage requirement. Alternatively, in a virtual machine environment, it will penalise a virtual machine demanding 'too much' time from the central processing unit (CPU). It might then happen, on an overloaded installation, that turn-round is severely degraded, even for jobs requiring modest amounts of computer time. So for even this fairly low level of activity there is a potential advantage to be gained in reducing a job's CPU requirement, in order to be able to enter a more favoured job class.

In the case of programs requiring more substantial amounts of time, perhaps an hour or so per day extending over many months, a significant improvement in the speed of the program could mean a reduction in the calendar time required to complete an analysis. Alternatively, users who have an almost unlimited load to offer the computer can obtain a greater throughput in a given elapsed time.

There are, in yet more extreme cases, some applications which a scientist may not even bother to analyse, because it is known in advance that the only available program is too costly to be used in the time allocations which could reasonably be obtained, and either no other solution is known, or no opportunity is available to write new programs.

In all these instances, the application of the techniques

considered in later chapters could possibly help to improve turn-round, reduce the total time of a long analysis, increase the total throughput, or make solving a problem practical at all, as the case may be.

The examples just cited are based on existing programs. When writing new programs, it is important to try to apply known optimization techniques, wherever this is thought worthwhile, during the design and coding processes. Since in many cases, however, there is no sound *a priori* knowledge of where the greater part of the time will be spent in new programs, a subsequent optimization may still prove to be necessary. In addition, it is certainly necessary to make regular checks on programs which are subject to continuous modifications. It is also clear that improvements can be made iteratively to a program. For example, when the benefit from a first optimization is significant but the advantages are slowly eroded because of a deterioration in the service provided by the installation, a further examination may reveal another set of improvements which can be made. These points will all be considered in more detail in Chapter 4.

2. The Management View

Computers, despite their relatively falling costs, are still expensive machines to purchase or to rent, and the management of a given installation may be in a situation in which it is unable to provide, at a given moment, a system upgrade for its users. This may be because no funds are available, or because there is a long delivery time for a machine which has already been ordered, or because it prefers to wait for imminent announcements of anticipated new models. The management may also, to make matters worse, be required to accommodate an increasing number of users, and therefore a greater workload, on its existing equipment. When all system tuning and resource scheduling expedients have been tried and been shown to be insufficient, the management can only, as a last resort, try to persuade or cajole users into considering the efficiency of their programs. By the process of providing selected large users with a trained consultant service, it may be possible to alleviate an unacceptable situation until more capacity is finally installed.

In an efficiency drive of this type, undertaken on a large installation at a research centre, and reported by Waldbaum (1978), it was shown that often dramatic improvements could be made to the programs of those comparatively few users who were consuming the greater part of the CPU time in the prime shift. In this instance, only a few percent of all users were responsible for consuming 50% of this particular resource, and it was a simple problem to identify them and offer them help.

On the other hand, computer management is often reluctant to involve itself with users' codes. It may not wish to vet, or police, its users' work, or may not have the trained manpower required to help the users. It may not even have, or be able to afford, or worse still, even be aware of the tools the users need in order to be able to help themselves. This would either reveal a serious lack of judgement, or a desire to purchase new equipment without strong justification. However, the investment involved in the provision of a task force of trained personnel, and of some simple timing tools, can pay for itself many times over in terms of the wasted resources saved. Training courses given to the users themselves can be of inestimable value, and may even be more useful than further tuning of an already well-tuned system, if the users are motivated to improve their code.

The ability of computer management to assist users in this way depends on their own access to measurement tools by which to establish just which, if any, resources are actually in short supply during substantial periods of real-time, and so are causing bottlenecks in the processing of the workload. It is not necessarily the case that inefficient programs are the only cause of poor performance. On an installation where no control is kept over the use of main memory, an over-indulgent use of this resource may be leading to poor utilisation of the CPU, as only an insufficient number of jobs can be kept active and these are unable to ensure its optimum use. An installation may be badly tuned at the level of input/output (I/O) channels, or may have too few peripheral devices, so that the CPU is kept unduly idle, waiting to receive or to send data. A thorough tuning of a complete system depends on a sure knowledge of the performance of all its critical parts, namely all those tending to degrade CPU utilisation (see, for example Beretvas, 1978), just as much as on ensuring that the application programs themselves are using as little of the CPU as is reasonably possible. However, whereas system tuning is clearly a task for an expert systems programmer, applications programs can be tuned by their authors, if a little trouble is taken, especially if some assistance is provided by the installation management.

For a given installation the true cost of optimization can actually be measured in terms of cash and computer resources by means of a controlled study of the amount of manpower required to produce a given reduction in workload on the computer. Such an exercise can give surprising results, especially upon a first application, and should be undertaken regularly at any cost-conscious computer centre.

It is equally true that any effort invested should be in areas where maximum returns are to be expected and small users, whose jobs are anyway in the fastest job class and who represent a trivial load on the computer, should be left in peace.

3. The Social View

A brief word is called for on the benefits to the rest of a computer installation's user community, which can be obtained by optimizing the few large programs which are using a substantial proportion of the computer resources, to the detriment of everyone else's turn-round. This applies especially in those cases where some users are given high priority to run large amounts of work, and the smaller users have access to only those resources which remain. This is a familiar situation in a university environment where students' programs often run with the lowest priority, competing with large number-crunching programs run by faculty members. If these latter programs can be improved, then the whole user community obtains a better service from the installation. This leads also to a better use of resources, which are often hard enough to fund, particularly in the case of non-commercial organizations.

4. The Cost of Optimization

It is often argued that optimization involves too great an investment of the time of an already busy and overworked programmer. In many cases this argument has to be regarded as short-sighted, for the reasons which have been outlined earlier in this chapter. It is, naturally, quite possible that a very productive scientist or engineer, full of ideas and ingenuity, and using Fortran merely as a tool in his more absorbing main field of study, will be more concerned with obtaining results than with anything approaching efficient use of his computer. In this instance he could, however, very well be causing havoc with the service provided to other users, and it may be quite desirable that he be given some part-time assistance by his management.

Where such a person, negligent of all principles of sound programming practice, can also cause himself harm, is in that he may actually require longer to arrive at his results using sloppy techniques, than if some moderate amount of care were taken.

An important aspect of working with the more recalcitrant users who object to anyone prying into their code is in the first approaches designed to win over their support for the investigation. Provided sufficient tact is employed, and an explanation is given of the mutual benefits to all parties concerned, no reasonable person can object to cooperating in a joint study.

An additional source of pressure which can be brought to bear in extreme cases is peer judgement. Where the computer centre regularly publishes lists of resources consumed by the principal users, it is to be expected that any given user will not wish to appear to be using an undue amount, especially when the resources are in short supply. It may even be that managers are unaware of the amount of resources used by those reporting to them, and will reconsider the desirability of carrying on with a program of work, if the benefits are not considered to be commensurate with the cost.

Another type of objection to optimization is that put forward by expert programmers who claim to have applied every possible improvement to their program already. In these cases, a discussion of the problem and its solution with another expert can nevertheless be expected to bring about improvements, as only then is a rigorous explanation of the methods really required, and it may be found to be wanting. It may even happen that coding errors, or errors of logic may be revealed.

A more valid objection to optimization may be raised when the hardware or compilers used are changing. It is clearly a mistake to over-optimize a long-lived program to a single mainframe or to a specific compiler version, as a change in either can cause a significant loss in optimization with respect to the original code. In order to help in this situation, Chapter 5 of this book is devoted to optimizations which are not, in principle, specific to any one environment, but which rather should help in most circumstances – machine-independent optimization. This level of optimization is one which can be carried out in all cases, before proceeding to more specific techniques, where this is warranted.

The danger of optimizing too assiduously for one machine, only to find that the program works less efficiently on another which is used just as often, is one which must be recognized. The difficulties associated with maintaining two separate versions of one piece of code are very real, and this should normally be attempted only in critical areas of code, and the differences clearly marked by means of comment lines.

5. Source Documentation

In order to be able to carry through an effective optimization of a given program or programs, running on a specific mainframe under a certain version of a compiler, it is necessary to have at least a basic idea of the architecture of the computer, of the degree to which the compiler will optimize code itself and of the working of the programs. It is clearly an impossible task in a book such as this to provide a detailed study of a large variety of mainframes and compilers. For a given installation, the manufacturer's own literature should normally describe adequately the principles of operation of the hardware and of the operating system. One is fortunate indeed, however, to discover in the Fortran manuals any but the most scanty advice on any programming techniques, especially optimization. Even if guidelines are published, they may no longer correspond to the installed version of the compiler, as documentation does not necessarily keep up with improvements to the product, nor do new versions of the documentation necessarily get distributed, even when it is kept up-to-date.

This book sets out rather to describe some of the more widely used hardware and compilers, such as the main-line IBM products — the System/370 architecture and the Fortran H compilers and their successor the VS compiler. The examples given are not to be taken as absolute truths, but as reminders of points which need to be borne in mind when writing new code, or optimizing existing programs. In all significant cases, the details need to be checked against the actual computer implementation being worked with, before embarking on major and possibly unnecessary changes.

Throughout this book, optimization is always taken to mean the methods by which some resource, usually the CPU, can be used more efficiently, normally considering only those changes or techniques which are available through the use of standard ANSI Fortran 77, or of certain extensions where explicitly stated. At the end of this time of transition between two standards, Fortran 66 and Fortran 77, and against a background of numerous and often undesirable manufacturers' extensions to those standards, the advice contained here is to be considered mainly as a prompt to some of the questions which should be considered when writing any type of Fortran programs.

Even when equipped with an extensive knowledge of both a particular computer model and its Fortran compiler, the path to a fully optimized program is still a difficult one. The complicated interactions between a source program, constituting the context in which a given section of code is placed, the complex workings of a compiler, and the intricate interconnections and synchronisations between the different parts of a CPU and its associated memory and peripherals, all combine to make predictions of the effect of a change to the source code hazardous. One of the early lessons to be learned is that often a change to the code can be detrimental, and attempts to perform optimizations can lead to a lessening of the ability of a sophisticated compiler to perform its own optimizations. The path to an optimized program is often paved with difficulty and studded with disappointments, but the journey is frequently a necessary one.

Questions

1. Examine the characteristics of your own programs. In what way would you benefit from optimizing them, and to what extent?

2. What is the history of your computer installation? What are the plans for future development?

3. What tools does your computer management possess to measure the workload on the system? Are the statistics available to individual users?

4. Is your computer system well-tuned? If not, in which respect?

5. Is any advice given to users at your installation to help them to improve their programming techniques?

6. Do you have access to adequate printed or on-line documentation about all aspects of your computer system? In what ways could this service be improved?

2 COMPUTER ARCHITECTURE

A computer consists physically of a large number of exceedingly complex electronic and mechanical components known collectively as the *hardware*. In order to be able to perform the tasks for which it is designed, the computer must be equipped with suites of programs which firstly ensure the correct functioning of all the component parts, the *operating system* in its broadest sense, and which secondly are able to interpret and execute the coded instructions which express the users' intentions. In the context of this book, this second group contains the compilers, loaders, linkage editors and system libraries which are necessary to ensure that these intentions are understood and carried out. These suites of programs are known collectively as the *software*.

Seen through the eyes of a programmer, a computer design may be viewed in terms of its *architecture*. By describing a computer in terms of its logical components and their interaction with one another, one is freed from the need to consider the details of the actual implementation of a computer design in physical components, and is able rather to consider the inherent logical capabilities of the system design.

In this chapter we shall introduce a number of architectural concepts which will pave the way to the later chapters on optimization, where some knowledge of the underlying machine architecture is often useful, and sometimes essential. In order to illustrate the principles involved, two actual computer architectures, those of the IBM System/370 and of the CDC CYBER series will be outlined. These two very different architectures will serve the practical purpose of conveying the principles involved, far better than any contrived design of a hypothetical machine.

1. Data Entities

A computer manipulates data. In order to be able to do this, the data must be stored within the computer, or on an external medium to which the computer has ready access. Depending on the type of storage and application, the data are referenced in different sized units, not all of which are directly available to a standard Fortran program.

The most primitive unit of data is the binary digit, or *bit*. This is simply a machine representation of the value '1' or '0', and is stored as the state of an electronic switch, or as the direction of magnetization of a tiny portion of a magnetic medium. Normally, an individual bit is manipulated and changed only within the computational heart of a computer – the Central Processing Unit (CPU). It is not directly addressable by standard Fortran code, nor by most assembly languages.

Nowadays most computers have what is known as a *byte* architecture. A byte is a sequence of bits forming a unit of transfer within the CPU, and by convention consists usually of eight bits. It is the element of storage of the entity known as a *character*, and is also the unit of logical transfer to and from magnetic tape and other external media. This architecture has become very widespread, following its original introduction in the IBM System/360 in 1964. On byte oriented machines the individual bytes are directly addressable through extensions to the Fortran syntax, and the byte is one of the storage data entities which are available to assembly languages (see Section 8.8). A byte is by convention assigned a value in hexadecimal notation, that is a value in the range 00 to FF (where each hexadecimal digit runs over the range which can be represented by four bits – 0 to 15 in decimal notation or 0 to F in hexadecimal).

On all computers a larger organized collection of bits, or alternatively of bytes, is the *word*. The number of bits in a computer word varies from eight on micro-computers to 64 on super-computers. Some other values which have been used are 12, 16, 18, 24, 32, 36, 48, and 60 bits, but the spread of byte oriented architectures means that increasingly the unit is two, four or eight 8-bit bytes. The computer word is the basic data entity of the Fortran language, and forms the elements which the programmer may directly reference and manipulate. The word is the unit of storage for the non-character data items: the integer, the real and the logical. The meaning assigned by the machine designers to the individual bits of a word varies from computer to computer, but for an integer on the IBM S/370, the pattern is

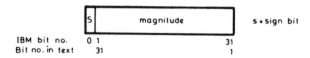

allowing the representation of positive integer values up to $2^{31} - 1$ as, apart from the sign bit, each set bit of the word, that is each bit with the value '1', carries a value of 2^{n-1}, where n is the bit position counting from the right (although IBM counts the bits from the left). A zero sign bit indicates that the number is positive. A one in the sign bit indicates that the number is negative, and in the range between -1 and -2^{31}. In the case of IBM integer representation, the magnitude of the negative value is stored in two's-complement notation, formed by inverting each bit in the corresponding positive number, and then adding one. It may thus be seen that the pattern of all ones represents the value -1. Other machines use a one's-complement notation in which the one is not added; this then allows a distinction between $+0$ and -0, as a pattern of all ones is simply the inverse of a pattern of all zeros:

$+1$ in 16-bit binary notation	0 000 0000 0000 0001	
		invert each bit
-1 in 16-bit one's complement notation	1 111 1111 1111 1110	
		add 1 to the string
-1 in 16-bit two's complement notation	1 111 1111 1111 1111	

To represent a real, or floating-point quantity, the bits of a word are partitioned in the following manner, taking the IBM representation as an example:

The first of the six hexadecimal digits of the mantissa (in bits 8 to 11) is normally non-zero, that is, it contains a value between 1 and F in hexadecimal notation. Such a number representation is called normalized, and is a method ensuring that as many bits as possible in the mantissa are actually used, giving the highest possible precision for what is almost always an inexact number representation. The sign of the mantissa is given by the sign bit. The exponent, in bit positions 1 to 7, is a number of the range -64 to

+63, to which is added a constant offset of 64, the so-called excess-64 notation. The actual value stored is then in the range 0 to 127.

In floating-point number representations, the radix point is considered to precede the mantissa, so that the value stored is

$$.\text{mantissa} \times 16^{\text{exp}}$$

with each bit carrying the value 2^{-n}, where n is the bit position within the mantissa, counting from the left.

Since the normalized mantissa lies between the values just less than 1 and 1/16, the range of values which may be stored is

$$16^{-65} \text{ to } (1 - 16^{-6}) \times 16^{63}$$

or approximately

$$5.4 \times 10^{-79} \text{ to } 7.2 \times 10^{75}$$

in decimal notation. (We note that 2^{-24} or 16^{-6} is the difference between 1 and the value of the mantissa with all bits set to one, its highest possible value).

Non-byte machines use similar representations, but normalize the mantissa so that its first bit is a one; this system is superior in that each bit of the mantissa is used, whereas in the byte representation up to three bits of precision may be lost. The exponent may also be differently represented, and even carry its own sign bit.

The representation of words of double-precision varies according to the machine. In all cases a second word is required to increase the precision. In some cases (IBM compatible computers), the whole of this second word is taken to extend the precision of the mantissa. In others, the second word is partioned exactly as the first, with its mantissa extending the precision of the first, and its exponent containing the value of the first exponent scaled down by an appropriate factor to take account of the smaller significance of the second word: if the second mantissa is the continuation of an n-bit mantissa from the first word, the second exponent is the first multiplied by 2^{-n}. In neither of these cases is the range of the number altered, as no extra significant bits are assigned to the exponent, but increased range is supported by some architectures, for instance the VAX.

The representation of logical values is a matter of convention within a compiler. For example, the logical value .TRUE. might be represented by an integer value 0, and the logical value .FALSE. by an integer value 1. To make explicit use of the knowledge of an actual representation of the logical values is a poor programming practice as it makes a program less portable, even possibly across different compilers on the same computer. Sometimes small logical arrays are packed into the bits of a word.

The manipulation of data by the computer is governed by *instructions* which describe precisely the operations to be performed by the hardware. Instructions too must be stored and, outside the CPU, are usually treated in exactly the same manner as data. Instruction formats, *i.e.* the way in which instructions describe the operations and in which they are packed into words of storage, vary enormously from computer to computer, and will be discussed further in Section 2.4. Full details are often given in the manufacturers' assembly language reference manuals. It is sufficient here to mention that an instruction may occupy either the whole or a fraction of a computer word, and short instructions are usually packed as densely as possible into words, in order to keep the total amount of space they occupy to a minimum, which in turn allows them to be processed faster.

As we shall see in the next chapter, instructions are usually generated by a compiler from the source code of a program. The instructions are not directly accessible to a Fortran program, and on some machines are even kept in a reserved area of storage; any inadvertent attempt by a program to access a storage location in this area leads to an execution-time error.

2. Levels of Storage

Within a computer system there are several different levels of storage, (see Fig. 1). These are characterized by an inverse relationship between the size of the store on the one hand and the speed of access and the cost per bit on the other; the larger the store the slower is the access.

The fastest stores are actually made a part of the CPU itself, and consist of two different types, one for data words and another for instructions. They are both referred to as *registers*. Data registers are used to hold the operands for the operations performed by the CPU and for addresses and indices. According to the nature of the data and the length of their elements, registers are organized into sets, a given set containing registers of equal length and intended to hold a certain type of data, for instance addresses in address registers or floating-point words in floating-point registers. Examples of sets of registers appear later in this chapter.

Instructions are held for use by the CPU in instruction registers.

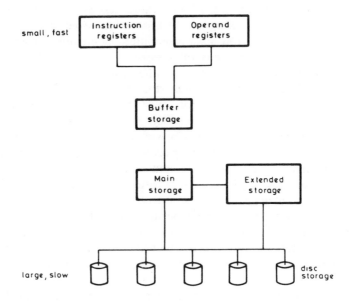

Fig. 1   Storage levels

These may also be organized into a set, which is then known as an *instruction stack*. The length of an instruction register is often the same as the length of a computer word.

Data and instructions are obtained from the next level of storage, which is larger and is accessible to the CPU only via a control unit. All computers have a level of memory known as *main storage*, which on older machines consisted of magnetic core storage, but is now usually semi-conductor storage.

According to the type of computer, there may be another level of storage intimately associated with the main memory. This may be smaller and faster, and act as a buffer between the main memory and the registers, and is then known as a *cache* store. Alternatively, it may be larger and somewhat slower, and known as an *extended* store, acting as a buffer between the main memory and the next level of storage, the *backing-store*.

The backing-store usually consists of magnetic disc storage, and may be of one of two types. In the first type, the discs are directly accessible to a user's program, and may contain data to be read and written with explicit read/write commands. Magnetic tape and other peripheral devices may also be used in this way.

In the second type of disc-based backing-store, a number of the disc units are fully integrated into the overall storage of the system.

A user program may address storage locations within an address range which is many times larger than the physical capacity of the main store, and all user programs together have access to a still larger address space. The operating system and hardware are responsible for performing the necessary manipulations to ensure that the areas of data actually being referenced by the CPU are brought to and from the backing-store to main memory as required. Since the user never knows the physical location of any given address, such an address is known as a *virtual address*, and such a storage system as a *virtual storage system*. Data in a virtual storage environment are transferred between backing-store and main memory in units known as *pages*, and sophisticated software and hardware *paging* algorithms are required to ensure that the most frequently referenced pages are those that are retained preferentially in the main memory. The actual physical address of a data word in a virtual location is at any given time known only to the operating system and is of no concern to the programmer, nor is it even under his direct control.

This type of storage system, first introduced in the Atlas computer (Kilburn *et al.*, 1962), has also become very widespread, and is a powerful extension of the environment in which a programmer works. Some potential drawbacks with regard to program speed will be discussed in Section 8.9.

3. The Central Processing Unit

The arithmetic and logical operations of a computer are performed by the central processing unit, according to instructions specified by the programs. The CPU in modern computers is a very complex device to which the following description can in no way do justice. Rather, the complexity will be hidden behind a simple breakdown into a few of the most obvious component parts.

The computations are performed by devices known as a *functional units*. There exist functional units which perform only a single type of operation, for instance additions or multiplications, and the CPU will then contain as many different functional units as it performs different types of operation, perhaps ten or so. A more usual scheme is the integrated functional unit, or arithmetic-logical unit (ALU), which is able to perform all the operations. The control of the operations within a functional unit is also of two types – hard-wired or micro-programmed. In the first case the control mechanism is built into the electronic circuitry, and can be modified subsequently only by appropriate modifications to the hardware itself. In the second case, the control is exercised by a small, complex control program which acts on the individual bits of the operands to obtain the desired result. This scheme was first proposed by Wilkes (1951). The speed of micro-programmed CPU's can be steadily improved by the introduction of better micro-programs which carry out a given operation in fewer steps. New micro-code is installed simply by changing the contents of the medium on which it is stored, and this technique allows a smoother evolution and even extension of the CPU's capabilities.

In order to be able to perform a single operation, say a floating-point add, a number of sub-operations will be required, each one of which is typically carried out during one clock-cycle of the machine, where a clock-cycle is the period of time required to complete a transition of the state of the CPU to its succeeding state. The sub-operations might be:

— compare the two exponents
— shift the mantissa of the smaller operand and increase its exponent, to make both exponents equal
— add mantissas
— normalize result or perform carry.

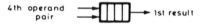

Fig. 2   A segmented functional unit (pipeline)

It may thus be seen that four clock-cycles are necessary to perform one complete operation. It is, however, possible to make use of the segmentation of the computation to increase the duty cycle of operations, using a technique known as *pipelining*. Instead of the functional unit waiting to finish the complete operation, a new pair of operands is accepted as soon as the first intermediate result is ready, after one clock cycle (see Fig. 2). In this manner, the functional unit is able to compute at one time on up to four operand pairs, provided the operands do not in any way depend on one another. This is, of course, not always possible and so the average rate is significantly less than the peak rate. Pipelining is one method which can be used to speed up a CPU. Another, used in CPU's which contain multiple functional units, is to increase the concurrency of computations by designing their control in a way which allows them to operate simultaneously on independent computations. This technique would permit, for instance, an add instruction to be issued to the add functional unit, and an independent multiply to be

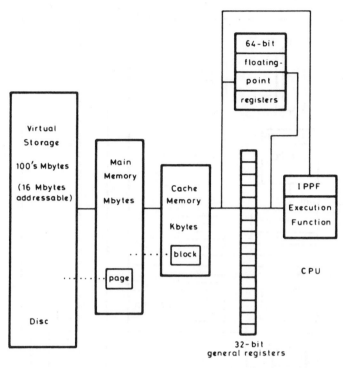

Fig. 3   The hardware organization of the IBM 3033

instruction execution, and the instructions from this active buffer are passed into an instruction register and decoded; these decoded instructions are placed in an instruction queue. The other two instruction buffers are filled with the instructions following any branches contained in the instruction sequence in the instruction queue. Should a branch be taken, the instruction sequence is switched to be taken from the appropriate buffer. The instruction queue may contain instructions which will not be executed, because of a branch, but by maintaining three buffers, and by choosing which buffer is to be active on the basis of design experience, the probability is increased that the next required instruction will actually be in the instruction queue, or at least in a currently inactive buffer, rather than in virtual storage. Should this latter condition occur, the program execution is interrupted by a wait.

The operand addresses contained in the decoded instructions are kept in operand address registers, whereas the instruction queue feeds directly into the E-Function; the placing of operand addresses in the operand address registers in the IPPF causes the operands to

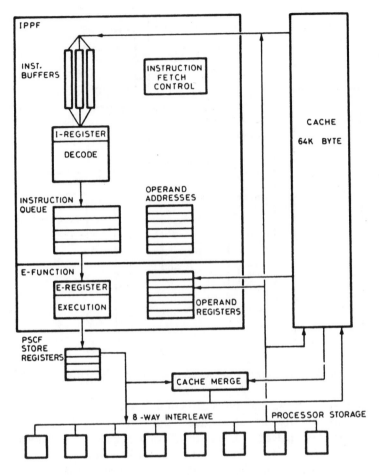

Fig. 4   The CPU of the IBM 3033

which they correspond to be fetched from cache memory or main memory under control of the PSCF and to be placed in the operand registers which form part of the E-Function. Should the operands not be correctly aligned, if for instance a 4-byte real quantity is stored half in one word and half in the next, the IPPF performs the necessary alignment. The flow of instructions into the E-function constitutes a pipeline, as it is overlapped with the execution of instructions which have already been issued.

Access by the E-Function to the general and floating-point registers is direct. These are the registers which are under program control; the 16 32-bit general registers are used to store integer operands, address constants and indices, and the four 64-bit float-ing-point registers may hold up to four single- or double-precision real operands. The movement of operands between registers and vir-tual memory is directed solely by programmed instructions acting via the E-Function. For instance, one machine instruction may cause a given data word to be stored in a general register, and the next may cause the contents of that register to be multiplied by a multiplicand still located in virtual memory. This second operand will be fetched under control of the IPPF and PSCF into an operand register in the E-Function, ready for the multiplication to be performed.

The flow of data (operands and instructions) between the CPU and the various levels of memory is of critical importance to the efficient functioning of the whole computer. This flow takes place concurrently with the operation of the CPU and the method by which it is controlled may be illustrated by following the operations which occur when a 4-byte operand is requested that is not available in the cache memory, a so-called cache-miss. If the operand is phys-ically located in the backing-store (*i.e.* is on disc) rather than in main memory, a so-called page-fault condition, then the 4 Kbyte page of data of which it is an element will be transferred to the main memory. It will usually replace the least recently used page. The main memory is divided into eight banks, and consecutive double-words (8-byte units) from the page will be stored in consecu-tive banks, and not in contiguous locations of one bank. This inter-leaving allows a subsequent faster transfer of the contents of contig-uous virtual locations to the cache, as each bank will be addressed in turn, rather than just a single bank having to satisfy the transfer request. The double-word containing the requested operand is next transferred to the operand register in the E-Function, and simultane-ously to a location in the cache. In following clock-cycles the next seven double-words of virtual storage will also be transferred from the page in main memory to the cache, and to the operand registers if required. This *block* will normally replace the least recently used block. It may therefore be seen that the fetching of any operand from main memory initiates a transfer of a complete 64-byte block to the cache, on the assumption that if one double-word of data or instructions is required, its following neighbours in virtual storage will also be required immediately afterwards. The cache may hold up to 1024 such blocks of 64 bytes.

At the same time as operands are being fetched, other operands may have to be stored. Fetch operations take priority over stores, in an attempt to keep the E-Function busy, and this is helped by the provision of store registers to hold the results from the E-Function while they wait to be stored in memory. The memory storage operation takes place in two stages: first the bytes to be stored are merged with the rest of the double-word in cache (unless the bytes constitute a complete double-word) and then the double-word is copied to the main memory. (If the double-word is not in the cache, it must first be fetched from main memory.) This procedure is known as store-through.

In the Amdahl 470V/6, and later in the 26 nsec cycle-time 3081, store-through was replaced by a more efficient procedure know as store-in, whereby the contents of main memory are not refreshed until the block position in the cache is required for new data, and only then is the whole block stored in memory. The longer blocks in the cache of the IBM 3081 are 128 bytes in size; the cache itself has a capacity of 32 Kbytes or 64 Kbytes. The main memory page size is 2 Kbytes with two-way interleaving. The 3081 contains two central processors each with its own cache, and sharing main memory. Within the CPU's the functioning of the instruction element (equivalent to IPPF) and execution element is such that there was no overlap between them in the original D model, so the instruction element issued no new instructions from the queue until the execution element had completed the processing of its current instruction; this revealed an area of potential improvement for the future, partially realised in the K model. Data addressing on the 3081 is totally byte oriented, so that no alignment of operands not falling on word boundaries is required.

6. The CDC CYBER System

The Control Data Corporation (CDC) has a long history of designing computers at the top end of the range used for large-scale scientific data processing. This began with the introduction of the CDC 6600 in 1965, and continued with the CDC 7600 in 1971, repackaged later as the CYBER 176, and culminating in 1982 with the dual processor CYBER 170-875. As a parallel development, CDC has designed a series of vector machines leading to the CYBER 205 (see Chapter 11). Apart from this last computer, the word-addressable machines of the past and current product lines share certain common features in their architecture, and these are illustrated here using the CYBER 176 as a model (Fig. 5). We note, however, that CDC is now breaking away from their word oriented architectures and is introducing byte oriented computers running with a virtual memory operating system, NOS/VE.

The speed of the processors is based on a clock-cycle of 25

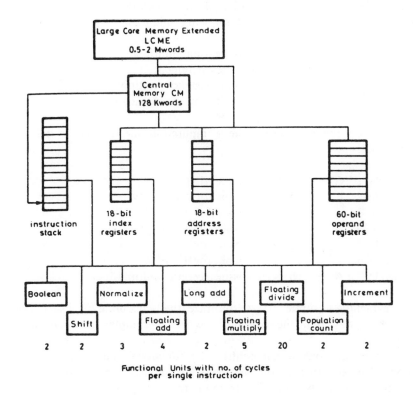

Fig. 5   The hardware organization of the CYBER 176.

nsec, and on a high degree of parallel operation of the functional units. All of the functional units are segmented into a number of micro-operations, each of which is executed each clock-cycle. The segmented functional units, except the multiply and divide units, accept a new operand or operands on each clock-cycle after the first operands have been delivered to the unit. This means that once a unit is primed with a set of operands, it can deliver a new result every clock-cycle. In the case of the multiply unit, the segmentation is based on a two clock-cycle period rather than one. The divide unit performs its operation using an iterative method, and only after 18 of the full 20 clock-cycles have elapsed can it accept a new pair of operands. It may be seen that the CPU can be used very effectively if this pipeline feature is well exploited.

Another important hardware feature is the ability of the functional units to operate concurrently on independent operations. It is therefore possible to issue an add instruction followed one clock-cycle later by a multiply, if the relevant operands do not depend on one another. A fast sequence might be

cycle 1   C = A*B   issue first multiply
cycle 2   I = J + K   issue increment
cycle 3   F = D*E   issue second multiply
                                (unit now ready again)

but data dependence within the computation means that a delay is introduced:

cycle 1   C = A + B   issue first add
cycle 2   F = D*E   issue first multiply
cycle 3   wait for C and F
cycle 4   wait for C and F
cycle 5   wait for F
cycle 6   wait for F
cycle 7   A = C*F   issue second multiply

It is evidently a subtle art to optimize the scheduling of instructions in such a way that the overall time for a complex computation is minimized.

The instructions which control the functional units are held in a 60-bit Current Instruction Word (CIW) register. Since instructions may be either 15 bits or 30 bits long, there may be either two, three or four instructions in this register. It is fed from the Instruction Word Stack (IWS), which holds 12 of the 60-bit instruction words. The IWS ensures that new instruction words are immediately available to the CIW, without having to wait for them to be fetched from memory, and provides an important means of reducing the amount of instruction word fetching required when executing tight loops. Only when a branch to an instruction not contained in the stack occurs, must the CPU wait for an instruction to be fetched from memory. Whether a given instruction word is or is not available in the stack is established by a comparison of the instruction address with the addresses in the Instruction Address Stack, which is a companion stack to the IWS, containing the instruction addresses on a one-to-one basis. During the sequential processing of instructions, a new instruction word is brought into the bottom of the stack each time its tenth word is accessed. All the other instruction words are moved up by one position to accommodate the new word, the top instruction word being lost. If we now imagine the execution of a short loop, its instructions will be brought successively into the stack from the bottom, and if it does not exceed 10 words in length, it will eventually be completely contained in the stack, and no further instruction fetches will be required during its subsequent iterations. The stack may be imagined as a fixed window through which the moving sequence of instructions is viewed.

The operands for the functional units are kept in three sets of registers; many of the machine instructions perform an operation on the contents of two registers and place the result in a third. The eight 18-bit index registers are intended for use as accumulators and for loop counters. The first index register contains the value fixed zero, and may not be written to. The eight 60-bit operand registers and the eight 18-bit address registers are logically connected, in that if an address is placed in one of the second to sixth address registers, the contents of that address location in main memory will be placed in the corresponding operand register. If an address is placed in one of the last two address registers, the contents of the corresponding operand register will be stored in the location in main memory designated by that address. The first registers of each of the two sets are not linked in any way.

The instruction and operand registers are loaded directly from main memory, or Central Memory (CM), with no intermediate buffering; address references to CM, however, go through a three word buffer. Only with the introduction of the model 875 has the user been provided with a CM greater than 128K 60-bit words – this model is addressable up to 1 Mwords. The earlier models backed the CM with a Large Core Memory Extended (LCME) of up to 2 Mwords. This memory has the same maximum transfer rate as CM, but a much slower access time. The 875 may be similarly equipped with an External Extended Memory. A 512 word buffer is provided, to help overcome the longer access time for references to localized areas of storage. Instruction words can be fetched by the IWS only from CM, whereas data words may be fetched under program control from either CM or LCME.

The CPU is used solely for computations, and does not have to be involved, as in most other computers, with performing the tasks associated with I/O operations. These are the responsibility of the up to 20 Peripheral Processor Units (PPU) which interface the two memory systems to the peripheral devices. Each PPU is an independent computer, with a processing unit and a 4K 12-bit word memory. This off-loading of I/O activity ensures the highest possible availability of the CPU to user programs.

The state of an executing program is described by the contents of all the addressable and control registers. These together are called an exchange jump package which is stored away when a job can no longer execute, for instance because it is waiting for I/O, and is restored when the job is resumed.

7. Summary

In this chapter we have introduced some of the computer architecture concepts which will figure in later chapters. These have been illustrated by describing the architecture of the most popular range of general purpose large-scale computers on international markets, and by another range which has found a large measure of success within the scientific computing community. These particular machines will be the subject of further study in Chapters 8 and 9 respectively, where the influence of their architectural features on program optimization will be examined.

Questions

1. In what manner are the various data entities of your computer represented? Is your computer word- or byte-oriented? Compare the advantages and disadvantages of the two systems.

2. What are the capacities, access times and transfer rates of each of the levels of storage on your computer?

3. Describe the basic architecture of your computer, with emphasis on the way in which the CPU functions.

3 COMPILING TECHNIQUES

1. The Task of a Compiler

At the deepest level of its hardware, a computer responds only to control information given in the form of strings of bits. The circuits in the CPU of a computer of the CDC CYBER series interpret the bit string

$$100100\ 001\ 010\ 011$$

as a command to divide the contents of operand register 2 by the contents of operand register 3 and to place the quotient in operand register 1. Almost all the earliest computers had to be programmed using this type of binary notation, but it rapidly gave way to the use of *assembly languages,* in which the bit strings are replaced by mnemonic codes, which are easier for a programmer to manipulate[+]; the above example becomes

$$FX1 \quad X2/X3$$

Since the hardware still requires its final directives in binary notation, a program known as an *assembler* is required to perform the necessary translation of the mnemonic codes into bit strings. An assembly language is referred to as a *low-level language,* as the programmer must know and understand the details of the computer architecture.

Around the early 1950's the need to relieve the programmer of

---

[+] In fact, an early computer, the EDSAC, already used an assembly language (Wheeler, 1950).

this burden was realized, and the first *high-level languages* began to be developed. These allow the expression of the programmer's intent in a direct way which is, in principle, independent of the hardware features of any particular computer, allowing perhaps the division to be written as simply as

$$X = Y/Z$$

In order to translate these more straightforward notations into binary form, a program known as a *compiler* is required. The compiler accepts as input the so-called *source code,* and may produce as output either binary code, or assembler code for subsequent assembly, or some other form of intermediate text which requires further translation. The final binary output is known as the *object code.*

The object code from a complete Fortran program normally contains address references relative to the beginning of each program unit (main program, subroutine or function) or to COMMON blocks. In order that the program be executed, it must first be placed in contiguous memory locations, the actual addresses substituted, and references to library routines satisfied. This task is carried out by another program, either a *loader* or a *linkage editor.*

The early compilers were based on *ad hoc* attempts to perform the necessary translation, but during the 1960's mathematically based theories of compilation techniques began to be developed, and some of the fundamental papers of that period have been collected together by Pollack (1972). An extensive treatment of the mathematical basis of compiling techniques is given in Aho and Ullmann (1972 and 1973); the second of these two volumes includes a detailed treatment of optimization techniques in particular. A more accessible volume by the same authors describes many of the design principles of modern compilers (Aho and Ullmann, 1977), and contains excellent bibliographic notes to guide the reader through the wealth of literature on the subject. Some simple code optimizations are described by Hanson (1983), and bibliographies on program optimization as such were given by Allen (1975) and Hansche *et al.* (1982).

In this chapter we outline the basic phases of compilers, indicating some of the more important methods they utilise. In practice, most Fortran compilers are based on a judicious mixture of theory and pragmatism to arrive at an acceptable product − a compiler which is itself reasonably fast and compact, producing object code which has the same desirable characteristics. We shall look first at the structure of a compiler, then at the way in which the source code statements are lexically analysed into their component parts. This is followed by a discussion of the syntax analysis, in which these components and their relationships are transformed into a text which the subsequent phases of the compiler will use as input. The need for adequate and comprehensible error diagnosis will be emphasised. Finally the principal optimization techniques, the code generation and the source listings and cross-reference maps will be treated. No particular compiler will be used as a model, as regrettably only one major manufacturer, IBM, actually publishes details of its modern Fortran compilers (see Chapter 8), although an early implementation for DEC appears in Abel and Bell (1972) and for UNIVAC in Busam and Englund (1969). Rather, the general techniques which are or could be employed will be described, with illustrative examples from actual implementations included where appropriate.

2. The Structure of a Compiler

A compiler is a program which, like any other, has initialization, input, processing and output phases. The common structure of compilers may be illustrated by the flow diagram of the IBM Fortran H Extended compiler, shown in Fig. 6. The compiler is invoked by a call initiated in the Job Control Language (JCL); it initializes its internal tables and starts to process the first program unit. Program units are compiled individually and separately; each time an END statement is encountered the compiler will complete its compilation of the current program unit, re-initialize itself, and begin to process the next. When all the program units have been compiled, control is returned to the operating system.

During the first stage of processing of each program unit, known as the lexical analysis, the individual statements are read in one at a time. The statement is scanned from left to right to remove any blanks, which are still without significance in Fortran (except in character strings), and the various variables and constants it refers to are entered into tables. At this stage the source text is broken down into its component parts, and in the case of this particular compiler, transformed into an intermediate text, in which each operator (not only arithmetic operators like *, but also punctuation marks like comma or parentheses) and each operand (such as variables and statement labels) are combined into pairs.

In the next stage, called syntax analysis, this intermediate text is transformed into another, which combines operations and operands into quadruples, which designate the operator, the operands and the

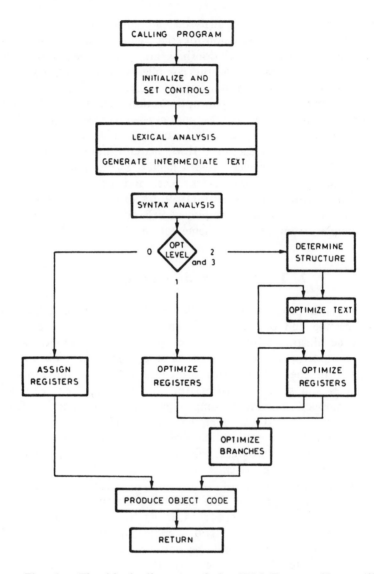

Fig. 6   The block diagram of the IBM Fortran H compiler

target. For instance, the simple statement

$$C = A*B$$

would now appear as

$$*,C,A,B$$

(see Section 3.5 below). During this transformation a check on the syntax is made; this new text is the one used by all subsequent phases of the compiler. It contains the results of other transformations between the two intermediate text forms, such as the expansion of subscript expressions into their component additions and multiplications, and the generated temporaries used to hold intermediate results of computations. Taking the optimization branch causes the compiler to determine the structure of the program unit by recording all branching information, and to set up the tables necessary to optimize the use of variables, constants and temporaries in the subsequent phases. The next three phases of this compiler, which are the optimizing phases, are described in more detail in Chapter 8. The last phase is the actual generation of the object code.

In the above description, the term *phase* has been used to describe each box in the flow diagram. Each phase performs a *pass* or passes, that is it reads the whole of one of the text files, often several times. A pass in compiler terminology implies a complete reading of a text stream, and its transformation for a subsequent pass. One-pass compilers are usually larger than multi-pass compilers and generate less efficient code, but are themselves fast. A multi-pass compiler can make better use of memory by overlaying its various phases, and can generate better object code because it has the opportunity to use the information generated in one pass in subsequent ones. It is, however, clearly slower.

3. Lexical Analysis

The purpose of this compiler phase is to read each source statement, and to separate it into its separate logical entities or *tokens*. A token may be a variable, a constant, a punctuation mark, an operator or any other entity defined by the language. For instance, in the statement

$$DO \ 10 \ I \ = \ 2,10$$

the following tokens may be identified: DO; 10; I; =; 2; , and 10. These tokens are passed to the following phase, the syntax analyser, for further processing, either in the following pass, but more normally in the same pass. We thus see how a phase is a logical concept, but a pass an implementation detail.

Each token may consist of two parts, the first being a code defining the type of the token, the second a pointer into a table listing the attributes of the token. This table is known as a *symbol table.* An entry in the symbol table for the statement label 10, when statement labels have been assigned the type 106 in the example, might be

106   label,   value = 10

whereas the constant 10 might have an entry

229   constant, integer,   value = 10

A keyword, like DO, would not require a pointer into the table, as its meaning is fixed, and it has no attributes.

The identification of tokens is a non-trivial task, especially in a large language like Fortran, which has no reserved words, that is words which have a predefined meaning and which may not be used for other purposes. This particular fact can lead to ambiguous situations which require the scanning algorithm to look ahead in order to be sure of a token's clear recognition. In the case of the DO, not until the first comma is reached during the scan is it possible to identify the DO with certainty as a keyword, rather than the beginning of an assignment like

DO10I = 2.10

This difficulty increased in Fortran 77 with the extension of the DO-construct to include expressions as parameters, and reals as control variables. The use of the optional comma between the statement label and the control variable is, therefore, a means by which programmers may speed the scan:

DO 10, AB = Q(1,I,5), A*B, −D**E

An example of this scanning difficulty and the extra work it causes appears in the subroutine IDENT at the end of Appendix B.

The algorithms used to identify tokens are based on *transition diagrams* and their formal representation, the *deterministic finite-state automata* (DFSA). The DFSA are beyond the scope of this book, and the interested reader is referred to the literature.

A transition diagram is similar to a flowchart, but using different symbols: the *states* of the diagram are represented by circles, which are connected by arrows called *edges*. Each edge bears a label describing the valid character which can appear on the transition between the two states it joins. Thus, the transition diagram for a

Fortran identifier, which consists of a letter followed by letters or digits followed by a delimiter (comma, parentheses, equals sign, *etc.*) is

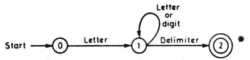

In analysing each new character, the diagram is traversed from one state to the next, until the successful identification is complete, and the identifier token recognized. We note that an edge can point to the state from which it originates, as when looping round state 1 in the example. When the identifier has been recognized, the scanner has already read the delimiter. In order that this character can itself be correctly identified, the scan needs to retract by one character, and this is indicated by the asterisk.

A lexical analyser has to contain all the relevant transition diagrams imposed by the definition of the language, and an efficient implementation of the analysis is essential for fast generation of the tokens for the next phase of the compiler.

4. Syntax Analysis

The syntax analysis phase is performed by a *parser* which, using the tokens as input, attempts to reconstruct the syntactical content of the source code, and to verify it. The *syntax* of a statement is correct if its construction adheres to the formal rules of the language, but at this stage no information about the *semantic* correctness of the statement is available, that is, the purpose or meaning of the statement. Thus, in Fortran

$$A = B + - C$$

is syntactically incorrect as two operators may not appear together, whereas the statement

$$A = B + C$$

is syntactically correct, but is semantically incorrect if either B or C has not been defined at a point in the program which logically precedes the assignment. (However, if B and C are local variables and never appear on the left-hand side of an assignment nor are passed as an argument to an external routine, some sophisticated compilers are able to signal a semantic error in a later phase.)

The logical output of the parser is a *parse-tree* for each statement. There are many methods by which such trees may be constructed, of varying degrees of efficiency and complexity, although typically a parse tree remains a purely notional entity, as it is represented indirectly in the form of an intermediate text for use by the remaining phases of the compiler.

The theory of parsing is based on the concepts of the *context-free grammar* or Backus-Naur Form (BNF) description of a language. In this notation the grammar of a language is defined recursively from basic elements. For instance, supposing an expression E consists, by definition, of one of

- an identifier I
- two expressions separated by an operator O
- an expression in parentheses
- the complement of an expression

and that an operator O is one of

$$+ \quad - \quad * \quad / \quad **$$

then using the vertical bar to represent an 'or', we can write

$$O \ ::= \ + \ | \ - \ | \ * \ | \ / \ | \ **$$

and

$$E \ ::= \ I \ | \ EOE \ | \ (E) \ | \ -E$$

We can then see, for example, that if E1 and E2 are valid expressions, then so too are E1*E2 and $-E1$.

If we now consider the assignment statement

$$A \ = \ B*C + D/E$$

the parser will produce the tree shown in Fig. 7, in which the level at which operands meet specifies the order in which they are to be processed.

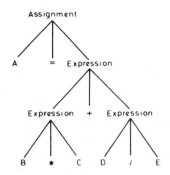

Fig. 7   A parse-tree

5. Intermediate Text

The way in which the trees produced by the parser are represented is important, as the description of the syntax that they contain will be subject to extensive manipulation by a compiler possessing optimization phases. Since these are the only compilers of interest in this book, only the usual representation they employ, the *three-address code* will be described.

The three-address code is a sequence of four entities, usually grouped into a *quadruple*. The entities are the three addresses of the two operands and the result, together with the operator acting on the two operands to form that result. Thus for

$$X = Y*Z$$

the quadruple might appear as

$$*,X,Y,Z$$

Since a quadruple contains one operator only, a whole expression will generate a series of quadruples, each possibly having as one or both operands an intermediate result of the expression evaluation. Returning to Fig. 7, the quadruples which are generated might be of the following form (where Ti stands for a compiler-generated temporary):

```
*,T1, B, C
/,T2, D, E
+,T3,T1,T2
=, A,T3,
```

In each case, the contents of the operand and result fields are pointers into the symbol table, prepared during the lexical analysis. During the parsing, this symbol table has to be extended to include the compiler-generated temporaries.

When the source code performs mixed-mode arithmetic, the parser will generate the quadruples required to *coerce* an operand of one type into the type of the other. For instance if, in the example above, B had been declared type INTEGER, an additional quadruple converting it to a real temporary would be generated.

6. Error Reporting

During the lexical and syntax analysis, the compiler is able to verify the formal correctness and consistency of the source code and the resulting intermediate text. In the interest of fast and efficient debugging, it is very important that the error reporting in these phases of the compiler be accurate, complete, clear and restrained, although these are not objectives which may be easily reached.

Taking each point in turn, the error messages should be related to the statement which is at fault, and not to another. Thus, if a DO-loop is not correctly terminated, this error should be reported at the line defining the beginning of the DO-loop, and not at a line correctly terminating another DO-loop containing the faulty one.

The error message should list all reasonable mistakes which the programmer might have made to cause an error. If a reference to A(I) appears on the left-hand side of an assignment statement, and if A has not been declared as an array, then the error message should mention not only the possibility that the assignment is a misplaced statement function, but also the possibility of a missing declaration. A compiler reporting an illegal character should remind a user at a terminal that the character in question may be an unseen one (such as a backspace). All available information should be provided. If a long DATA statement or FORMAT statement contains an illegal terminator, the message should point to the last correct component of the statement.

Error messages should state their meaning in clear, if concise, English, and not in some obscure internal gibberish, or only by reference to an error number which requires further reference to a manual.

A single error should not trigger a whole avalanche of error messages. Once a forgotten COMMON declaration has given rise to its first dozen or so error messages, it is time for the compiler to suppress further diagnostics about array references which have already been diagnosed several times.

A further requirement is that the compiler should try to complete the compilation of the program unit as well as possible, at least through the lexical and syntax analysis phases. Only in this way is it possible to correct the largest possible number of errors after each attempted compilation. What the compiler should never do is to try to 'correct' errors which it detects, and to carry on into the execution step of the job. The true intention of the programmer is known only to him, and he alone should have the duty of correcting mistakes. For example, in which of the four possible positions is the missing right parenthesis supposed to be:

$$A = (B + C*D/E \qquad ?$$

Or is there still more of the statement missing?

7. Optimization Techniques

A compiler is able to perform optimization of the object code at three main levels. At the first level, the source code is manipulated during the generation of the quadruples in order to perform small local improvements. For instance, the syntax analyser might read $2.*A$ but generate $A + A$ if it is known that addition is significantly faster than multiplication. It may also perform *constant folding*, replacing $2*3$ by 6, for example. The second level at which optimization may be performed is by appropriate manipulation of the intermediate text, to eliminate, for instance, common expression evaluations. This type of optimization is independent of a particular processor. The third level is concerned with the optimization of the object code for a particular processor, and in particular with register allocation, choice of instructions and possibly instruction scheduling. The last two levels are the subject of this and the following sections.

Clearly, no compiler is ever able to produce perfectly optimized code, if only because many of the variables have ranges of values which can never be known to the compiler. It may, therefore, optimize an inner loop whose index goes from 1 to N where N, in fact, never exceeds three, at the expense of an outer loop which actually goes through 1000 iterations. The compiler must also run in a time which is judged to be reasonable by the user, and this precludes it making a very large number of passes, each giving a smaller net improvement. Optimized object code is, then, not optimized in the true sense of the word, but is ideally the result of an optimal combination of compile- and execution-time considerations, and of the need to limit the manpower investment in compiler writing to a realistic level. Thus it cannot be assumed that a given compiler contains all the optimization procedures described below; instead the methods may be limited to those described, for instance, in the references given at the end of Section 3.1.

The first task of any optimizing phase is to divide the program unit into *basic blocks*. A basic block is defined as having a single entry through which the block must be entered, and a single exit. The following fragment of code consists, then, of two basic blocks:

```
        SUM  = 0.                    Block 1
        PROD = 0.                          1
        DO 1,I = 1,20                Block 2
            SUM  = SUM + A(I) + B(I)       2
            PROD = PROD + A(I)*B(I)        2
    1   CONTINUE                           2
```

It is possible to define relationships between basic blocks; a block is a *predecessor* to another if it is possible to execute the second block immediately after the first. In this case, the second block is then called a *successor* to its predecessor. A block may be a predecessor to more than one block, or a successor to more than one block. In the example above, block 1 is a predecessor to block 2, its successor.

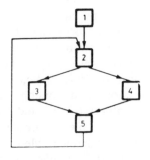

Fig. 8   A block structure (flow graph).
Each block points to its successors.

Given a block structure or *flow graph* expressing these relationships, as shown for example in Fig. 8, we can now define the concept of *dominance*. A block I is said to dominate another block K if every path along a sequence of successors, starting from the entry block of the program unit through to block K, always passes through block I. In the block structure above, it is then possible to see that block 1 dominates all the other blocks and that block 2 dominates blocks 3, 4 and 5, as control to any of these blocks always passes through this block. Block 3 does not dominate block 5 as control may pass through block 4 instead. If a given block J is dominated by several other blocks, then one of these dominating blocks, L, is dominated by all the rest. This block L is called the *immediate dominator* of the block J.

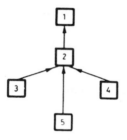

Fig. 9   Dominance relationships.
Each block points to its immediate dominator

The block structure of Fig. 8 can now be transformed into the immediate dominance relations of Fig. 9.

With these dominance relationships now established, it is possible to identify all the *loops* in the program. We note here that a loop is any kind of loop, not just a DO-loop; the importance of loop optimization is evident, as most time in program execution is spent inside them. A loop can be defined as a set of connected blocks which has a single entry block dominating all other blocks in the loop, and in which any block can pass control only to another block in that loop. We see that the blocks 2, 3, 4 and 5 of Fig. 8 satisfy these two conditions.

The beginning of a loop is normally preceded by some initialization of quantities required in the loop, for instance the control parameter of a DO-loop. This initialization is performed once only for each entry into the loop, and we therefore require that a block containing this prologue be added before the loop entry block. We now obtain a block structure for the loop of Fig. 8, as shown in

Fig. 10.

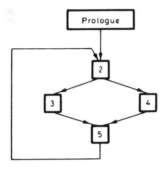

Fig. 10   A block structure for a loop

It is clear from this definition that not all of the statements of a Fortran DO-loop will necessarily fall within a loop. Consider this DO-loop, which contains an unconditional branch outside its range:

```
      DO 1,I = 1,10              Block 1
         IF (Y(I).GT.O.) GO TO 2        1
         X(I) = Y(I)+Z(I)               2
         GO TO 1                        2
    2    X(I) = X(I)+4           Block 3
         GO TO 3                        3
    1 CONTINUE                  Block 4
      :
    3 ........
```

The loop for this DO-loop includes blocks 1, 2 and 4 (Fig. 11), but not block 3. Blocks such as block 3 cannot participate in the loop optimization procedures.

Based on this loop analysis, it is now possible to determine for each variable and for each point at which it is referenced whether or not it is *busy*. A variable is busy at a point in a program if at that point it contains a value which will be required later in the logic flow. For instance, in the sequence

```
    1   X = Y+1.
    2   Z = X+1.
    3   P = Q+4.
    4   X = P+Q.
```

the variable X is busy after line 1 and possibly line 4, but not after

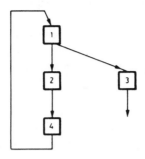

Fig. 11   The block structure of a DO-loop containing an
unconditional branch outside its range

lines 2 and 3 as its current value is no longer required. This information is useful in determining which variables must have their values retained when exiting from a loop, and is useful too in register
allocation (see next section).

The actual manipulation of the intermediate text can now begin,
during which three principal transformations can be performed –
common expression elimination, backward code motion, and induction variable optimization.

Common expressions can be expressions explicitly appearing in
the source text, but are more usually the common expressions generated by the syntax analyser for common subscript expressions inside
DO-loops. The search for an expression common to one appearing
in a given basic block need take place only among blocks in the
same loop as the block in question. If the search is performed starting with the innermost loop, common expressions can be moved into
the prologue of the loop. On a subsequent pass through the next
outer loop, this expression can be combined with any identical
expression in that loop, and so moved progressively outwards. The
scan for common expressions must take into account any store into
one of the operands which might occur between two instances of the
same expression. If such a store is detected, the expression cannot
be considered common with the earlier one. If blocks 2 and 5 of
Fig. 8 were both to contain the expression $X + 3$ but either of block
3 or 4 contained a redefinition of X, the expression could not be
considered common. If, on the other hand, no such interfering redefinition is present, the first occurrence could be used to define a
compiler-generated temporary variable for subsequent use in block 5,
or the result of $X + 3$ could even be used directly if it is not itself
redefined in between the two references.

Since the search for common expressions could grow roughly as the square of the program size, various strategies are required to limit the search time; a simple limitation contained in an IBM compiler is to restrict the search to a maximum of 10 dominating blocks. Others search only within the equivalent of a few source statements.

Loops may contain *invariant* code, that is expressions which do not depend on the loop variable. In unoptimized programs, such expressions would be evaluated on each iteration of the loop (if we ignore branches within the loop). Once again, by progressing successively through the loops starting with the innermost, it is possible to move any invariant expression which can be identified into each loop prologue, whence it may be moved out further still, if it is invariant also to the next outer loop. If the block 4 of Fig. 10 were to contain the array references A(I)*B(I), where I does not depend on the loop, A(I) and B(I) could be fetched and multiplied in the prologue of the loop, and the result kept for use during each iteration. We note that if, for whatever reason, the branch to block 3 is always taken, the program will be less fast than before; but on average this optimization brings a net gain in execution time. It may also be seen that in a loop containing tests on division by zero, the movement of an invariant division without its accompanying test can lead to a potential error condition. This so-called unsafe optimization should always be contained in the very highest optimization level of a compiler, so that a programmer may select a lower level without losing the benefits of safe optimization.

The third major optimization performed on loops is that concerning *induction variables,* which are variables which at one and only one point in a loop are always incremented or decremented by a fixed amount. Examples of induction variables are DO-loop control variables. In

```
    DO 1,I = 1,10
        A(2*I + 3) = B(J,I)
  1 CONTINUE
```

the induction variable is I which is incremented by one at each iteration, and which is used in the subscript expressions 2*I + 3 (which contains an implicit increment by two) and J,I (which contains an implicit increment by the column length of B). These two expressions contain multiplications if they are evaluated explicitly each time, but they are reduced to additions by this optimizing phase. This technique was first used by Babbage. This is an example of *strength* *reduction,* replacing a strong operation by a weaker and faster one.

Allen *et al.* (1974) have shown how strength reduction may be applied to a wide variety of expressions containing induction variables, including exponentiation, polynomials and trigonometric functions. An example is shown in the successive stages of Fig. 12 for the loop fragment

```
    DO 1,I = 1,K5,K2
     A = B(I*K1)
  1 CONTINUE
```

given by Lowry and Medlock (1969) for the IBM compilers.

Prologue

I = 1	I = 1	I = 1
	I2 = K1*I	I2 = K1*I	I2 = K1
	K3 = K1*K2	K3 = K1*K2	K3 = K1*K2
		K6 = K1*K5	K6 = K1*K5

Loop

T1 = I*K1	T1 = I2	T1 = I2	
A = B(T1)	A = B(T1)	A = B(T1)	A = B(I2)
I = I+K2	I = I+K2		
	I2 = I2+K3	I2 = I2+K3	I2 = I2+K3
I ⩽ K5	I ⩽ K5	I2 ⩽ K6	I2 ⩽ K6

Stage 1   Stage 2   Stage 3   Stage 4

Fig. 12   The successive transformations in induction variable optimization

The loop depicted in stage 1 contains an induction variable I which is incremented by K2 during each iteration. The loop completes when I exceeds K5. I is multiplied by K1 to reference an array element.

In stage 2, the multiplication has been replaced by an addition within the loop, using a new variable I2 which is incremented by K3

(= K1*K2) during each iteration. In stage 3 the original induction variable I is removed from the loop, as I2 can be used to test for completion against a new constant K6 (= K1*K5) which ensures the same number of iterations (K5/K2). In the last stage, a procedure known as *subsumption* has replaced the reference to T1 by a reference to I2, and the reference to I by a reference to 1 (I is then deleted). A variable is said to be subsumed by another variable if all its references may be replaced by references to the other. Subsumption is a standard optimizing technique; when performed in a short sequence of code, it is an example of a common technique known as *peephole optimization* (McKeeman, 1965).

There is one other transformation which might be applied to the intermediate text. Using the flow graph and dominance relationships, it is possible to determine points in the program at which certain expressions are *very busy*. An expression is very busy at a point in the program if between that point and the appearance of every next occurrence of the expression there is no intervening redefinition of one of the operands involved. In Fig. 13, representing alternative paths through a section of code, the expression B*C appears on two disjoint paths; the code may be *hoisted* to a higher point in the program flow to define a compiler-generated temporary variable for subsequent use, even though it is not required at that higher point.

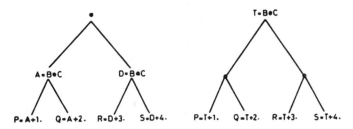

Fig. 13   An example of code hoisting

8. Code Generation

The final output of a compiler is the object code. For each program unit the compiler produces an object module containing all the information required by the loader or linkage editor to combine the module with others in order to build a load module for final execution. An example of the internal structure of an object module, for CDC compilers, is given in Fig. 14.

The generation of the machine instructions themselves is highly machine dependent, since the instruction sets and CPU architectures

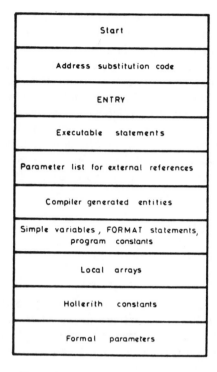

Fig. 14 A CDC load module

of individual computers are so radically different. On machines which have a restricted number of registers it is important to minimize the number of operand fetches and stores by maintaining only the most used variables in registers, and fetching and storing the less used ones. The number of store operations can be reduced by using the information obtained in an earlier phase, about whether a variable is busy or not at a point in the program where the register it occupies is required for another variable. If it is not busy, its register may be overwritten directly with no store required. An example of the way in which register allocation is carried out is given in Section 8.4 for the IBM compilers.

Another consideration is the choice of instructions. Some machines have instructions which allow a quantity to be incremented by one or to be incremented by one and tested. This is clearly superior to using an explicit addition by a constant 1. Similarly, addresses may be constructed by implicit additions of address fields inside an instruction, rather than having to perform explicit additions.

On machines in which the instructions enter a pipeline and are executed overlapped with one another, the order in which instructions are issued can be decisive in the overall efficiency of the object code. Guidelines for IBM type register-based architectures with pipelined instructions have been given by Rymarczyk (1981). A particular problem arises if the instructions not only enter a pipeline, but if they can operate in parallel in independent functional units, a feature of CDC CYBER computers. This problem has been illustrated in Section 2.6. In this case it is important to schedule instructions to perform a slow operation well before its result is required, allowing other faster operations to be performed in the meantime. For instance, in the sequence

$$D = Q + 4.$$
$$I = I + 1$$
$$A = B/C$$
$$E = A + 1.$$

it is possible to re-order the three first operations so that the instructions to calculate D and I are issued after the slow instruction to calculate A. In this way the evaluation of E will not have to wait so long for its operand A, and D and I can be calculated in the waiting period.

9. Cross-reference Maps

During its various phases the compiler generates a large amount of internal information about the structure of the program units it compiles. Some of this information is normally made available to the programmer in the form of optional source listings and cross-reference maps. To be useful, the maps should be presented in a readable fashion, and should include all the information required to enable the program to be debugged quickly, with the minimum number of runs. The error messages have been discussed earlier, so here only the standard listing is considered.

The maps should list alphabetically each variable referenced, giving a list of the line numbers where it is defined and where it is referenced. A local variable which does not appear on the left-hand side of a statement or in an argument list should be signalled as undefined. A local variable which has been found to be *dead,* defined but never referenced, should also be signalled. Similarly, a block of code which is dead, that is can never be entered because it is preceded by an unconditional branch and bears no statement label, should be indicated. All these conditions can arise because of typing or logical errors, and this information allows a fast desk-check of the code, especially during early compilations.

The compiler should list all the files and external routine names which are referenced in the program. This too allows typing errors to be detected early, without having to wait for mysterious fatal errors at execution time.

The relative location within the program unit of at least each statement label in the relocatable code generated should be given, together with the relative location of each local variable, and the relative location of all COMMON variables in their respective COMMON blocks. Possibly the relative location of each statement should appear alongside it in the source listing. This information would help with the diagnosis of any possible execution-time errors, in the absence of a *post-mortem* dump analyser, or other debugging tool.

The references to each statement label should be listed, and labels which are not referenced at all should be marked. Spurious labels may degrade optimization and may be the result of a coding error.

Information on DO-loop nesting should be given. In particular, the reason for the compiler possibly not being able to perform a full optimization of an inner loop should be stated. On machines with instruction stacks, the length of the loop should be given referenced to the stack size, so that it may be seen whether any small improvement could just ease a loop into the stack. Ideally, any backward code motion should be indicated, as a source of error can be transferred from the body of a loop into its prologue, giving unexpected execution time diagnostics.

Finally, in the interests of portability, any statements which do not conform to the ANSI Fortran standard should be suitably flagged.

10. Summary

In this chapter we have outlined the basic purpose and structure of Fortran compilers. The techniques they employ to transform the source code into tokens, intermediate text and finally optimized object code have been described, and references to more detailed treatises have been given. Compilers differ very much in the details of their implementation, the degree of optimization they perform and the attention they receive from their vendors. It is in the compiler users' own interests to find out how the compilers they use work, and to cooperate with their manufacturer's representatives in designing improvements to these products.

Questions

1. Describe the way in which the compiler you use operates. Which types of optimization does it perform?

2. Compare the speed of compilation and of execution of a complete program with which you are familiar, using each optimization level of the compiler in turn. How does the storage requirement vary?

3. Which aspects of the compiler would you like to see improved?

4. Does your computer management cooperate with your computer vendor to improve the compiler?

is given as

```
      S = 0.
      DO 1 I = 1,N
        S = S+(-1)**I*I
    1 CONTINUE
```

The algorithm proposed to replace this direct transcription of the formula is

```
      S = 0.
      DO 1 I = 1,N,2
        S = S-I
    1 CONTINUE
      DO 2 I = 2,N,2
        S = S+I
    2 CONTINUE
```

which is claimed to require only 4.9% of the original time for $N = 100,000$. However, by inspection, the simple code

```
      S = N/2
      IF (MOD(N,2).EQ.1) S = S-FLOAT(N)
```

is almost independent of N in its execution time, and so is about 100,000 times faster still (based on a count of the operations), and is incidentally immune to any problems of precision which might occur when manipulating large values in loops, and also avoids the totally unnecessary integer to real conversions (see Section 5.4). In addition, the final algorithm is *robust* in that no intermediate result is generated which is larger than N, and so if N is a valid number on a given machine, then so is S, and no overflow can occur.

Another example of robust code, where this is of greater importance than efficiency, is in the algorithm in Ex. 1 for the square root of the sum of two squares, due to Moler and Morrison (1981). This code is robust in that it does not generate any intermediate result greater than roughly the larger of A and B. This makes it invaluable for avoiding overflow conditions on machines with a restricted range. However, its authors make no claims that it is particularly fast, and indeed its deceptive simplicity hides the fact that it is several times slower, on an IBM 3033, than the standard SQRT function. (The algorithm converges to machine-precision accuracy in three iterations on a 32-bit machine).

An amusing account of the need to examine the algorithms

```
        FUNCTION PYTHAG (A,B)
*
*  PYTHAG (A,B)  =  SQRT(A**2 + B**2)
*
        P  =  MAX(ABS(A), ABS(B))
        Q  =  MIN(ABS(A), ABS(B))
        IF (Q.EQ.0.) GO TO 20
*
    10 R  =  (Q/P)**2
        T  =  4. + R
        IF (T.EQ.4.) GO TO 20
        S  =  R/T
        P  =  P + 2.*S*P
        Q  =  S*Q
        GO TO 10
*
    20 PYTHAG  =  P
*
        END
```

Example 1

before starting on optimization has been given by Samet (1975). A program which failed to complete in 30 minutes finally executed in less than three minutes after successive improvements, the major one being to replace a tortuous algorithm for calculating a remainder (code slightly modified)

```
        DO 6 J  =  1,1000
            IX(J)  =  IDAYS  −  IP(I)*J
            IF (IX(J).LT.0) GO TO 9
    6   CONTINUE
    9   IREM(I)  =  IP(I) + IX(J)
```

by the single statement

```
        IREM(I)  =  MOD(IDAYS,IP(I))
```

In general, of course, algorithms are far more complex than these trivial examples, and the search for the most suitable one can be undertaken only by an expert in the particular field. The sources of algorithms are diverse, but when working in a given field it belongs to a specialist's professionalism to be aware of them. When solving a new problem, the first source of algorithms is in code which has been used locally to tackle similar problems. Such code will exist in the libraries of colleagues, or in the program libraries which all computer centres provide for their users. These central libraries will often contain very efficient code, as frequently library routines which are known to be heavily used will have been written in optimized assembly language. It is important, on the other hand, to be careful not to use a sledge-hammer to crack a nut, and to ensure that the solution is well matched to the problem. If, for instance, a library routine is able to perform a linear interpolation between function values in an arbitrarily high number of dimensions, it might be very inefficient to use it for interpolations in one dimension, as the general code is ill-suited to the particular problem. Similarly, iterative procedures should not be required to converge to an unnecessarily small tolerance.

The next level of search is in the commercial libraries like those provided by IMSL (1979) and NAG (Ford et al. 1979). These contain well tested and reliable code, and provide an excellent point of departure for algorithm choice. However, it must not be assumed that the code itself is highly optimized to a given computer, and some further work may be required in this direction.

In most specialist fields there now exist extensive algorithm libraries, for instance those in physics published in *Computer Physics Communications,* and in mathematics in the ACM *Transactions on Mathematical Software,* and these libraries are presumably known to people working in such fields. Manufacturers often provide catalogues of mainly Fortran programs in science and engineering which are available commercially from named suppliers (see, for example, DEC, 1982, IBM, 1981b, and Prime, 1980). The relevant journals and books also often contain algorithm supplements, and it is then important to avoid the 'not invented here' syndrome, and choose to copy existing algorithm implementations rather than to begin oneself from scratch. Only after proper testing and comparison of the algorithms under typical run conditions and with the whole range of data expected (Howden, 1982), need the following step in the optimization procedure begin − the identification of the hot-spots in the newly constructed code.

2. Profiling Tools

In this section we shall examine the various ways in which it is possible to identify those areas of a program which actually deserve to be subject to any optimization effort. There exists a supposedly widely applicable '10-90 rule', that 10% of the code of a program uses 90% of the time. If we assume that this rule is valid, what are its consequences? A program of 500 lines will need to have 50 lines optimized, when they have been located, which is a modest task. A program of 50,000 lines will involve a far greater amount of work, on 5,000 lines of code. If the program is written with no *a priori* knowledge of where the time is likely to be spent, then it is probably less effort to optimize those 5,000 lines than to write the whole 50,000 with a conscious effort to optimize them all. On the other hand, it is normally possible to recognize the potential hot-spots in large programs in advance, and it is then worth coding these areas very carefully from the outset. That it is wasted effort to invest too much time in the remaining 45,000 lines may be seen by a simple example: if the time spent in the 5,000 lines is reduced by a large factor, say three, then the new version of the program will still spend 75% of its new total time in those 5,000 lines, and only 25% in the remainder. We see that even if these 45,000 lines had been coded better by a factor of two, the overall gain to the final version would be only 12.5%, which is hardly worth the effort in most cases. We may then conclude that the larger the program the more important it becomes to apply some optimizing techniques to the presumed areas of intense activity at the design and coding stages, whereas for small programs it is often better to optimize when they are working and tested.

Another factor is the ultimate purpose of the program. Those which are heavily used, especially as parts of widely distributed libraries, require far more attention than those used infrequently. It is of little use trying to optimize an application program if the library routines it calls are themselves using a large fraction of the time, are inefficient and perhaps inaccessible in source form.

When timing algorithms, it is essential to time them over the whole range of their input data. A DO-loop beginning with a statement such as

DO 1 I = 1,EXP(P)

will not be executed at all for small values of P, but the number of iterations will rise dramatically as P increases, and proper attention must be given to timing for a typical set of its values.

There are a number of procedures by the which the hot-spots of a program may be identified. Should none of the tools described in the rest of this section really be available, an initial guess for small programs may be made by counting the nesting levels of the

```
      DO 1 I = 1,L1
         DO 2 J = 1,L2
            (6 operations)
2        CONTINUE
         DO 3 J = 1,L3
            (20 operations)
3        CONTINUE
1     CONTINUE
```

Example 2

DO-loops, and then multiplying the number of iterations over each loop by an estimate of the number of operations within each one. For instance, in the fragment of code in Ex. 2 we see that the loop over 2 contains L1xL2x6 operations, and the loop over 3 contains L1xL3x20 operations. If L2 is usually 1000, and L3 usually 10, then the loop over 2 is 30 times more time-consuming than the loop over 3, independent of the value of L1, and is the loop which should be optimized. This type of static analysis is rather tedious and error-prone, especially in the presence of IF-loops, and should be used only as a last resort. It is helped considerably, however, by a source listing in which the DO-loops are indented, and a program to reformat a source program in this fashion is offered in Appendix B. This program also indents any IF-blocks, in order to improve the readability of the code, and the nesting level of each of these two constructs is inserted into the comment field of each statement.

If a static analysis is not possible, an alternative is a primitive dynamic analysis obtained by inserting counters at strategic points in the program, and printing their values upon program completion:

$$KOUNT(1) = KOUNT(1) + 1$$
$$\vdots$$
$$KOUNT(2) = KOUNT(2) + 1$$
$$\vdots$$

Fosdick (1974) and Lyon and Stillman (1975) have described schemes to insert such counters automatically by program at the beginning of each basic block, and the second reference also contains a classification of profiling tools.

Most computer centres make available a library subroutine which provides the CPU time used by an executing progam in some unit determined by the actual computer being used. This is useful for timing short sections of code, in the way shown in Ex. 3. In this example, the two initial calls determine the overhead of the calls themselves, and this is used to correct the value TIME measured for the subroutine being timed. Timing information is often provided in rather large units, and in this case care is needed to ensure that the time spent in the area being tested is large compared with that unit. In order to achieve this, it might be necessary to enclose the section of code under test in a DO-loop over a large number of iterations, but this must be done carefully, as an optimizing compiler may then promptly move some of the invariant code out of the loop, and thereby invalidate the timing data (see Section 3.7). Timing subroutines are themselves often sources of substantial overheads, as a system interrupt is generated to gain access to the system clock, and calls of this type should not be heavily used if they are incorporated into production programs.

```
        :
    CALL  CLOCK(T0)
    CALL  CLOCK(T1)
    TD  =  T1 − T0
        :
    CALL  CLOCK(T0)
    CALL  TEST
    CALL  CLOCK(T1)
        :
    TIME  =  T1 − T0 − TD
        :
```

Example 3

Using such a subroutine, it is possible to confirm intuitive ideas about which areas of relatively small programs are the most intensively used, and to measure the effect of any changes to the code (as long as they result in differences of time significantly larger than the basic timing unit). Normally in these timing measurements it is desirable to separate any program initialization and termination phases from the main processing phase.

Another type of timing tool is provided by the CFT compiler of Cray Research. Using a compiler option, it is possible to insert into the object code the necessary instructions to count the number of entries and the percentage of the total time spent in each subroutine. Only if a significant amount of time is spent in library subroutines does this method suffer from the disadvantage of not giving the complete timing statistics. Another disadvantage of such a tool is that no information is available about the timing distribution within each subroutine, and one must resort to informed guesses.

A further tool requiring compilation of all the subroutines under investigation is a product known as FETE (Ingalls, 1971) available for IBM mainframes, which inserts into the object code a counter for each executable statement, and for each logical IF a counter for the number of times the branch was taken. A tool of this type is invaluable for identifying localized hot-spots, and for revealing possibly unexpected paths through the program logic. The effect of any change to the code is immediately measurable, and a modified example of its output is given in Fig. 15. Tools of this type have the additional advantage that they allow a test on whether every possible path through a program has been taken at least once.

```
STATEMENTS        *** FETE 370 ***    EXECUTIONS

        DO 14 I1 = 1,N                              2
          MAIN = N+1-I1                             9
          LPIV = INDEX(MAIN)                        9
          IF (LPIV-MAIN) 12,14,12                   9
12        ICOL = (LPIV-1)*IDIM+1                    6
          JCOL = ICOL+NMIN1                         6
          IPIVC = (MAIN-1)*IDIM+1-ICOL              6
          DO 13 I2 = ICOL,JCOL                      6
            I3 = I2+IPIVC                          48
            SWAP = A(I2)                           48
            A(I2) = A(I3)                          48
            A(I3) = SWAP                           48
13        CONTINUE                                 48
14 CONTINUE                                         9
        DETERM = DETER                              2
```

Fig. 15   A sample of FETE output

Tools which do not require any special compilation are also available. It is possible on some CDC computers to inspect the address of the current program instruction at a frequency which allows the address to be entered into a histogram covering the address space of the program. The resulting histogram shows peaks, and the addresses corresponding to the peaks can be used in conjunction with a load-map to locate the areas requiring attention. A similar product for use on IBM computers (Johnson and John-ston, 1976) assumes control of the object code and runs it as a sub-task. An ideal tool of this type would relate the histogram auto-matically to the load-map, making the investigation simpler for large programs. A histogram produced by one of these tools is shown in Fig. 16.

```
LOW  HIGH TOTAL   %    EACH * REPRESENTS 0.2332%

05000 – 05037   928  8.46  ********************************
05040 – 05077   768   .94  ****
05100 – 05137    38   .05
05140 – 05577              – – – – –  GAP  – – – – –
05600 – 05637   883  5.96  *************************
05640 – 05677   780   .95  ****
05700 – 05737   992  3.65  ****************
05740 – 05777   185   .23  *
06000 – 06037   388   .47  **
06040 – 06077   602  1.96  ********
06100 – 06137   996  1.22  *****
06140 – 06177   611   .75  ***
06200 – 06237   343   .42  **
06240 – 06277   155   .19  *
06300 – 06377              – – – – –  GAP  – – – – –
06400 – 06437   307   .37  **
06440 – 06477     2   .00
```

Fig. 16   Extract from a timing histogram

Large programs present a difficulty when being timed if they are in overlay form (see Section 5 of this chapter), as a given instruction address will be occupied by different instructions in the course of the test. To overcome this problem, the program must be restructured without overlays for the test, or the program logic altered in such a way that only one overlay at a time is used and tested.

When the timing information is finally available, in whatever form, the clear object of the exercise is to try to reduce the size of the timing peaks. If these are very narrow, it might be sufficient to examine the relevant few lines of code for some obvious improvement, perhaps one suggested in the following chapters. For broader peaks a further analysis of the algorithm may be a better approach. A successful attempt to reduce the peaks will naturally lead to the other parts of the program becoming of greater relative significance, and one is faced with a battle on a wider front and with a law of diminishing returns, as each step in the optimization is likely to bring a smaller percentage improvement.

An aspect of timing which can easily be overlooked is to examine the relationship between the real-time and CPU time of the program. For a given installation running under typical load conditions there should be some factor which is considered to be 'normal'. If the actual factor obtained is much larger than this reference value, it may indicate that the program is being slowed down in real-time by some unsuspected inefficiency in the program's I/O activity. A good computer system will provide the relevant statistics on resource utilization upon request, so that the necessary check can be carried out, and corrective action taken.

3. Clarity

It is commonly regarded as a desirable attribute of a program that it is clear to read. The program statements should be written in an obvious way, and the overall purpose of a section of code should be intelligible to any competent reader. Appropriate comment lines should guide the eye through the logic flow, and the general appearance of the program enhanced by a tidy layout. In this way a program becomes easier to understand, maintain and modify.

It might be asked why a section on clarity appears in a book on optimization, and there are, in fact, three immediate reasons for being concerned with this topic. In the first place, clarity in the program statements and simplicity in the logic flow and control structure of a subroutine have a direct and profound effect on the ability of optimizing compilers to perform their task effectively. We have seen in the previous chapter how code is often divided into basic blocks and loops, and optimized at those levels. If the blocks are short and the logic flow tortuous, with few obvious loops, there is little opportunity for the compiler to identify common sub-expressions, to move invariant code and to perform the other procedures we have outlined. An early investigation by Knuth (1971) revealed that in fact most programs do have a fairly simple and even trivial structure. In the programs studied, 68% of all assignment statements contained no operation, and nearly 60% of all DO-loops contained only one or two statements. Over 50% of the

DO-loops were singly nested. Almost all the sources of inefficiency he identified resulted from poorly optimized inner-loops, but advances in compilers since then invalidate many of the results, as they are now able to optimize badly written code better, unless the control structures are too inhibiting. This still remains a principal reason for avoiding the 'spaghetti' style of programming, with many branches, and especially backward ones. In short, clear logic, apart from its other advantages, has the effect of increasing the ability of the compiler to analyse and optimize a program.

The second aspect of clarity with respect to optimization is the positive effect it has on anyone dealing with the program. Any attempt to optimize the code is made simpler by the greater ease of understanding, whereas untidy code is not only difficult to understand, but it is less easy to find a way to improve it. The changes are less safe because of unforeseen side-effects and the person responsible may lose all motivation at the mere thought of having to tackle the work, and prefer to write a new program.

The third aspect of clarity is in contrast to the previous two. The process of optimizing code may sometimes lead to a program becoming less clear as a result of the changes made to it. Fortran has the great advantage of being a language in which mathematical expressions can be written in a very direct way (hence its name, FORmula TRANslation), but the re-arrangements required to optimize can lead to the Fortran statements becoming far removed from their obvious origins, with the negative consequences which have been indicated above. It is the opinion of some mathematicians that clarity should reign supreme and optimization be left to compiler writers (and the purchasers of equipment!), but this attitude, expressed already in the early 1970's as computers became cheaper, takes no account of the seemingly inexhaustible increase in demand for computer time.

Optimizing may also mean consciously abstaining from using certain powerful Fortran constructs, like the function reference, and this is indeed another negative effect of optimization. What must be clearly stated here is that any optimization involving such a loss of clarity should be envisaged only in sections of the code which warrant this treatment. In general, it is possible to counteract some of the negative effects by inserting suitable comment lines at the points where clarity has been affected, and full use should be made of them.

4. Portability

In Chapter 10 there appears a fuller discussion of the vexed question of program portability. This section serves as a reminder of a further negative aspect of optimization, namely the reduction in program portability which inevitably results. There are many desirable programming facilities which are absent from standard Fortran (ANSI, 1978), and which have to be emulated using awkward methods, manufacturer extensions or local libraries. There are, for instance, many applications which require the ability to manipulate the individual bits of a computer word. To set a bit is simple enough:

$$I = I + 16$$

sets the fifth bit from the right, but the assignment will go seriously wrong if the bit is already set, as it will unset the bit and set a higher one instead. To test the same bit requires the strange

$$MOD(I/16,2)$$

and the extensions to handling small groups of bits of arbitrary length is a tricky exercise which reduces many skilled programmers to counting on their fingers. It is then no small wonder that compiler writers have introduced into their products facilities to mask bits and shift words. The most powerful of these is perhaps the FLD function of Sperry. However, use of any special facilities on grounds of efficiency and ease of use immediately renders a program non-portable to computers using other compilers.

Another approach is to write bit handling functions as part of a local library in assembly language, and to translate them into the assembly language of any other computer which might be used. This solution is portable at the expense of some work, but highly inefficient, as it implies the use of external code rather than in-line sequences.

A similar situation arises with respect to I/O facilities, as the fastest implementations are often those using asynchronous I/O which is not defined in the standard (Section 5.11).

For a program which has to remain highly portable, the only way to resolve the conflict between portability and efficiency is to be sure to use any special facilities only in those areas of a program which will definitely benefit from their introduction, and to use comment lines to show how they should be written in standard

Fortran, in case that information should ever be required.

5. Space Optimization

The introduction of fast and cheap semi-conductor technology for constructing computer storage systems has meant that the former problem of fitting programs into tiny core memories is a thing of the past. No longer is it necessary to save a word in core by adopting dangerous practices like letting a given constant stand for two separate purposes, just because by coincidence, for instance, a logical unit number was the same as a histogram bin-width.

There are, however, still perfectly valid reasons for wanting to reduce the overall size of a program, and some of these are discussed in this section. It is first useful to point out that there is very little conflict between time and space optimization. An optimizing compiler produces faster code mainly because its transformations of the source and intermediate texts and its superior choice of machine instructions actually result in fewer and faster instructions being generated in the object code, which therefore requires less storage space, often by a considerable amount. Anything which can be done to help the compiler produce better code, even at the expense of a few extra data words in some cases, is likely to produce fewer machine instructions. There are some obvious exceptions, the heavy use of in-line code instead of external functions, for example. In general, the simplest way to keep the space requirement low is to use an optimizing compiler at its highest level.

If still more space must be saved, in order to fit into available memory or to enter a more favourable job class, there are several principal methods which can be applied. The first is to use scratch COMMON blocks in order to allow large arrays in different subroutines to share the same storage location. This can be a dangerous practice in incompletely tested programs, as a spurious dependence between subroutines may be introduced. It is necessary to make sure that the program's logic flow is not such that a subroutine called by another, directly or indirectly, uses storage locations whose values are required by the calling routine after control is returned to it. Overwriting is a difficult bug to locate. The inherent dangers of this approach mean that it should be used only for a few, selected, large arrays, if at all. In no circumstances should it be used for large numbers of local scalar variables, as this increases the danger of overwriting and degrades optimization (see Section 7.4). Similar arguments apply to the use of the EQUIVALENCE statement within a single subroutine.

Another method which may be applied in certain programs, is to place infrequently used large arrays onto a backing-store, either disc or magnetic tape, and to read in only portions of them as required. Direct access files are ideal for this treatment.

If large arrays are nevertheless proving to be a significant problem, it may be necessary to ensure that they do not contain large amounts of redundant information, for instance many zeros, or repeated items;   a more appropriate data structure might be called for.

Another possibility is to keep the data packed in some way, several items to one computer word, and to accept the overhead of packing and unpacking the data as they are required. In the case of CHARACTER data, this possibility is provided by the language and one should avoid using CHARACTER arrays of unit element length, thus

CHARACTER * 1000 C

is better than

CHARACTER C(1000)

A more sophisticated way of sharing storage between different parts of a program is to use a *dynamic memory manager*. Use of a dynamic memory manager involves keeping the data in a program in so-called *banks*. Each time new data are generated, the system is asked to provide storage for the new bank;   when a bank is no longer required the system is informed and the space occupied by the bank may then be re-used. In this way the problem of overwriting is completely overcome, and the total space requirement is reduced, provided the program logic is such that it never requires access to all the banks ever defined simultaneously. The use of a dynamic memory management system allows more advanced data structures to be constructed than are available in standard Fortran, but the code can become more obscure as the banks cannot bear meaningful variable names. Banks also provide a convenient means of communication between program modules, if the program has been structured in this way.

An example of how dynamic memory managers are used is given in Ex. 4, based on a system proposed for use in high-energy physics experiments (Brun *et al.,* 1982). In this system, all the data which it organizes are kept in blank COMMON. The system is initialized to define the boundaries of the area of this COMMON

```
        COMMON / / USER1(1000),FIRST,
     +     G(100000),
     +     LAST,USER2(2000)
*
*       INITIALIZE SYSTEM
        CALL GINIT(FIRST,LAST)
*
*       GET ONE BANK
        CALL GRQUST(NWORDS,IADDR)
        :
*
*       USE BANK
        G(IADDR + n) = ......
        :
        X = G(IADDR + m)
*
*       DELETE BANK
        CALL GDLETE(IADDR)
```

Example 4

which is available to it, and to define its own system variables. In order to obtain NWORDS of working space, a bank of length NWORDS is requested, and the location of the corresponding contiguous data area is returned. Subsequent use of this area requires this variable as a base address. When the bank is no longer required it may be deleted to free the space. More complicated applications allow banks to be named or numbered, to be linked logically to one another by pointers to form chains or trees, and to be grouped together in larger structures of sets of banks.

Another method of saving space is provided by many operating systems in the form of an *overlay loader*. Most programs can be divided into sections which form closed modules which require to communicate only *via* COMMON variables. As an example, a program may consist of an initialization section, a processing section and a termination section. Each section is called in turn by a main program. It is possible to place the routines belonging to each section together into units known as overlays; the main program is placed in the root overlay, and typically calls each of the other overlays in turn. A subroutine in one overlay cannot call a subroutine in another overlay at the same level, either directly with a call or indirectly through a call into the root and a call from there, as only one overlay other than the root overlay can occupy space in

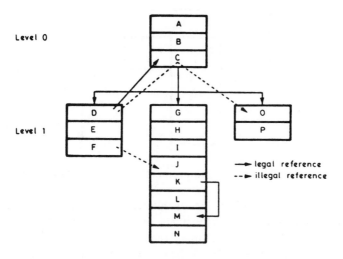

Fig. 17   A schematic diagram of an overlaid program

main storage at any one time. The other overlays are kept in a backing-store until they are required. Thus in Fig. 17 we note that each overlay is called in turn by the main program, that subroutine calls from low level overlays to subroutines in the root are permitted, but that references in the opposite sense and between subroutines in overlays of the same level are illegal. It is often possible to break up the overlays into primary and secondary overlays in the same manner, allowing the construction of a tree of overlays. In this way the maximum space requirement is the sum of the space required by the root plus the longest overlay, or longest combination of primary and secondary overlays (Fig. 18). When constructing overlays, care needs to be given to balancing the tree by reducing the length of the longest overlay by an appropriate use of secondary overlays, where available, and by consolidating short overlays until all overlays are of similar length.

Great care is required in the design of an overlaid program, as communication between overlays can take place only through COMMON blocks at the next higher level or above. Any subroutine which is required by two or more overlays should be considered for positioning in a higher level overlay, in order to avoid loading it repeatedly each time the overlays containing it are called. This will not change the space required if the subroutine is moved from the longest branch. A major drawback of overlay systems is the real-time overhead of loading them into main storage from the

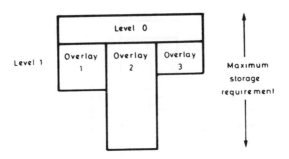

Fig. 18   The space requirement of an overlaid program

backing-store, and this can be prohibitive if the overlays need to be refreshed frequently. Normally it is necessary to ensure that the main processing overlay, for example, remains resident in main storage. Gentleman and Munro (1979) have described an algorithm for an optimal generation of overlay structures, but this has not been implemented in existing linkage editors.

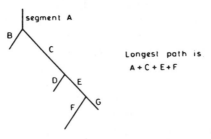

Fig. 19   A segmentation tree

A simpler and less restrictive method than overlaying is provided by the so-called *segment loaders*. The program is divided into modules known as segments, which may reference one another. Each time a segment is referenced which is not in main storage, it is brought in from the backing-store. The maximum space occupied is determined by the longest active path in the segmentation tree (Fig. 19). This method leaves the management of the calling and loading of segments to the operating system, and is far simpler to implement for a monolithic program which already exists and needs to be reduced in size, since overlaying such a program can often be a daunting task if the calling patterns are very complex.

Lastly, many compilers define large buffers for the I/O files referenced by the program, and it may be possible to reduce this requirement by changing the blocking of the files or by making similar machine-dependent modifications, details of which may normally be obtained from the manufacturer's documentation.

Questions

1. What steps do you take to select algorithms for any new program you write? In which publications are algorithms associated with your own field of interest to be found?

2. Using a program with which you are familiar, attempt to improve or replace the principal algorithm. Assess the robustness of the new code.

3. Use and compare all the profiling tools to which you have access. Are the results as you expected? Does the ' 10-90 ' rule hold?

4. Assess the clarity of a program with which you are unfamiliar.

5. To what extent do you compromise on efficiency in order to write portable code?

6. Use some of the techniques described in Section 4.5 to reduce the storage requirements of a program. Compare the difficulty of using each method.

5 BASIC OPTIMIZATION

1. Compiler Independent Optimization

There are certain factors which influence the efficiency with which a program runs regardless of the compiler used, and these form the subject matter of this chapter. For a particular installation they might include the fact that certain peripheral devices are in short supply or ill-matched in speed to the CPU, and should be used sparingly. There are also computers which suffer from a shortage of main memory either because the configuration is simply too small, or because of the basic architectural design, for instance when the address fields of machine language instructions do not encompass a sufficiently large range.

Other examples are, however, of a more general nature than these, and concern, for instance, a knowledge of the speed at which basic computational operations are performed. A good optimizing compiler may well generate fewer operations than a non-optimizing compiler, or try to substitute a fast operation for a slow one by an appropriate transformation of the source text, but in general, Fortran still does give the programmer a certain 'feel' for the way in which the code is going to execute.

However, when the object code executes, it might well be noticed that some basic optimization rules have been ignored, and that no degree of automatic optimization can cure the problem, as it is impossible for a compiler to analyse the intention of the author of the source text, or to know which of a multitude of possible values may enter into the calculation to be performed. Each potential source of such a loss of optimization is dealt with, point by point, in the following sections. Observance of the guidelines mentioned will help to improve execution speeds, even when the source code is compiled by the most primitive of compilers, but in examples in which expressions are re-ordered, a check might be necessary to ensure that no loss of precision has occurred. Of course, precision might just as well have been improved.

2. Initialization of Variables

It is a common feature of many programs that some fraction of the variables used needs to be initialized at the beginning of the program. In addition, some variables may require initialization at the beginning of each of a repetitive or iterative loop in the program logic flow. In the former case, it is normally more efficient to use a DATA statement than an explicit assignment at execution time:

```
INTEGER KOUNT(100)        INTEGER KOUNT(100)
:                         DO 1 J = 1,100
DATA KOUNT/100*0/             KOUNT(J) = 0
:                       1 CONTINUE
:                           :
:                           :
KOUNT(I) = KOUNT(I)+1     KOUNT(I) = KOUNT(I)+1
```

Example 5

In the first part of Ex. 5, the initialization of KOUNT will occur during the compilation itself, and if the number of variables to be initialized is very large, and the number of executions of the object code is also large, significant savings of execution time can result. In addition, the constants used for initialization do not have to be stored by the compiler in separate locations in the object code; the assignment

$$AWKWRD = 4.96623$$

requires a constant which is unlikely to be used elsewhere in the same program unit, and it will occupy its own memory location, just for this single assignment.

One warning is required. For the initialization of very large arrays, it might happen that the object code generated requires a significant amount of space at load-time, and so becomes counter-productive in reducing turn-round time, because of an excessively large load-step memory requirement. In this case, especially when the initialization is to a constant value, the use at execution time of a fast move or copy routine, supplied as part of most installation libraries, should be considered.

```
PARAMETER (LEN = 10000)
REAL A(LEN),B(LEN)
CALL ZERO(A,LEN)
CALL FILL(B,1.,LEN)
```

Example 6

In Ex. 6, the elements of the array A are set to zero by a presumed fast routine able to zero elements of an array, and B is filled with the value 1. by a fast fill routine.

In cases where large arrays must be repeatedly initialized and where no such fast library routines are available, the use of initialization loops can still be completely avoided if at least a fast copy routine is available.

```
      PARAMETER (LEN = 100)
      REAL A(LEN),SAVE(LEN)
      DATA SAVE/LEN*3.0/
      DO 1 ITER = 1,NITER
         CALL COPY(SAVE,A,LEN)
         :
    1 CONTINUE
```

Example 7

In Ex. 7, the presumed fast copy routine substitutes for a loop, setting the elements of A back to 3.0 at the beginning of each iteration.

This type of inefficiency is not present in all loaders, but interleaving data array initialization will invariably generate large loader tables, thus

```
DATA (A(I),B(I),I = 1,250)/500*0./
```

is less efficient than

```
DATA (A(I),I = 1,250),(B(I),I = 1,250)/500*0./
```

in which the data elements are in contiguous storage locations.

Execution time can always be saved by the complete elimination of unnecessary operations. In the case of an initialization it is necessary to consider whether it is actually needed at all. There is a widespread programming habit of setting all variables initially to zero, and this unwise practice is compounded by the fact that many loaders perform this same task for all data words not explicitly defined in DATA statements. In the former case, the user deprives himself of the protection afforded by some machines of having words preset to a bit pattern which is recognized as undefined if used inadvertently during execution. For instance, an error in the logic of the program may fail to place into a variable the value which is expected, and subsequent use of that variable will cause a wrong result to be calculated, rather than generating a run-time error and diagnostic. The wrong result may well escape detection. In the latter case, the user loses not only the protection just mentioned, but finds also that any mis-typed variable has a defined value, and can again generate wrong results. In addition, if code is written assuming memory initialization to zero, the program is difficult to transport to other machines where this is not the case. The ideal default method is for the loader to generate a bit pattern which is directly recognizable as undefined by the hardware, as is the case with many CDC systems. Alternatively there are bit patterns which generate an interrupt if used in a calculation (because their value gives an underflow or overflow), or an address error if used as an index (because their value is outside the address range of the computer). On IBM and similar computers, the value 81818181_{16} has this property, but this feature is unfortunately not available as a standard feature.

3. Arithmetic Operations

When writing code it is important to understand that there are usually great differences in the speed at which the various arithmetic operations are performed. For the basic operations the order is normally, beginning with the fastest:

$$
\begin{array}{rl}
\text{addition and subtraction} & +\ - \\
\text{multiplication} & * \\
\text{division} & / \\
\text{exponentiation} & **
\end{array}
$$

Whenever the opportunity arises to rearrange code so as to substitute fast operations for slow ones, it should be taken. This procedure is known as *reducing the strength* of operations. A well known instance of this is the use of Horner's Rule for polynomial evaluation, in which exponentiation can be completely eliminated: to evaluate

$$y = a_0x^n + a_1x^{n-1} + a_2x^{n-2} \ldots\ldots a^n$$

with $n = 5$, and with the coefficient array A dimensioned A(0:5), we may rewrite

```
Y =
  + A(0)*X**5 + A(1)*X**4 + A(2)*X**3 + A(3)*X**2 + A(4)*X + A(5)
```

as

```
Y = (((((A(0)*X + A(1))*X + A(2))*X + A(3))*X + A(4))*X + A(5)
```

which has the same number of additions and multiplications, but no exponentiations.

Another example of the elimination of an exponentiation is in an alternating series like

$$(-1)^{**}I*F(I)$$

which can be summed in a single inefficient loop (see Section 4.1), but is better handled (for even N) by a loop such as

```
      SUM = 0.
      DO 1 I = 1,N,2
         SUM = SUM - F(I) + F(I + 1)
    1 CONTINUE
```

Of course, if the difference between the two terms is known in terms of I, this quantity may be directly substituted for the two function references.

Arithmetic operations can often be saved by factoring expressions, thus

$$A = B*(E + F) - C*(E + F) + D*(E + F)$$

can be rewritten as

$$A = (B - C + D)*(E + F)$$

using fewer operations. In general, expressions should be written in a direct way, avoiding the use of necessary temporary variables:

$$A \ = \ B + C + D*E$$

not

$$T1 \ = \ B + C$$
$$T2 \ = \ D*E$$
$$A \ = \ T1 + T2$$

thus saving assignments which can be as costly as operations.

A complication in this area is the need to consider the difference in speed between operations on various data types. On a given machine, and especially on scientific ones, the floating-point hardware may be faster than the hardware used to perform integer arithmetic. On very small machines, on the other hand, there may be no floating-point hardware at all, and these operations will be performed by calls to Fortran library functions. Yet other machines have no integer multiply or divide units, and will convert integer operands to reals before performing the operation, and convert them back to integer after, leading to these operations becoming slower on integer operands than on reals. There is a great disparity between machines which perform all floating-point operations in double-precision at the hardware level, such as large IBM systems, and those which perform the operations by software, such as CDC systems. In the former case, explicit double-precision operations are carried out at the same speed as single-precision ones, whereas in the latter case a double-precision addition can require nearly 20 separate instructions (see Section 9.3).

In general, divisions are very much slower than multiplications (by factors of up to five or more), and are particularly to be avoided. An example of the poor use of divisions is contained in Ex. 8, where two arrays of equal length N are merged into a third array, using division for the subscripting inside a loop. The alternative code using a counter executes far more efficiently.

```
                                     J = 1
      DO 1 I = 2,2*N,2               DO 1 I = 2,2*N,2
         C(I-1) = A(I/2)                C(I-1) = A(J)
         C(I)  = B(I/2)                 C(I)  = B(J)
    1 CONTINUE                          J = J+1
                                   1 CONTINUE
```

Example 8

It needs to be remembered that the MOD function contains a hidden division, and should be used with care. Repeated division can be eliminated by consolidating the divisors. For instance

$$A = B/C/D/E$$

should appear as

$$A = B/(C*D*E)$$

For exponentiation large differences arise depending on whether the exponent is an integer constant, an integer variable or a real variable. In the first case compound multiplications are often substituted, whereas in the other two cases calls to Fortran functions are required, preceded if necessary by a conversion of an integer base to a real value (which is a negligible operation compared to the exponentiation itself). For integer exponents, the speed may depend strongly on whether the base is integer or real, in those cases where integer and floating-point arithmetic are performed at very different speed.

A special case of exponentiation is the constant exponent value 0.5 – in this case the SQRT function normally provides a result faster, as it typically uses a special purpose algorithm, and does not have recourse, as is the case for other real exponents, to several additional functions to perform the intermediate ALOG and EXP operations required for general exponentiation (see, for example, IBM, 1981d).

Taking all these points together, we arrive at a typical ordering as shown in Table 1, whose contents must be verified for each computer, as even different models of the same type may have different characteristics.

Table 1

The approximate order of arithmetic operations, starting with the fastest. Some special cases are discussed in the text.

Operation name	Symbol	Example
Integer addition and subtraction	+ –	I + J; I – J
Floating-point addition and subtraction	+ –	A + B; A – B
Integer multiply	*	I*J
Floating-point multiply	*	A*B
Floating-point divide	/	A/B
Integer divide	/	I/J
Exponentiation to a positive integer constant	**	A**3; J**4
Exponentiation to an integer variable	**	A**I; J**I
Exponentiation to a real variable	**	A**B

4. Mixed Mode Arithmetic

The rules of Fortran 77 allow mixed mode arithmetic. The general conversion rule is that the result of any valid sequence of operations is the type of the least simple operand. Thus, if I is an integer, A a real, C complex and D double-precision, then the result of $A + I$ is real, of $A + D$ is double-precision, and of $I + A + C$ is complex.

The intermediate steps of a computation are carried out according to the left-to-right rule, after the evaluation of expressions in parentheses, and they are performed in an implicit type governed by the types of the operands at that step of the computation. Thus, in the expression

$$I + (A + J) + C$$

the first step is the addition of A to J, yielding a real result, the second step is the floating-point addition of I to the first result, and the final step is the complex addition of C to the second result, yielding a final complex result.

When the final result is used to define another variable in an assignment statement, a conversion to the type of that variable is required if the two sides of the assignment are of different types. Thus

$$I = A + D$$

produces an integer conversion of a double-precision result, rounded down to the nearest whole number.

Each time such a conversion is performed during the evaluation of an expression or in an assignment, a serious overhead is incurred, as additional instructions are required for every conversion. These instructions, when converting to or from type integer, perform the non-trivial task of reformatting the data word, which often also involves a normalization when the conversion is from type integer. The conversion can actually take more time than the arithmetic operations carried out in the computation of an expression. This can be appreciated by considering the usual integer data word format (see Section 2.1):

and comparing it with the usual, more complex, floating-point data word format:

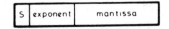

On IBM computers, for instance, five instructions must be executed to perform one conversion, and this number is typical.

Normalization is a procedure used to preserve the maximum amount of precision during computations, by keeping the significant bits of the mantissa away from its low-order end, where they would be subject to possible rounding errors. The mantissa is stored in such a way that no zero bit (or zero hexadecimal digit on some byte machines) is kept at its left-hand, or high-order end. To achieve this, an unnormalized mantissa is shifted left by the appropriate number of positions and the exponent adjusted accordingly.

It should by now be clear that avoiding mixed mode arithmetic is both desirable and difficult; desirable since execution speed is thereby improved, and difficult as it is so easy to write in mixed mode. One way to make the use of mixed mode arithmetic at least visible is to use explicitly the Fortran conversion functions, that is to write, for instance

$$A = FLOAT(I)$$

rather than

$$A = I$$

The use of such functions in no way impairs the execution speed, as they are compiled in-line (in the place where the call is made rather than jumping to a function supplied by the loader), but they make the use of mixed mode arithmetic very obvious, and might thereby act as stimulus to tackling the problem.

REAL I
:
$A = B/Q + 14. - I$
$D = A - I + Q*4.$

Example 9

The elimination of conversions can be approached by one of three methods:

a) The conversions can be avoided by an appropriate typing of variables. If an integer quantity appears only in expressions involving variables of other types, it should be promoted to that other type, as shown for the variable I in Ex. 9, (assuming that I is nowhere defined in an integer arithmetic expression containing divisions). However, overriding Fortran implicit types is not normally to be encouraged, as it can lead to some confusion when reading code, and the use of a more appropriate variable name for I is to be preferred if the problem is already spotted when the code is being first written. Correct typing of constants is equally important. In

IF (Y.EQ.4)   J = 10.

one and possibly two conversions are required, whereas

IF (Y.EQ.4.)   J = 10

involves none.

b) It is sometimes possible to use a duplicate variable name, as shown in Ex. 10(a). In the second version, the extra increment of X can actually be faster than the conversion of I contained in the first version. In this particular case, Fortran 77 allows yet another alternative, Ex. 10(b), but this is just as slow as the first version, because of the conversion of X to type integer in the subscript calculation.

```
                              X = 1.
    DO 1 I = 1,N              DO 1 I = 1,N
       A(I) = I                  A(I) = X
  1 CONTINUE                     X = X+1.
                             1  CONTINUE
```

Example 10(a)

```
    DO 1 X = 1,N
       A(NINT(X)) = X
  1 CONTINUE
```

Example 10(b)

c) The number of mixed mode conversions occurring in a mixed mode expression can be kept to a minimum by appropriate grouping of the variables. Comparing

$$X = A+I+B+J+C+K$$

with

$$X = FLOAT(I+J+K)+A+B+C$$

we note that the number of integer to real conversions has been reduced from three to just one.

5. Character Variables

Fortran 77 introduced the new data type CHARACTER to provide a convenient means of manipulating strings of literals. The new operator // denoting concatenation was introduced to enable two character strings to be joined together into one contiguous string. A set of new functions was also provided, allowing the conversion of characters to their positions in a collating sequence and *vice versa*, to locate one string in another, and to test on the relative position of one character in a collating sequence. All this was intended to replace the old Hollerith constants of Fortran 66.

Unfortunately, the new data type cannot always be used in the way that was possible with Hollerith constants, as the standard defines no mapping of a character into a computer word, and it is therefore not possible to mix characters with other data types, for instance in a COMMON block or through an EQUIVALENCE statement. Concepts such as null (*i.e.* empty) strings and variable length strings are not included in the language, nor is even a complete collating sequence defined (see Section 10.3).

All this is bad enough, but what is especially significant in the context of this book, is the apparently widespread view of compiler writers that character manipulation is an activity of little interest to Fortran programmers, and one that can safely be implemented inefficiently. For example, an external call is likely to be generated for any character operation, rather than an in-line sequence of instructions, and the IBM VS Fortran compiler performs no optimization of character expressions, even in loops.

This attitude ignores applications such as source text management, computer typesetting and compiler writing itself, where in each case there exist examples which have been written in Fortran, and which in their own contexts all need to be very efficient to be useful. The program in Appendix B is such an example.

As there are, in fact, some efficient implementations (*e.g.* the VAX compiler), there will be vast differences in character processing speeds on different computers as long as the present situation persists. Depending on the application involved, any programmer who is concerned with efficient character handling, and who has confirmed that the remarks made above are indeed valid for his compiler, has no other alternatives than either to make use of the obsolete features, which are implemented in most compilers as an aid to backward compatibility, or to have recourse to any totally non-standard facilities which may be provided by his local installation, or to select a more appropriate language, such as SNOBOL.

Where CHARACTER variables are used, some local inefficiencies can be avoided by defining the lengths of variables to be no longer than absolutely necessary, otherwise hidden overheads can arise in assignment statements. Thus, in

```
CHARACTER *80 LINE
    :
LINE = 'KEY'
```

the assignment will blank fill LINE with 77 blanks. On the other hand, this implicit blank filling is superior to explicit filling in a DO-loop:

```
LINE = ' '
```

is more efficient than

```
    DO 1 I = 1,80
       LINE(I:I) = ' '
  1 CONTINUE
```

The use of the concatenation operator should be avoided where possible, as fewer character manipulations can be achieved by other means. For instance, the combined length of two strings is obtained more efficiently by

$$LEN12 = LEN(STR1) + LEN(STR2)$$

than by

$$LEN12 = LEN(STR1//STR2)$$

Another example is the use of the sub-string notation, where we can compare the assignment

$$A(I:I) = '*'$$

with the clumsy concatenation

$$A = A(:I-1)//'*'//A(I+1:)$$

6. DO-Loops

Most of the execution time in programs is spent in the execution of DO-loops, and it is here that the greatest gains in optimization are to be achieved. This fact has led compiler writers to devote their greatest efforts to the optimization of loops, both DO-loops and simple IF-loops, and we shall return to this topic in the following chapters. In this chapter on compiler independent optimization, we confine ourselves to some basic considerations concerning loop usage.

To begin with we need to consider the difference between a DO-loop as defined by the 1966 Fortran standard and the new 1978 standard. The form of the DO-loop has been generalized from

DO *sl iv* = *m1,m2,m3*   *sl* = statement label
iv = integer control variable
m1,m2,m3 = loop parameters

to

DO *sl v* = *exp1,exp2,exp3*   *v* = control variable

$$exp1,2,3 \;=\; \text{any expression}$$

Where necessary, *exp1*, *exp2* or *exp3* are converted to the type of *v*; they may be any of the types REAL, INTEGER or DOUBLE PRECISION.

The status of the control variable has also changed: whereas the value of *iv* was not previously available on completion of the loop, under the new standard the most recent value of *v* is available after completion or on exit from the loop.

Previously the number of iterations was normally determined by adding *m3* successively to *m1* until the value *m2* was exceeded. Only on the CRAY-1, under the CFT compiler, was a test on loop completion made at the beginning of the loop; all others allowed one iteration through the loop whatever the initial values of *m1, m2* and *m3*. Under the new standard, the number of iterations is defined at the beginning of the loop as exactly

$$\text{MAX}(\text{INT}((exp2 - exp1 + exp3)/exp3),0)$$

and as can be seen, the number of iterations may well be zero, giving rise to the concept of the *zero-trip loop*. The loop parameters may be modified in the loop without having any effect on the number of iterations.

The third parameter, *exp3*, may be either positive or negative. Some compilers will generate more efficient code if its sign is known at compile-time, and this fact should be borne in mind in critical loops.

6.1 Loop avoidance

Considering now the case of loops under a compiler conforming to the Fortran 77 standard, we can see that the following steps are necessary to secure correct execution of the body of the loop:

step 1   calculate number of iterations
step 2   test for zero (and branch if necessary)
step 3   keep value of control variable
step 4   execute body of loop
step 5   decrement iteration counter, increment control variable
step 6   test for completion (and branch to step 3 if necessary).

Compared with the execution of a section of equivalent straight-line code it can be seen that steps 1 to 3 constitute a loop

initialization overhead, and steps 5 and 6 a loop completion overhead. The magnitude of these overheads is such that the first rule of
DO-loops can now be enunciated, namely to avoid trivial loops
completely, as the cost of their overhead is likely to be comparable
with or even exceed the cost of executing the body of the loop. This
means particularly that quite short loops such as Ex. 11 should not
be used.

```
      DO 1 I = 1,2
        A(I) = 0.
    1 CONTINUE
```

Example 11

Other loops with a small number of iterations such as Ex. 12
should be replaced by their explicit equivalent:

$$Y = ((A(0)*X + A(1))*X + A(2))*X + A(3)$$

In the case of such a short loop as this, which contains some
expressions requiring evaluation, the compiler may impose the additional penalty of reserving some registers for intermediate results, at
the expense of using them where they are more urgently needed, for
instance in the surrounding code.

```
      Y = A(0)
      DO 1 I = 1,3
        Y = Y*X + A(I)
    1 CONTINUE
```

Example 12

6.2 Loop nesting

This question of register usage depends, of course, on the context in
which such loops are placed. In particular, to position a trivial loop
as the deepest of a set of nested loops can cause the loss of registers for the possibly more significant second deepest loop, as the
greatest degree of optimization is usually reserved for the innermost
loop.

The way in which loops are nested is subject to other considerations. In Ex. 13 the total number of initializations could be reduced
from 1101 to 23 and the number of tests on completion from 3100

to 2022, if the three loops were to be nested in the reverse order.

```
      DO 1 I = 1,100        No. of initializations  =        1
        DO 2 J = 1,10                                       100
          DO 3 K = 1,2                                     1000
            :                                             -----
            :                 Total                 =     1101
            :                                             =====
3           CONTINUE          No. of tests on
            :                 completion            =     2000
2         CONTINUE                                        1000
1       CONTINUE                                           100
                                                          -----
                              Total                 =     3100
                                                          =====
```

Example 13

From this example of inefficient nesting, it can be seen that loops should be nested, where the problem allows it, such that the most repeated loops are the innermost ones. This requirement has indeed become more important with the advent of Fortran 77, as the standard requires that the value of the control variable be available outside the range of the loop, and its value therefore needs to be stored every time the loop is completed, which is an additional overhead. (In fact, many Fortran 66 compilers did this anyway).

A further consideration in nested loops occurs when the inner one is executed only for certain combinations of loop indices, as in Ex. 46(a), where the body of the innermost loop is executed only if the sum of all the indices is equal to N. These loops will execute many times faster rewritten as shown in Ex. 46(b), where better use of the loop parameters eliminates huge overheads.

```
      DO 1 I1 = 0,N
        DO 1 I2 = 0,N
          DO 1 I3 = 0,N
            DO 1 I4 = 0,N
              IF (I1 + I2 + I3 + I4 .NE. N) GO TO 1
              :
1 CONTINUE
```

Example 14(a)

```
DO 1 I1 = 0,N
   DO 1 I2 = 0,N − I1
      DO 1 I3 = 0,N − (I1 + I2)
         I4 = N − (I1 + I2 + I3)
         :
1 CONTINUE
```

Example 14(b)

6.3 Loop parameters

The use of the third loop parameter which determines the *stride*, or iteration increment, through array elements referenced in the loop, is sometimes neglected, and as a result explicit subscript calculations are performed quite unnecessarily. Comparing the two loops in Ex. 15, it can be seen that a subscript expression is eliminated when all three loop parameters are used to control the loop, which in addition expresses the actual intention of the programmer more directly.

```
DO 1 I = 1,10                DO 1 I = 7,34,3
   J = 3*I + 4                  X(I) = Y(I) + C
   X(J) = Y(J) + C        1 CONTINUE
1 CONTINUE
```

Example 15

6.4 Loop manipulation

```
DO 1 I = 1,N                 DO 1 I = 2,N,2
   A(I) = B(I)*C(I)             A(I − 1) = B(I − 1)*C(I − 1)
1 CONTINUE                      A(I) = B(I)*C(I)
                           1 CONTINUE
```

Example 16

In critical situations it can be useful to *unroll* a loop in order to reduce the number of overheads per operation. The loop in Ex. 16 can be rewritten as shown, obtaining two multiplications per loop test. This can be especially effective on machines where the multiplications are pipelined, and the loop can be unrolled even further (but should not go beyond the stack size of a machine with an instruction stack). Care must be taken if N is not a multiple of the chosen degree of unrolling; in this case some extra code is necessary after the loop.

Another example of unrolling is the elimination of a short outer loop based on an explicit constant: compare the two loops

```
DO 1 I = 1,3                    DO 1 J = 1,N
   DO 1 J = 1,N                    X(1,J) = Y(1,J)+Z(J,1)
      X(I,J) = Y(I,J)+Z(J,I)       X(2,J) = Y(2,J)+Z(J,2)
1 CONTINUE                         X(3,J) = Y(3,J)+Z(J,3)
                                1 CONTINUE
```

The important effect of loop unrolling has been measured by Dongarra and Hinds (1979).

In a similar way, loops can be combined to save on overheads as shown in Ex. 17, but combinations of loops should be used with care if the combined loop is no longer short enough to fit into the stack of a stack machine, or if optimization is otherwise adversely affected.

```
DO 1 I = 1,100                  DO 1 I = 1,100
   A(I) = B(I)*C(I)+4.             A(I) = B(I)*C(I)+4.
1 CONTINUE                         D(I) = E(I)+5.
   DO 2 J = 1,100               1 CONTINUE
      D(J) = E(J)+5.
2 CONTINUE
```

Example 17

The reverse technique is *unswitching*, useful in the case of loops containing an invariant logical test, as shown in Ex. 18. The second version avoids repeated testing of the invariant, and increases the possible degree of optimization by creating shorter loops.

6.5 Elimination of common operations in loops

Short summation loops sometimes contain an operation which is applied to each term of the sum. Such loops should be examined to determine whether the operation can be removed entirely from the loop. In Ex. 19, a multiplication is removed, saving $N-1$ multiplications, and in Ex. 20, $N/2-1$ subtractions can be saved (for even N).

There is sometimes a possibility to re-use certain common sub-expressions, even though they are loop dependent. In Ex. 21(a),

```
      DO 1 I = 1,100              IF (FLAG) THEN
         IF (FLAG) GO TO 3           DO 1 I = 1,100
         A(I) = B(I) - 2.*C(I)          A(I) = B(I) + 3.*D(I)
         GO TO 1                        B(I) = X*D(I)
  3      A(I) = B(I) + 3.*D(I)     1 CONTINUE
         B(I) = X*D(I)            ELSE
  1 CONTINUE                       DO 2 J = 1,100
                                      A(J) = B(J) - 2.*C(J)
                                 2 CONTINUE
                                   ENDIF
```

Example 18

```
      SUM = 0.                    SUM = 0.
      DO 1 I = 1,N                DO 1 I = 1,N
         SUM = SUM + X*A(I)          SUM = SUM + A(I)
  1 CONTINUE                     1 CONTINUE
                                   SUM = X*SUM
```

Example 19

```
      ISUM = 0                    ISUM = 0
      DO 1 I = 2,N,2              DO 1 I = 2,N,2
         ISUM = ISUM + L(I) - 2      ISUM = ISUM + L(I)
  1 CONTINUE                     1 CONTINUE
                                   ISUM = ISUM - N
```

Example 20

we note that the values of $A(I)$ and $A(I+1)$ are both used with a common factor in the loop. It is possible to rearrange the code such that the value of $A(I+1)*C$ is used a second time on the second and subsequent iterations in the definition of $B(I)$, by introducing a temporary variable as shown in Ex. 21(b).

6.6 Elimination of redundant tests

It is important to remove from loops any redundant tests, as they cannot be removed as dead-code by a compiler. In Ex. 22, the logical IF condition can clearly never be satisfied, and should be

```
DO 1 I = 1,10                  T01 = A(1)*C
  B(I) = A(I)*C+Q              DO 1 I = 1,10
  D(I) = A(I+1)*C                B(I) = T01+Q
1 CONTINUE                       T01 = A(I+1)*C
                                 D(I) = T01
                             1 CONTINUE
```

       (a)   (b)

Example 21

eliminated, saving a test each time through the loop.

```
DO 1 I = 1,N
  X(I) = A(I)**2
  Y(I) = -B(I)**2
  IF (X(I).LT.0.) GO TO 1
  Z(I) = X(I)
1 CONTINUE
```

Example 22

7. Invariant Code

Within a loop there may be expressions or sub-expressions whose components do not depend in any way on the control variable of the loop. Such code is known as invariant code, and it will be considered in the following two chapters. Here we are concerned with a type of invariant code which cannot be eliminated by an optimizing compiler and which has to be treated explicitly by the programmer, namely invariant arrays, or their equivalent.

In Ex. 23, a fragment from a minimization program, we notice that the elements of A and R are recalculated on each pass through the outer loop, but that the array C remains unchanged. If N is large, and space is not an important consideration, but if the division is proving to be a hot-spot in the program, then a temporary array RC can be defined outside the outer loop. Its elements have all to be set to the reciprocal of the corresponding elements of C, and the division can then be replaced by a multiplication by RC(I,J).

```
    DO 1 M = 1,N
       :
    DO 2 J = 1,K
       DO 2 I = 1,L
          R(I,J) = ...........
          A(I,J) = ...........
2   CONTINUE
       :
       :
    RN = 0.
    AN = 0.
    DO 3 J = 1,K
       DO 3 I = 1,L
          RN = RN + R(I,J)*R(I,J)/C(I,J)
          AN = AN + A(I,J)*A(I,J)*C(I,J)
3   CONTINUE
1   CONTINUE
```

Example 23

8. Branches

Table 2

The rough order of branch statements, starting with the fastest

Branch	Example
Unconditional GO TO	GO TO 1
Assigned GO TO	ASSIGN 1 TO K
	:
	GO TO K,(1,2,3)
Logical IF	IF (I.EQ.0) GO TO 2
Arithmetic IF	IF (I) 1,2,3
Computed GO TO	GO TO (1,2,3), I − 2
(see text)	

Just as with the arithmetic operations, it is essential to be aware of the fact that the various branching control statements execute at rather different speeds, and to make use of this knowledge when choosing the type of branch for a particular control structure, although a possible loss in clarity must also be guarded against. The typical but by no means general order, starting with the fastest, is given in Table 2. A slight variation in this order is that on some computers the arithmetic IF-statement is somewhat faster than the logical IF. The arithmetic IF does, however, present its own problems in comprehensibility, especially when used as a two-branch IF. For example,

     IF (I – 2) 2,1,2
  2 ....

is less obvious than

     IF (I.EQ.2) GO TO 1

and tracking down errors caused by wrongly programmed arithmetic IF's can be a programming overhead which nullifies any slight gain in raw efficiency. In many cases, where the arithmetic IF is nevertheless used, the fastest execution is obtained if the first of the three possible branches is the one normally taken. When used as a two-branch IF, some compilers will treat it as the equivalent logical IF, provided one of the statement labels immediately follows the test. Hence,

     IF (I – J) 1,1,2   becomes   IF (I – J.GT.0) GO TO 2
  1 ....   1 ....

Another variation is that some computers use a fast instruction when testing against zero, thus avoiding a load of the constant zero. In this case, when I can take only the value 0 or 1,

     IF (I.NE.0) GO TO 1

is faster than

     IF (I.EQ.1) GO TO 1

Although the computed GO TO is, in principle, the slowest of these control statements, it becomes faster than a sequence of IF tests when the number in the sequence exceeds about six. In Ex. 24 the sequence might well work faster written as

     GO TO (1,2,3,4,5,6),I

especially if the different values of I are evenly distributed amongst the different possibilities. Under Fortran 77, I in this example may be an expression, whose speed of evaluation must also be taken into account.

```
IF (I.EQ.1) GO TO 1
IF (I.EQ.2) GO TO 2
IF (I.EQ.3) GO TO 3
IF (I.EQ.4) GO TO 4
IF (I.EQ.5) GO TO 5
IF (I.EQ.6) GO TO 6
```

Example 24

Looking again at Ex. 24, it is possible to save some tests on I if the frequency of occurrence of the various tested values is known in advance. If, for instance, I normally has the value 6, and only infrequently any of the other values, the test

```
IF (I.EQ.6) GO TO 6
```

should appear as the first in the sequence, avoiding redundant testing against all the other values. The same remark holds for the order of testing using the Fortran 77 block IF:

```
IF (test1) THEN
    statements
ELSEIF (test2) THEN
    statements
ELSEIF (test3) THEN
    statements
ENDIF
```

With some compilers, this is true also for a multiple condition logical IF. The components of an IF test separated by .OR. operators should be ordered such that the condition most likely to be satisfied is placed first in the sequence. When logical expressions are separated by .AND. operators, the condition most likely to fail should come first. Because of this, it is also better to use statements containing only either .OR.'s or .AND.'s, rather than combinations of the two.

When using a compiler which does not contain this feature, it is possible to decompose a test into its component parts for individual testing; the expression

IF (I.EQ.1.OR.J.EQ.9.OR.K.EQ.15) GO TO 1

can be more efficiently written as in Ex. 25, since the testing is broken off as soon as the required condition is fulfilled.

IF (I.EQ.1) GO TO 1
IF (J.EQ.9) GO TO 1
IF (K.EQ.15) GO TO 1

Example 25

Compound tests, especially those containing the .NOT. operator, usually take longer to evaluate than their simpler equivalents obtained by the application of de Morgan's theorem, which states that the complement of a logical condition is obtained by reversing the sense of the individual tests, and by changing each .AND. to an .OR., and *vice versa*. Thus

IF (.NOT.(I.EQ.0)) GO TO 1

is equivalent to

IF (I.NE.0) GO TO 1

and

IF (.NOT.(I.NE.K.OR.J.EQ.4.AND.L.GT.0)) GO TO 1

may be written more simply as

IF (I.EQ.K.AND.(J.NE.4.OR.L.LE.0)) GO TO 1

Note that the precedence of the .AND. operator in a compound expression has to be maintained in the rewritten version by the use of parentheses. In this example, the logical expression using the .NOT. operator contains one additional logical operation, and will have to be completely evaluated. In its revised form, an optimizing compiler may produce object code which breaks off the evaluation immediately if I is found not to be equal to K.

Also to be avoided is the inadvertent splitting of a relational operator into its two components:

IF (I.LT.0.OR.I.GT.0)   J = I+2

is obviously inferior to

IF (I.NE.0)   J = I+2

Another source of branching inefficiency which needs to be avoided is the use of mutually exclusive tests, or of repeated tests in sequences. For instance,

```
IF (I.EQ.1)   J = K+2
IF (I.EQ.1)   L = 0
IF (I.NE.1)   J = K-3+N
```

may be replaced by

```
IF (I.EQ.1) THEN
   J = K+2
   L = 0
ELSE
   J = K-3+N
ENDIF
```

thereby exploiting fully the power of this Fortran 77 construct, and reducing also the number of tests required.

Another example, shown in Ex. 26 (a) and (b), demonstrates the way a complex series of IF-statements may be replaced by more efficient block IF's, to simulate a decision table.

```
IF (I.GT.0.AND.J.GT.0.AND.K.EQ.0)   L = 2
IF (I.GT.0.AND.J.GT.0.AND.K.EQ.2)   L = 2
IF (I.GT.0.AND.J.LT.0.AND.K.EQ.1)   L = 2
IF (I.EQ.0.AND.J.LT.0.AND.K.EQ.2)   L = 2
IF (I.EQ.N.AND.J.GT.0.AND.K.EQ.1)   L = 2
IF (I.EQ.N.AND.J.GT.0.AND.K.EQ.3)   L = 2
IF (I.EQ.N.AND.J.LT.0.AND.K.EQ.0)   L = 2
IF (I.EQ.N.AND.J.LT.0.AND.K.EQ.3)   L = 2
```

Example 26(a)

Yet another inefficient practice is to use complicated logical tests to steer various paths through a single section of code. If the tests form a substantial fraction of the statements, it would be better to

```
IF (I.GT.0) THEN
    IF (J.GT.0) THEN
        IF (K.EQ.0.OR.K.EQ.2) L = 2
    ELSEIF (J.LT.0.AND.K.EQ.1) THEN
        L = 2
    ENDIF
ELSEIF (I.EQ.0.AND.J.LT.0.AND.K.EQ.2) THEN
    L = 2
ELSEIF (I.EQ.N) THEN
    IF (J.GT.0) THEN
        IF (K.EQ.1.OR.K.EQ.3) L = 2
    ELSEIF (J.LT.0) THEN
        IF (K.EQ.0.OR.K.EQ.3) L = 2
    ENDIF
ENDIF
```

Example 26(b)

write out the various sequences of code explicitly, which would also
ease the task of an optimizing compiler in analysing the logic flow.
The IF...THEN...ELSE construct of Fortran 77 provides a powerful
means of expressing complicated logical conditions, while at the same
time simplifying flow analysis in the compiler by reducing the number of statement labels required.

Finally, it might be mentioned that IF-statements can be completely eliminated from sequences such as

```
IF (X.EQ.Y) THEN
    COND = .TRUE.
ELSE
    COND = .FALSE.
ENDIF
```

which is more efficiently written as

```
COND = X.EQ.Y
```

9. Calling Sequences

Fortran permits two possible ways of passing information between
subprograms, if we ignore the very costly use of intermediate I/O
files. One method is to place the variables in question in a
COMMON block, and to reference this block in all routines, not

forgetting possibly an appropriate SAVE statement if this Fortran 77 feature is installed according to the standard. To pass the value of a variable, the relevant assignment is made in the calling routine, where the address calculation may possibly be performed at compile time, and the called routine can access and modify the value directly from the memory location defined by the variable's position in the COMMON block. Using different variable lists with a single COMMON name allows more complicated mapping of variables onto memory locations, and even a change of data type in a limited number of cases, but this is normally regarded as a bad programming practice, and in the general case all appearances of a given COMMON block should be identical. There are various systems outside the Fortran language, and extensions to it like the INCLUDE statement of VAX and IBM, which make such a discipline simple to implement; they allow a single definition of each block, which is then distributed unchanged throughout the program to any subprogram which contains the relevant reference.

The second method of transferring information between routines is by the use of arguments. The calling routine defines a list of parameters which is passed to the called routine, which in turn refers to them through dummy arguments. The arguments in the called and calling routines must correspond in type and number, and in the case of character arguments in element length too. Arguments can be used, additionally, to pass the name of a function for use in the called routine, and to provide the linking necessary for the alternate RETURN feature of Fortran 77. Arguments are especially convenient for references to library routines.

```
COMMON/BLOCK/A,B,C,X
A = 1.                          A = 1.
B = 2.                          B = 2.
C = 3.                          C = 3.
CALL SUB                        CALL SUB (A,B,C,X)
Y = X+4.                        Y = X+4.
```

Example 27

The ways in which arguments are passed vary widely from compiler to compiler, even on the same machine, and so general statements are hard to make. Nevertheless, it is often true that the passing of arguments is more costly than the use of COMMON variables, except in certain cases involving optimizing compilers which will be dealt with later. The reason for this greater inefficiency lies in the fact that the calling routine first has to store away the values in question, just as in the case for COMMON variables, but then has to perform additional work in order to set up and store a table of addresses and a pointer to that table. This table will be retrieved and used by the called routine to locate the required variables. The two systems are shown schematically in Fig. 20 for the code in Ex. 27.

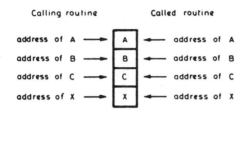

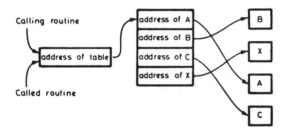

Fig. 20   Two schemes for passing data between subroutines

It may be seen that passing a scalar variable involves fetching two quantities from memory, one for the address of the variable, the other for the variable itself. In the case of arrays, $N+1$ fetches for N elements are required, one for the base address of the array, and one for each array element. Thus we see that where an argument list is referenced many times, it is more efficient, where applicable, to consolidate scalar variables into a single array in order to save some address fetching. The indirect addressing of scalars means that it might sometimes even be better to store them into a temporary variable in the called routine, especially when they appear in a loop, and indeed some compilers do this automatically.

With some compilers, when the number of arguments passed is below some fairly small limit, the scalar arguments may be kept ready in registers, whereas a larger number requires the indirect addressing just described.

```
REAL  A(10,5)                REAL  A(10,5)
CALL  SUB(A)                 CALL  SUB(A,10,5)
:                            :
SUBROUTINE  SUB(A)           SUBROUTINE  SUB(A,N,M)
REAL  A(10,5)                REAL  A(N,M)
```

Examples   28(a)   28(b)

```
REAL  A(10,5)                REAL  A(10,5)
CALL  SUB(A,10)              COMMON/SIZE/N,M
:                            N  =  10
SUBROUTINE  SUB(A,N)         M  =  5
REAL  A(N,*)                 CALL  SUB(A)
                             :
                             SUBROUTINE  SUB(A)
                             COMMON/SIZE/N,M
                             REAL  A(N,M)
```

Examples   28(c)   28(d)

Depending on the nature of the arguments, a still greater loss of efficiency may occur. It is possible to pass array arguments by one of four different methods, as shown in Ex. 28. In the first method, 28(a), the dimensions of A are given explicitly in both calling and called subroutines, and the knowledge the compiler has at compile-time of the actual dimensions of A allows it to make many subscript calculations already at the compilation stage, (see Chapters 6 and 7 for more details of subscript calculations). This early use of explicit constants is known as early *binding*. In the second method, 28(b), the compiler does not know the actual dimensions, and all subscript calculations will contain the variable N, the column size, rather than the constant 10, and the necessary computations may even be performed by a separate hidden Fortran library call, each time the routine is called (*cf.* IBM VS Fortran). The third method, 28(c), new to Fortran 77, is similar; in this case the row size is not given at all, but this is anyway not a component of any subscript calculations. The fourth method, 28(d), is also part of Fortran 77, and is similar to the two previous examples in terms of inefficiency.

An additional overhead is incurred in all these cases under some options of certain compilers which at execution time substitute for each dummy array base address reference in the coded instructions, the actual array base address passed in the calling sequence. In other words, the symbolic address of the array in each machine language instruction referencing it is replaced by the number representing the actual location in memory of the passed array. This can represent an unexpected overhead if only a short fragment of the called routine in question is ever actually executed, as address references throughout the whole routine will be substituted for at each call.

In the case of character arguments, it may be more efficient to use an implicit length specification rather than an explicit length:

```
SUBROUTINE VARCHR(C)
CHARACTER *(*) C
```

and not

```
CHARACTER *10 C
```

This is because the length may be passed efficiently in a register, but otherwise will be accessed only *via* a hidden function call at execution-time.

Further overheads are incurred by any subprogram call, as usually registers will be loaded with new quantities by the called routine, and the original contents must be restored when the return to the calling routine is made. These overheads make it generally necessary to avoid writing very tiny routines which are called frequently to perform rather limited tasks. In this case, and especially inside loops, the code should perhaps be written out in-line, or the use of a statement function considered (see below). This practice does, however, conflict with the principles of good program structuring, and should be used only sparingly, where it is really warranted, namely where the overhead of the call is significant compared to the time spent in the body of the routine, and when that area of the whole program is a hot-spot. This is shown in Ex. 29. An alternative in some cases is to place the loop inside the called routine.

It might be noted that one modern compiler, the Perkin-Elmer Fortran VII Z, attempts to overcome the overheads involved in calling sequences by performing a so-called universal optimization across subprogram references, treating them optionally as macro references and expanding their code in-line.

```
        DO 1 I = 1,N              DO 1 I = 1,N
          :                         :
        CALL  SUM(A(I),B(I),C(I))   C(I)  =  A(I) + B(I)
          :                         :
    1   CONTINUE            1   CONTINUE
          :                         :
        SUBROUTINE SUM(X,Y,Z)
        Z  =  X + Y
        END
```

Example 29

10. Functions

Functions in Fortran represent a means of structuring programs well. Like subroutines, they are subject to all the foregoing considerations with respect to the use of variables in COMMON blocks or arguments, with the exception that functions have to have at least one argument under Fortran 66, and require a null list as a minimum requirement under Fortran 77. However, their ease of use can make them a hazard in the context of optimization. The overhead of the call itself is about the same as for a subroutine call, although some compilers do not store the value of the function directly in memory, but leave the value in a predetermined register. This saving is, however, minimal for all but the most trivial applications.

On many machines, some Fortran standard intrinsic functions, usually those corresponding to the intrinsic functions of the old Fortran 66 standard, have the advantage that they generate in-line code rather than an external call, and this represents an enormous saving if the application allows their use. They are listed in Table 3, and may also be used in place of slower equivalent tests and assignments; for example

IF (I.LT.0) I = 0

is often slower than

I = MAX (I,0)

and

IF (A.LT.0.) A = −A

is less efficient than

$$A = ABS(A)$$

Some compilers, for example that of Fujitsu, allow optional expansion of other longer intrinsic functions, such as SQRT.

Table 3

Intrinsic functions normally generating in-line code

Type conversion	INT REAL DBLE CMPLX
Truncation	AINT
Absolute value	ABS
Remaindering	MOD
Transfer of sign	SIGN
Positive difference	DIM
Largest value	MAX
Smallest value	MIN
For complex variables	AIMAG CONJ

A similar advantage to that of intrinsic functions holds for statement functions, and these should be preferred to external functions when a number of individual calls are required, all originating in a single subprogram. Where an external function is called from a single point inside a nested loop, it might be considered for direct substitution by in-line code.

On the other hand, great caution is necessary in substituting in-line code for the standard Fortran functions, such as SQRT, as the standard algorithms employed are usually very efficient (see IBM, 1981d, for example), and are additionally written in highly optimized machine language. To replace a standard function by in-line code will certainly save the overhead of the call, but it is an unequal battle in terms of some or all of: speed of execution, precision and robustness of code. For instance, the code in Ex. 1 (Section 4.1) for extracting the square root of A**2 + B**2, does have the important characteristic that it is robust, but its authors make no claims that it is particularly fast.

There are, however, occasions when a known approximation to a function is quite permissible, and a substitution can be made in a critical area of code. For instance, the ATAN function can be approximated to better than 0.3% by

$$X/(1.+0.28*X**2) \qquad\qquad |X| < 1.$$

and

$$SIGN(0.5*PI,X) - 1./(X*(1.+0.28/X**2)) \qquad |X| > 1.$$

and similar approximations can be found in the literature.

Another possible substitution, for the square root of a number A known to be close to 1., a situation sometimes occurring when renormalizing computed quantities, is based on the binomial expansion of $\sqrt{(1+x)}$:

$$ROOT = 0.5*(1.+A)$$

(where $x = A-1.$).

All such attempts to replace reliable code with either in-line Fortran code or alternative functions are to be undertaken with great care, and are certainly to be considered only where their use is proven to be safe as well as faster.

There are, on the other hand, occasions when it is possible to dispense with some function calls completely. For instance, if the SQRT function is employed to test whether a point X,Y is inside a circle of radius R, centred at the origin, the code

$$IF \ (SQRT(X**2+Y**2).LT.R) \ GO \ TO \ 1$$

is better replaced by

$$IF \ (X**2+Y**2.LT.R**2) \ GO \ TO \ 1$$

Similarly, algebraic reduction of the number of function calls may be possible. For example,

$$X = LOG(A) + LOG(B)$$

should appear as

$$X = LOG(A*B)$$

and

$$X = SQRT(F)*SQRT(G)$$

as

$$X = SQRT(F*G)$$

It may also be worth saving the result of an expensive function call in a temporary variable, if it is called often with an identical argument.

Another way in which costly functions can be dispensed with in an effective way is to replace them completely by tables. Imagine a function which is to be used between input values in the range 1 to 100. As a preliminary step in the program, the function is called for all whole number arguments in this range, and the values stored in a table dimensioned TABLE(100). For each value of the function actually required during program execution, either the nearest value in the table is taken,

$$TABLE(NINT(X))$$

or an interpolation is made, depending on the accuracy required. If the table required is large, the preliminary evaluation of the function values can be performed as a separate step, and the values stored permanently on an appropriate storage medium. Smaller tables can be stored in a DATA statement. This table look-up method can sometimes bring improvements of an order of magnitude in program execution time, but care in the choice of algorithm is required.

11. Input/Output Operations

The proportion of execution time spent in input/output (I/O) operations varies tremendously between programs. At one end of the range are those computation bound programs which read one data value, compute for hours and print out one number. The other end of the range is occupied by programs which are solely engaged in manipulating large files of data. For any program which spends any appreciable amount of time performing I/O, a number of basic rules are applicable, but more detailed ones are strongly dependent on the actual peripheral devices used, and therefore beyond the scope of this book. Only the guidance offered by the manuals published by the manufacturers of the equipment can help in these cases, and often this guidance will apply to the way in which the job control language should be used to increase efficiency. Here the definition of efficiency is widened to include such additional concepts as the packing density of data on a recording medium, the choice of peripheral types and recording media, real-time considerations concerning data-transmission rates, and the effective use of a limited number of physical units.

Examples of these points might be:

a) the correct choice of recording density and block size and type for magnetic tape;
b) the decision whether to use disc or drum storage rather than a large amount of main memory;
c) whether to use directly a relatively slow device, such as a magnetic tape unit, or to spool the data to or from intermediate disc storage;
d) how to make the most efficient use of a limited disc space allocation, by perhaps packing and unpacking data at the cost of an execution time overhead.

The overriding consideration is to achieve a good match between the rate at which the program reads or writes data, and the performance of the peripheral devices used, bearing in mind that this match has to be made with reference to real-time and not CPU time.

Returning from the program environment to the level of the Fortran program and its CPU efficiency, one major gain in optimization can always be realized by preferring unformatted to formatted data for all numerical data streams which do not have to be seen by the human eye.

There are two reasons for this, involving speed and precision. A value stored in a computer word or words, whatever its data type, is transferred unmodified to or from the external storage medium when processed by an unformatted I/O statement. When processed by a formatted I/O statement the data have to be converted into character strings suitable, for instance, for printing. Thus the hexadecimal digit string

BE1D7DBF

corresponding to the exact value -0.00045 on an IBM, when converted under the format specification E7.1 becomes the character string

$$-.5E-03$$

involving a significant number of operations for the conversion, and involving additionally a loss of precision should this value ever be read back by a subsequent program or program step. Formatted data can also occupy more space on an intermediate file than unformatted data, unless large quantities of small integer values are involved.

The efficiency of I/O operations is also influenced by the exact form of the I/O list being processed, and once again this tends to be compiler dependent. A simple rule is to keep the lists themselves simple, as each item in the list generates a call to the Fortran I/O library routines, which in turn call system supervisor routines. Less sophisticated compilers may additionally generate a loop containing a call to the I/O routines for each element of an array, if the reference to the array elements is made using an implied DO-loop. I/O operations normally carry an overhead consisting of calls to initiate and terminate the processing of the list.

```
   REAL A(50), B(50), C(50), D(150)
   EQUIVALENCE (A,D), (B,D(51)), (C,D(101))
   :
 1 WRITE (NOUT) A
 2 WRITE (NOUT) (A(I),I = 1,50)
 3 WRITE (NOUT) (A(I),I = 1,50),(B(I),I = 1,50),(C(I),I = 1,50)
 4 WRITE (NOUT) (A(I), B(I), C(I), I = 1,50)
 5 WRITE (NOUT) D
```

Example 30

In Ex. 30 the first WRITE statement, for a whole array, will generate a single call to the output routine (ignoring the overhead just mentioned). Depending on the compiler, the second statement, performing exactly the same function as the first, will generate perhaps one call, but possibly 50. Similarly, the third statement may generate either three calls or 150, although some compilers will block the list to give a single call. In the fourth statement, the three arrays A, B and C are written interleaved, and 150 calls, one per element will be required. Finally, the fifth statement, by means of the EQUIVALENCE statement, writes all three arrays with just a single call. When in doubt, it is often convenient to write variable length arrays using a call to a short output routine, as shown in Ex. 31, where the actual WRITE statement uses a single array reference.

A difficulty arises if an array needs to be written or read using a set of indices which does not correspond to the Fortran default,

```
      REAL A(100)
      :
      LEN = ....
      CALL OUTPUT(A, LEN, NOUT, *10)
      :
*     ERROR RECOVERY
 10   .............
      :
      SUBROUTINE OUTPUT(ARRAY,LENGTH,NOUT,*)
      REAL ARRAY(LENGTH)
      WRITE (NOUT, ERR = 100) ARRAY
      RETURN
100   RETURN 1
      END
```

Example 31

as in

        WRITE (NOUT) (A(I), I = 1,49,2)

where only some elements are selected, or in

        WRITE (NOUT) ((B(I,J), J = 1,M), I = 1,N)

where the two-dimensional array B is written out in row-major order, rather than in column-major order. In such cases the use of an intermediate storage array should be considered. The data can be transferred to this array with explicit DO-loops, and can then be written with a simple WRITE statement, as shown in Ex. 32.

```
      REAL B(5,10), C(10,5)
      DO 1 I = 1,5
        DO 1 J = 1,10
        C(J,I) = B(I,J)
  1   CONTINUE
      WRITE (NOUT) C
```

Example 32

In an analogous way, the character output statement

        WRITE(NOUT) C(:N)

is often more efficient than

WRITE(NOUT) (C(I:I),I = 1,N)

An I/O statement which is quite frequently used and which can lead to gross inefficiencies in real-time is the BACKSPACE statement. Many files are organized using system control words which indicate the length of the record at which the file is positioned, ready for a forward read, but do not have the information available to be able to move backwards across the record which has just been processed. In order to perform the backspace operation, the file may be rewound and re-read up to the position required, an exceedingly inefficient sequence of operations. If magnetic tape is used, frequent backspaces cause the forward motion of the tape to be halted and reversed, leading to a huge loss in the average data transfer rate.

A similar difficulty can arise in the over-use of the REWIND statement. For magnetic tapes this is evident, but even with rotating mass storage devices, the system may possibly close and reopen a file every time it is rewound.

When designing programs which need to jump around inside a data file, the Fortran 77 random access features should be considered, as they permit access to any given numbered record of a direct access file, usually on disc. Another possibility, when a formatted record needs to be processed several times, is to read it into a Fortran 77 internal file for repeated processing. An example is shown in Ex. 33, where the choice between one of three different formats is made without any re-reading from the external file.

```
       INTEGER IN(78)
       CHARACTER LINE*78, FORM (3)*6
       DATA FORM /'(78I1)','(39I2)','(26I3)'/
*
       READ (NIN,'(I1,A)', END = 100) KEY, LINE
       N = MAX (1, MIN(KEY,3))
       READ (LINE, FORM(N)) (IN(I), I = 1,78/N)
       :
*      NO DATA ENCOUNTERED
  100 .....
```

Example 33

It should be noted in this example that the in-line format is defined in the source code, and converted into an appropriate internal form at compile time. This compile-time conversion occurs also for FORMAT statements and format specifications in PARAMETER statements. When formats are read in or otherwise defined at execution-time, this conversion of the format itself also needs to be performed at execution-time, resulting in a further overhead.

Other inefficiencies which can occur in FORMAT statements result from over-complicated specifications. The specification

    1 FORMAT (10F11.3)

is more efficient than either

    1 FORMAT (1X,F10.3,1X,F10.3,.....)

or

    1 FORMAT (10(1X,F10.3))

as the space is included in the edit descriptor, and the repeat count is explicit. Embedded blanks in FORMAT statements are removed at compile-time, but this operation can only be carried out at execution-time for formats which are defined dynamically and they should, therefore, contain as few blanks as possible.

For programs which, in spite of every effort to optimize the I/O using standard Fortran facilities, still remain unacceptably I/O bound, there may be no other alternative than to use non-standard I/O facilities. Some installations provide these in their local libraries, for both sequential and direct access files, but one which is found frequently in Fortran extensions is the asynchronous read/write feature which often uses faster system routines than standard I/O does; an additional reason for using it. This feature, often called BUFFER IN/BUFFER OUT, enables I/O operations to be initialized before the input data are required, or before the output data buffer needs to be refilled with fresh output data. It allows the data transfers to proceed while the program itself continues to execute normally, and a means is provided for finally testing whether the I/O operation is complete, before processing the contents of the input buffer, or refilling the output buffer.

A program using an asynchronous read (Ex. 34) typically makes an initial call to fill the buffer, copies it to a workspace, and then initiates a new input operation. The data in the workspace can then be processed while the new input operation proceeds. After processing the first set of data, a branch back to the beginning is made, where a check is required that the buffer is now filled, and the sequence can continue. No copy procedure is necessary if only access to the fast I/O is required.

```
      REAL  BUFF(1000),WORK(1000)
*
*       INITIAL READ
      I = 1
      READ (NUNIT,ID = I) BUFF
*
*       EXECUTION LOOP
   1  WAIT (NUNIT,ID = I,COND = ITEST) BUFF
      IF (ITEST.NE.1) GO TO 2
      CALL COPY (BUFF,WORK,1000)
      I = I+1
      READ (NUNIT,ID = I) BUFF
      :
      :
      GO TO 1
*
*       ERROR EXIT
   2  RETURN
```

Example 34

Input using IBM asynchronous read statements.

12. Summary

Not all the points touched on in this chapter are equally important, either generally or for a given program. The following list places them in a rather subjective order of overall decreasing importance:

Eliminate overhead of external references in critical loops.
Use in-line code instead of external references.
Nest DO-loops in an optimal fashion.
Unroll short loops.
Reduce strength of operators.
Eliminate mixed mode arithmetic.
Use unformatted I/O in preference to formatted.
Use simple I/O lists.
Use efficient FORMAT statements.
Avoid type CHARACTER (on many computers).
Use efficient IF-statements.
Use COMMON rather than arguments to transfer data between subprograms.
Use DATA and PARAMETER statements to initialize variables.

Questions

1. Write a short program to test the efficiency of character handling on your computer. What is your conclusion?

2. Write short programs to test the relative speeds of the five arithmetic operators +, −, *, / and **, the last with different types of base and exponent.

3. Using a program with which you are familiar, test the effect of applying some of the techniques described in this chapter. Do your results agree qualitatively with the rating given in the summary?

4. Repeat Question 3 using an unfamiliar program. Was this second exercise more difficult than the first? If so, why?

5. Are any of your programs I/O bound? How can they be improved in this respect?

6 NON-OPTIMIZING COMPILERS

Nowadays almost all Fortran compilers offer some degree of built-in optimization. In some cases this can be switched on or off by means of a parameter in the call to the compiler, changing the default which either is set by the compiler itself, or is an installation parameter chosen by the computer management. Other compilers offer the possibility of choosing between a number of different optimization levels, where once again one level is set as a default. The decision to choose to use a compiler at its lowest optimization level is one which would normally be taken only to achieve a very fast compilation at the expense of an often much slower execution, mainly for debugging purposes. In cases where the time spent in the former step is greater than that spent in the latter, there may actually be a gain in the total time of compilation plus execution, and this can be very useful in an interactive or real-time environment, where wall clock time may be the user's primary concern, as this determines how long is spent waiting at the terminal.

On a small computer, the only compiler which is available may contain just rather basic optimization options, or even none at all. There may also be some other obstacle to achieving any significant degree of optimization, if, for instance, insufficient memory is available to perform an optimization pass.

If, then, most of the work with a compiler is being performed without using any significant degree of optimization, whether voluntarily or involuntarily, it may become desirable to improve the execution time efficiency of the program, in order to decrease further the overall run-time of the whole job. The purpose of this chapter is to give hints on how to achieve this aim, a procedure which might be termed 'hand-optimization'. It must be stated at the outset that much of the advice given is completely redundant, or worse still, counter-productive, if the resulting source code is, some time later, compiled and run often under an optimizing compiler, as will be seen in the next chapter. The effort of hand-optimizing for a non-optimizing compiler should be undertaken only if that represents the permanent environment in which the program will be run.

The steps outlined here can, in principle, be partially automated, and an attempt to perform such an automatic optimization of source code has been described described by Schneck and Angel (1973) for their Fortran-to-Fortran Optimizing compiler. This consisted of a large program, itself written in Fortran, which attempted just that analysis of program flow and expression evaluation which a true compiler might perform, but in this case it modified the original source code to produce a new source stream, to be passed subsequently to the compiler proper. The disadvantage of this approach is that the resulting code often bears little resemblance to the original source statements, and this presents problems at the debugging stage, where diagnostic messages refer to the line numbers of the intermediate text and not to those of the original code. A further disadvantage is the uncertainty that such a program is itself free of errors. (This reasoning is valid also for true compilers, but their widespread use and the support given by the manufacturers normally ensure that errors are found and corrected on an acceptable time-scale.)

A program of this type suffers also from the fact that it needs to be partially rewritten every time a new standard is introduced, and needs to incorporate the extensions to the standard which are available under the given true compiler for which it is modifying the code. In addition, as it is itself a large slow program, it is unsuitable for use on a small machine anyway. For these reasons, this approach has not found any degree of acceptance, especially as the large programs for which it might be most useful are invariably run under an optimizing compiler. The hopes expressed by the authors, that the future approach to program optimization might follow their path of automatic machine-independent source code optimization rather than that of using machine-dependent optimizing compilers, have not been realized.

The basic assumption when working with a non-optimizing compiler is that each statement will be executed exactly as it is written, and any effort required to save on the number of operations performed must be expended by the author of the code. Optimization in these circumstances means rewriting or restructuring the program so as to minimize the number of operations performed at execution time, at the expense of perhaps no little effort on the part of the programmer. To perform a full flow analysis of a complicated routine by hand, as it is done by automatic optimizers, is probably a task which most programmers would be very reluctant to undertake, and we restrict ourselves here to local optimization, that is over short sections of code, and leave global optimization to the more obvious cases. It is further assumed that the optimization procedures described in the previous chapter have been investigated and applied where necessary.

1. Elimination of Dead Variables

The code should be carefully examined to see whether any local variables are defined by their presence on the left-hand side of an assignment statement, and are then subsequently never referenced. These so-called dead variables would often be indicated by a sophisticated compiler, and it may be a worthwhile test to compile code on another computer, just to get this sort of information if it is not otherwise normally available. A dead variable occurs either because of a typographical error, which simply needs correcting, or because the variable really is not required, and the relevant assignment statement and any on which it depends and which themselves become redundant should be removed. In Ex. 35, the removal of the assignment to the dead variable X makes Y a dead variable, and its own assignment can also be dispensed with.

```
      SUBROUTINE SHOW (A,B,C)
      REAL A(*), B(*), C(*)
      Y = A(1) + B(1)
      DO 1 I = 1,100
         B(I) = A(I) + 5.
    1 CONTINUE
      X = Y + B(2) - 4.
      DO 2 I = 1,100
         C(I) = A(101 - I) + B(I)
    2 CONTINUE
      END
```

Example 35

Dead variables often crop up in code which has been heavily modified by several different people, and are relics of computations no longer contained in the code. This happened frequently under Fortran 66, where expressions calculated for an output list had to be explicitly assigned to a variable, as expressions were not permitted in an output list. These assignments would subsequently survive longer in the code than the WRITE statement for which they were intended.

2. Elimination of Redundant Variables

A similar technique is required for redundant variables, *i.e.* those which are defined and then used just once, and whose assignment can be incorporated into the statements in which their single reference occurs. In the fragment

$$I1 = I + 1$$
$$R2 = R(I1)**2$$
$$AREA = PI*R2$$

both I1 and R2 are redundant variables (assuming neither is used elsewhere in the subprogram), and the three lines can be collapsed to

$$AREA = PI*R(I + 1)**2$$

saving two stores and two loads, as well as the space required to store the two variables and the instructions required for the assignments.

3. Elimination of Constant Expressions

It is often desirable, as a means of internal documentation, to write out explicitly any constant expressions, so that the derivation of the expression is clear to a reader. With a non-optimizing compiler, such expressions will be evaluated each time they are encountered, and consideration should be given to their evaluation by hand, or to moving them to a place where they will be evaluated only once. To retain their value as documentation, the original statement can be left in the form of a comment card. This serves also as a means of checking a hand calculation, should that later prove to be necessary. Thus

$$PERIM = 2*4.1 + 2*10.1$$

could become

```
***** PERIM  =  2*4.1 + 2*10.1
      PERIM  =  28.4
```

saving additionally two integer to real conversions. Similarly,

    IF (R2.LT.3.**2) GO TO 1

could become

    IF (R2.LT.9.) GO TO 1

A standard method of calculating π to the accuracy of the computer being used is to use ACOS(-1.). If any such expression appears in loops, it should be removed, and a variable used instead:

```
PI  =  ACOS(-1.)
:
AREA(I)  =  PI*R(I)**2
```

Constant expressions which are repeated, or whose values are used several times, are better placed in a PARAMETER statement, as a symbolic constant may not appear on the left-hand side of an assignment statement, and can never inadvertently acquire an incorrect value (unless used as an argument in a call to a subprogram which overwrites its value!):

    PARAMETER (PERIM = 2*4.1 + 2*10.1)

If the value is required in more than one subprogram, it may alternatively be stored as a COMMON variable, so that all of its appearances use the same value.

4. Elimination of Common Sub-expressions

An attempt should be made to divide the source listing of the code into basic blocks, each of which starts with a statement label and finishes at the statement preceding the following statement label. Depending on whether it redefines any of the variables referenced in the block, an external reference or an I/O statement may also act as a terminator. This must be checked for each such occurrence.

Having identified blocks in this way, a simplification of the more complex analysis made by a compiler, the code should be examined for expressions or sub-expressions which occur several times, including subscript expressions. If, between two such occurrences, there is no redefinition of any of the variables involved, the expressions or sub-expressions can be replaced by a new temporary variable which needs to be evaluated once before its first appearance. Thus, the expressions

$$A = (X*Y + 4.)/S$$
$$B = (X*Y + 2.)/S$$
$$C = (X*Y + 2.)/S$$

can be rewritten as

$$T01 = X*Y + 2.$$
$$T02 = 1./S$$
$$A = (T01 + 2.)*T02$$
$$B = T01*T02$$
$$C = B$$

and the expression

$$X = A(2*I + J, \ 2*I + J)$$

can become

$$IT02 = 2*I + J$$
$$X = A(IT02, \ IT02)$$

At this stage particular attention should be given to the substitution of multiplications for divisions, but it is necessary to ensure that the substitutions are not simply trivial and confusing, and a count of the number of saved operations should first be made. A check that precision is not adversely affected is also required.

It is possible, in principle, to perform a more complex block analysis than the simple one described here, for instance following the scheme of Schneck and Angel, in which the relationships between the basic blocks are examined to see whether they contain common expressions which lie on a common path, such that no redefinition of the variables involved occurs between their various appearances in the blocks. These common expressions can then be evaluated at a single point in the program. An analysis of this type, if performed manually, is tedious and likely to be prone to error, and should be attempted only if really necessary. An example is given in Fig. 21, where the expression A + B is common to blocks 1

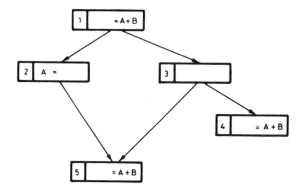

Fig. 21   A block dependency analysis

and 4, but may not be re-used in block 5 due to the redefinition of A in block 2.

5. DO-loops

With whatever version of a compiler a program is run, it is most likely that the greatest part of the execution time is spent inside DO-loops. In order to save both on loop overheads and subscript calculations, the lowest possible number of dimensions should be used in array declarations, and scalars should always be preferred to vectors whenever possible. In Ex. 36(a), the compiler will generate code to address each element of the arrays, using the standard Fortran formula

$$(J - 1) * \text{column length} + I$$

This calculation can be avoided by the EQUIVALENCE statement shown in Ex. 36(b), and if AA and BB were used throughout the program, without having to perform explicit subscript evaluations equivalent to those generated by the compiler for A and B, further savings would be possible.

Attention should be paid to the presence inside loops of invariant expressions, that is any form of expression or sub-expression, including subscript calculations, which remains unchanged during the successive iterations of the loop. In Ex. 37(a) the sub-expression /B, the function call SQRT(PI) and the subscript evaluation $2*J + 4$ can be removed either from the innermost loop, or from the nested

```
      REAL  A(10,5),  B(10,5)
      DO 1 J  =  1,5
         DO 1 I  =  1,10
            A(I,J)  =  B(I,J)**2
    1 CONTINUE
```

Example 36(a)

```
      DIMENSION  A(10,5),  J(10,5),  AA(50),  BB(50)
      EQUIVALENCE  (A,AA),  (B,BB)
      DO 1 I  =  1,50
         AA(I)  =  BB(I)**2
    1 CONTINUE
```

Example 36(b)

loops entirely, as shown in Ex. 37(b). Any removal of divisions or functions from a loop is an especially important improvement.

```
   DO 1 J  =  1,5                    T01  =  1./S
      DO 1 I  =  1,10                T02  =  SQRT(PI)
         A(I,J)=C(2*J+4)*SQRT(PI)    DO 1 J  =  1,5
         B(I,J)  =  A(I,J)/S+D(I)       T03=C(2*J+4)*T02
 1 CONTINUE                             T04  =  T03*T01
                                        DO 1 I  =  1,10
                                           A(I,J)  =  T03
                                           B(I,J)=T04+D(I)
                                   1 CONTINUE
```

Examples   37(a)   37(b)

It is necessary to examine the possible use of scalar temporary variables to replace array references inside loops. This is often possible in summation loops, where subscript calculations can be saved by making a substitution of the type demonstrated in Ex. 38(a) and 38(b).

Lastly, a further example of the technique used in recursive loops (Section 5.6.5), is found in the evaluation of the Fibonacci series

$$F(1) = F(2) = 1.$$
$$F(J) = F(J-1)+F(J-2)$$

```
      DO 1 K = 1,5
        DO 1 J = 1,5
          S(J,K) = 0.
          DO 1 I = 1,10
            S(J,K) = S(J,K) + A(I,J,K)
1   CONTINUE
```

Example 38(a)

```
      DO 1 K = 1,5
      DO 1 J = 1,5
        T01 = 0.
        DO 2 I = 1,10
          T01 = T01 + A(I,J,K)
2       CONTINUE
        S(J,K) = T01
1   CONTINUE
```

Example 38(b)

The straightforward code of Ex. 39(a) might be replaced, for large N, by the code of Ex. 39(b), saving on subscript evaluations.

```
      F(1) = 1.                    F(1) = 1.
      F(2) = 1.                    F(2) = 1.
      DO 10 J = 3,N                FJM1 = 1.
        F(J) = F(J-1) + F(J-2)       FJM2 = 1.
10 CONTINUE                          DO 10 J = 3,N
                                     FJ = FJM1 + FJM2
                                     FJM2 = FJM1
                                     FJM1 = FJ
                                     F(J) = FJ
                                  10 CONTINUE
```

Examples   39(a)   39(b)

7   OPTIMIZING COMPILERS

Almost all modern computer systems offer a Fortran compiler which possesses the ability to perform optimization of both the intermediate source text, and of the object code which is intended for execution. In most circumstances, such compilers will be used at their highest possible optimization level when producing object code which is to be run either many times, or once for a single long run. The former case is typified by the production of an object library or of load-modules, and the latter by the initial compilation of a shorter program requiring a large amount of CPU time. A lower optimization level would normally be used only for fast test runs in which the compilation time is the predominant part of total time, or in those more unfortunate but nevertheless real instances, in which the higher levels contain errors which can be demonstrated to produce defective code.

The first basic assumption of this chapter is that the programmer is attempting to obtain the maximum possible degree of efficiency from his program, and is running with the highest compiler optimization level selected. Some compilers offer options to generate the additional object code instructions which are required to produce traceback or other diagnostic information, such as *post-mortem* dumps, in the event of the program terminating abnormally. It is assumed either that this option is deselected, or that it has been demonstrated to produce no significant slowdown in program execution, or that the possible loss of CPU time caused by running without it, and then being unable to perform a necessary recovery, outweighs the overhead of running with the option. For a fully tested program it is also inefficient to run with array bound or character sub-string range checking switched on, if it is available, and this option is assumed also to be deselected. (But we note that Allen *et al.* (1974) have quoted this practice as being akin to wearing a seat-belt while a car is warming-up, and removing it for the actual drive).

When reading through this chapter it must be kept in mind that any modification to the source code is likely to have a totally unpredictable effect on the efficiency of the object code produced, as optimizing compilers themselves subject the code to various types of optimization, and the final result depends not only on the few lines which may be under consideration, but also on the surrounding code in the same subprogram. When modifying code in these conditions, it is important to be aware of this difficulty. It is especially important to avoid making the task of the compiler more difficult by attempting to perform hand-optimization in areas where it is able to carry out the same task more efficiently. This advice contrasts sharply with that given in the previous chapter, which is based on the opposite assumption, namely that the object code produced by any given line of code is completely predictable. It cannot be overstressed that trying to achieve the ultimate degree of source code optimization involves thoroughly testing every change made, and being prepared for rude surprises when measuring their effect, and watching also for any change in the required precision which may result from reordering of expressions.

The sections which form this chapter are intended to be read in conjunction with the corresponding sections of Chapter 5, and it is assumed that the recommendations of that chapter have been examined.

1. Arithmetic Operations

In Section 5.3 the arithmetic operations were discussed in a general fashion. An optimizing compiler will normally try to reduce the strength of operations in a number of ways. These might include:

i) Replacing divisions by multiplications, as in

$$X = Y/2 \quad \text{which becomes} \quad X = Y*0.5$$

This particular expression corresponds to the 'division-by-two' instruction of some computers.

ii) Replacing any exponentiation by a constant integer power by a repeated multiplication:

A**5   becomes   (A*A)*(A*A)*A

where the term in parentheses is calculated just once and
re-used.

iii) On machines which generate more efficient code for additions
than subtractions, the compiler might generate for

$-A-B$ the more efficient $-(A+B)$

or for

$-(B-C)$ the equivalent expression $C-B$

iv) A multiplication by two might be replaced by an addition:

2.*X   becomes   X + X

The important point here is to be aware of the improvements
attempted by the compiler being used, and to structure the expressions to take advantage of them. If, for instance, repeated multiplications are generated for constant integer exponents, this form of
exponent should be used in preference to an integer variable. In
general, it is more efficient to use explicit constants or symbolic
constants (ones defined in PARAMETER statements), rather than
variables, but, in the former case, this does have the severe disadvantage of making code difficult to maintain and, therefore, full
use should be made of the PARAMETER statement.

2. Common and Constant Sub-expressions

Modern compilers make an attempt to identify repeated calculations
and to remove the repetitions. It falls to the programmer to help the
compiler by writing such expressions in identical forms, thus

A = X*Y + 2.0 + SQRT(Y*X)

should appear as

A = (X*Y) + 2.0 + SQRT(X*Y)

and

$$A = B*B*C*C$$

as

$$A = (B*C) * (B*C)$$

and in

$$A = B - C$$
$$\vdots$$
$$D = C - B$$

the second statement should be

$$D = -(B - C)$$

Parentheses are often needed to identify such repeated calculations, and should be used liberally.

This type of optimization may be inhibited by the presence of statement labels in the sequence of code, as this indicates a possible alternative path into the basic block and, therefore, possibly other values of the variables involved.

Subscript expressions are included in this optimization, and hand-optimization of the type

$$IP1 = I + 1$$
$$IM1 = I - 1$$
$$X = A(IP1,IM1) + A(IM1,IP1)$$

should not be used in the place of

$$X = A(I + 1, I - 1) + A(I - 1, I + 1)$$

as this creates unnecessary temporary variables and assignments.

Another example of regrouping which can save a division is

$$X = Y*Z/A$$
$$T = Y*V/A$$

rewritten as

$$X = (Y/A)*Z$$
$$T = (Y/A)*V$$

and this type of regrouping should be attempted wherever it is considered useful. A similar consideration applies to constant sub-expressions which can actually be evaluated directly at compile-time if they are evident to the compiler. Thus

$$Y = 180.*ACOS(V)/3.141$$

should appear as

$$Y = (180./3.141)*ACOS(V)$$

A symbolic constant is equivalent to an explicit constant in this respect.

3. DO-loops

In Section 5.6 we considered the ways in which sometimes significant improvements in program performance can be achieved by devoting attention to the manner in which DO-loops are written. The question of the calculation of array subscripts which depend on the control variable was not discussed, as the considerations depend vitally on whether or not an optimizing compiler is used. In Ex. 40, the array element $A(I,J)$ is referenced by adding the offset $(J-1)*10+I$ to the base address of the array. However, since this offset is incremented by one at each iteration through the inner loop, the subscript expression is replaced by a new variable which is defined to be $(J-1)*10$ at the beginning of the inner loop, and incremented by one each time the loop is executed. A variable of this type is known as an induction variable (see Section 3.7). The same method is used if the loops are nested in what is conventionally regarded as the wrong order. In this case the offset would be incremented by 10 each time, and there is no loss of efficiency in executing the loop with this nesting order, except in some particular cases.

The most important of these is that in a lengthy section of code the constant value 1 may well be required for other purposes, and the larger number of references to it, compared to those to the column length of 10 (in this example) could mean that the constant 1 is more likely to be a candidate for retention in a register throughout the range of the loop, whereas the constant 10 may be kept only in main memory, and will have to be loaded each time it is

```
      REAL  A(10,5)
      DO 1 J  =  1,5
        DO 1 I  =  1,10
        A(I,J)  =  0.
  1  CONTINUE
```

Example 40

required.

Secondly, at least one family of compilers, the FTN compilers of CDC, is more likely to cause operands to be pre-fetched in loops when the increment is one, than for any other value, for fear of generating an address well beyond the program's field length.

The last reason for retaining the conventional nesting order concerns the arrangement of main memory in banks. Consecutive words in address space are kept in consecutive banks, rather than in consecutive words of one bank, so that the fetching and storing of elements of arrays is interleaved between the banks, instead of referring only to a single bank. If the offset increment is inadvertently equal to the memory interleaving factor, the purpose of the hardware interleaving is defeated, and all memory references are made to a single bank, resulting in what can be a dramatic drop in the transfer rate of data to or from the CPU. The most efficient way to dimension arrays, if this is likely to be a problem, is in multiples of $(N-1)*n$ or $(N+1)*n$, where N is the interleaving factor and n the number of words transferred per bank reference. This ensures the longest possible interval between two successive references to the same bank. A similar consideration will be met when dealing with paging machines and cache memories in Section 8.9.

Even if none of these three conditions may occur, it is still advisable for code which is to be run on several different types of computer to retain the safe nesting order. If this is done, and if we remember the requirement to nest the loops also in an order which minimizes the loop overheads, we obtain the further rule that arrays should be dimensioned with their largest dimensions first.

When several arrays are referenced in the same loop, the compiler will use the subscript expressions several times if they are written identically and if the arrays in question are dimensioned identically in all but the last dimension, although it is clearly not always possible to achieve this with real problems.

In summary, an ideal loop in this respect is of the kind shown in Ex. 41, with conformable arrays sharing identical subscripts in optimally nested loops.

```
      REAL  A(50,10,2),  B(50,10,2)
      DO 1 K  =  1,2
        DO 1 J  =  1,10
          DO 1 I  =  1,50
            A(I,J,K)  =  A(I,J,K) + B(I,J,K) + 1.
    1 CONTINUE
```

Example 41

It is often thought that the artificial substitution of an array by a vector, for which the subscripting is performed explicitly, will improve run time efficiency. This is usually quite definitely not the case, as the compiler can no longer detect the relationships between the more complex subscript expressions, and is likely to generate slower code. Thus an expression like

$$AA(2*I + 2 + (2*I + 1)*10)$$

is slower than the equivalent

$$A(2*(I + 1), 2*(I + 1))$$

(where 10 is the column length), although this represents an extreme case of inefficient explicit subscripting.

```
      DO 1 J  =  1,10
        DO 1 I  =  1,10
          A(I,J)  =  C(J)*B(I,J)
    1 CONTINUE
```

Example 42

The treatment of invariant code in loops has to be handled with some care in the presence of an optimizing compiler, as it is all too easy to inhibit the optimizations it could produce when presented with cleanly written code. Considerable efforts have been invested in devising algorithms for the detection and removal of invariant code from loops, and when this occurs it is likely to be effected in the most efficient manner possible. This contrasts with the result of any clumsy hand-optimizations, which can actually degrade the efficiency of the loop. In Ex. 42, an optimizing compiler will detect that C(J) is invariant to the inner loop, and in all probability will assign the new value of the element to a register each time the inner loop is entered. A hand-optimization using the same technique would require an explicit temporary variable, whose value would occupy a word in memory, and in most circumstances some memory reference would be required. We note that the compiler is helped by placing the invariant at the beginning of the expression.

In fact, it is often necessary to order terms and use parentheses in order to help the compiler to recognize invariant expressions; in

$$DO \ 1 \ I \ = \ 1,10$$
$$B(I) \ = \ 2. + A(I) + Y$$
$$1 \ \ CONTINUE$$

the right-hand side of the assignment should be rewritten as

$$(2. + Y) \ + \ A(I)$$

Another example is

$$A(I,J) \ = \ 2.0*PI*X*Y(J)*B(I,J)$$

where the constants and the invariants are correctly grouped together, and are in the optimum order for recognition: constant − invariant − variant.

To ensure that invariant divisions are always recognized as such

$$(A(I) - B(I))/S$$

for example, should appear as

$$(1./S)*(A(I) - B(I))$$

A compiler usually assumes that the whole of the innermost loop is the most intensively used part of the program and, as we have seen, moves invariant code backwards out of the loop accordingly. There are, however, cases where this assumption is wrong, and steps need to be taken to guard against an optimizing compiler producing less efficient code than a non-optimizing one. In Ex. 43(a), the SQRT function call may well be moved into the outer loop and executed N times, whereas in the inner loop it may never have been called at all, if all the elements of A were positive. To prevent this backward movement where an inefficiency is likely to be produced, the right-hand side of the assignment needs to be written as a separate function containing the SQRT and addition (Ex. 43(b)). The compiler will then be inhibited from removing the reference.

```
     DO 1 I = 1,N
       DO 2 J = 1,M
         IF (A(J,I).GE.0.) GO TO 2
         A(J,I) = SQRT(FLOAT(I)) + B(J,I)
   2     CONTINUE
   1 CONTINUE
```

Example 43(a)

```
     A(J,I) = FUNC(I,B(J,I))
     :
     :
     FUNCTION FUNC(I,B)
     FUNC = SQRT(FLOAT(I)) + B
     END
```

Example 43(b)

A similar situation can arise when the code contains protection against calling SQRT with a negative argument, or against performing a division by zero, and the operation is then nevertheless performed outside the loop resulting in an execution-time error:

```
     DO 1 I = 1,N
       B(I) = 0.
       IF (A.NE.0.) B(I) = C(I)/A
   1 CONTINUE
```

In this case, the invariant division by A needs to be moved out of the loop explicitly. In both of these examples, selecting a lower level of optimization might be a simpler solution to adopt.

The degree of invariant code optimization performed in a loop containing external references depends on the extent to which the invariant code is obscured by references to variables in COMMON or in an argument list. In

```
     DO 1 I = 1,10
       A(I) = Y/Z
       CALL SUB(A,Z)
   1 CONTINUE
```

where Z is a local variable, the division cannot be removed from the loop because SUB may change the value of Z; the reference

$$CALL\ SUB(A,Z + 1)$$

however, cannot change the value of Z and the invariant can be removed. In a difficult case, this is a situation in which a temporary variable can be used to good effect. For the same reason, COMMON should not be used for the scratch storage of strictly local variables, as the compiler must assume that any COMMON variable can be changed by a call to an external routine, and therefore cannot treat any expression containing a COMMON variable as an invariant in the presence of a call.

This demonstrates one circumstance in which the use of COMMON variables may result in less efficient code, if there is a large number of them being referenced and kept in registers. Their values need to be stored away for each call, in case they are required by the called subprogram. In this case, and where they are not in fact referenced by the external, such variables should possibly be kept in temporary local variables over the range of the loop, although this is not normally a recommended programming practice, as the code becomes more difficult to read, and dangerous to modify. References to functions in the vendor supplied Fortran library should not generate this overhead, as they clearly do not contain user-defined COMMON blocks.

Inside short loops it is better to use scalars on the left-hand side of statements, rather than array references, as the scalar can be kept in a register during the loop, whereas the array reference may be stored for each iteration:

```
        SUM = 0.
        DO 1 I = 1,100
          SUM = SUM + A(I,J)
      1 CONTINUE
        B(J) = SUM
```

is better than

```
        B(J) = 0.
        DO 1 I = 1,100
          B(J) = B(J) + A(I,J)
      1 CONTINUE
```

We note also that Ex. 38 in the previous chapter should be treated in the same way with an optimizing compiler as with a non-optimizing one, but for a different reason.

Often the most serious loss of optimization in loops occurs because of the presence of an external reference, however trivial and perhaps disguised in the form of an exponentiation or a print statement. The compiler must assume that the registers it is using will be overwritten by the external routine, and has to ensure that their contents are saved and restored before and after each external reference. In short loops this overhead can exceed the processing of the rest of the loop, and causes possible inefficient register allocation, as the loop is split into at least two basic blocks. Replacing function calls by statement functions, in-line code or tables (see Section 5.10), can bring dramatic gains. Another approach is to push the part of the loop containing the calls into the called routine. For instance, where a random number function is called inside a loop it may be more efficient to call first a function capable of providing a whole vector of random numbers, and to reference the vector rather than the standard function inside the loop. In this context any I/O, RETURN or STOP statement has the same effect as an external reference, and they should be removed from loops as far as possible. The RETURN and STOP can always be eliminated easily by an appropriate branch. This type of loss of optimization obviously occurs even in the presence of external references which are never executed:

IF (FLAG) PRINT *,I,J,K

where FLAG is false.

A last consideration in the case of loops is that if they are kept short and simple, the compiler is usually able to make a better job of optimizing than if they are long and contain many branches, especially backward ones. A loop which consists of a single basic block is the ideal at which to aim, even at the cost of a somewhat greater number of loops and therefore increased loop overheads. As has been seen in Section 3.7, the presence of an unconditional jump out of a loop can cause some of the preceding statements to be excluded from the loop optimization.

4. Data Interference

Data interference is the interaction between memory references which prevents the elimination during optimization of at least one reference. For instance, in

```
REAL A(5)
:
X  =  A(2)
A(I)  =  1
Y  =  A(2)
```

the possible values of I are unknown at compile time, and the second fetch of A(2) cannot be eliminated.

In

```
    K  =  N+1
    DO 10 J  =  2,N
        A(J)  =  A(K)/A(1)
10 CONTINUE
```

A(K)/A(1) should be evaluated once before the loop and used as a temporary variable. The compiler cannot recognize the fact that K is greater than N and that the loop cannot therefore change the value of A(K), and hence does not remove this section of invariant code from the loop. Similarly

```
    DO 10 I  =  1,N
        X(J)  =  X(J)+X(J+I)*B(I)
10 CONTINUE
```

should be re-written as

```
    T  =  X(J)
    DO 10 I  =  1,N
        T  =  T+X(J+I)*B(I)
10 CONTINUE
    X(J)  =  T
```

since the compiler cannot recognize that J+I may not equal J, and will not assign a register for X(J).

Unintentional   data   interference   may   be   introduced   by over-zealous use of the EQUIVALENCE statement. If there are two separate equivalence classes located in a COMMON block, the compiler may merge them, as well as any intervening block members, into one large class. Thus the practice of equivalencing simple variables such as DO-loop control variables and parameters into a scratch COMMON is false economy.

In the following example

```
COMMON/SCRATCH/A(100)
INTEGER ITEMP(50)
EQUIVALENCE (ITEMP,A),(ITEMP(51),N),(ITEMP(52),M)
DO 1 N = 1,M
    IF (ITEMP(N).EQ. – 1) GO TO 10
    ITEMP(N) = 0
  1 CONTINUE
 10 ...........
```

there is unintended data interference between the store in ITEMP(N) and the use of N and M. This interference prevents loop optimizations such as the assignment of loop counters to registers throughout the loop. Similarly, in

```
COMMON//A(4),N,M,B,C(4)
REAL AA(11)
EQUIVALENCE(A,AA)
:
X = A(I)
B = 1.
Y = A(I)
```

the second fetch of A(I) may not be eliminated because of data interference with B, introduced by the EQUIVALENCE statement.

In general, variables kept in EQUIVALENCE classes frequently become unoptimizable and the use of this statement should normally be avoided. Especially bad are the use of scalars equivalenced to array elements, the equivalencing of loop indices or parameters, and the equivalencing of variables of differing type.

5. Summary

The following points should be regarded as a continuation of the list given in the summary of Chapter 5.

Do not hand-optimize, in the style of Chapter 6.
Group common expressions clearly.
Order the parts of an expression: constant – invariant – variant.
Use parentheses freely.
Avoid storage bank conflicts.
Use conformable arrays in loops.
Use scalar accumulators in loops.
Avoid the EQUIVALENCE statement.

Questions

1. Repeat Questions 3 and 4 of Chapter 5.

2. What is the storage bank interleaving factor of your computer? Does any program you use contain addressing patterns which might lead to bank conflicts (see also Section 8.9)?

8 THE IBM COMPILERS

1. Background

The first Fortran compiler ever written was the one produced to the original language specification of Backus at IBM in 1957 (Backus *et al.*, 1957). Even for this first compiler, one of the design objectives was to provide a high-level language which retained at least some of the efficiency which could normally be achieved only by use of machine language. Since that time, IBM has produced a number of other Fortran compilers, the principal ones being the Fortran H optimizing compiler (Lowry and Medlock, 1969), the Fortran G and G 1 non-optimizing debug compilers, the Fortran H Extended Optimization Enhanced compiler, sometimes known as the Q compiler (Scarborough and Kolsky, 1980), and finally the VS Fortran compiler (IBM, 1981a and c). Apart from the G compilers, the emphasis has always been on providing a very high degree of optimization, and the H compiler was the result of an application of extensive theoretical techniques to producing text optimizations, and was one of the most advanced compilers of its time.

There are two main IBM compilers in current use – the now obsolete Q compiler, which was itself written largely in Fortran and which accepts an IBM extension to the Fortran 66 standard, and the modern VS compiler, which accepts an extension to the Fortran 77 standard.

The Q compiler was used to optimize itself, thereby generating a compact and efficient product. The combination of techniques it utilises are the principal ones outlined in the following sections, which should be regarded as a continuation of the optimization discussion, begun in Chapter 3, on the principles of optimizing compilers. Here we describe, however, an actual implementation, and the source code considerations which derive both from that implementation, and from the architecture of IBM System/370 machines, in particular the IBM 308X (see Section 2.5).

IBM was the last major computer company to provide its users with a Fortran 77 standard conforming compiler, and its late introduction of the VS compiler to some extent retarded the acceptance of the new standard. This new compiler is written in an IBM internal system programming language PLS, itself a derivative of PL/1, and it replaces all the previous compilers, as it may be run to compile either Fortran 66 or Fortran 77 programs, according to which of two options is chosen; it also contains the debugging features of the G compilers. The compiler has four optimization levels – 0, 1, 2, and 3. Level 2 does not perform the unsafe type of backward code movement mentioned in Section 7.3, whereas level 3 does, and level 2 differs in this respect from level 2 of the Q compiler. The optimization techniques described by Scarborough and Kolsky have been largely carried over into the VS compiler; they resulted from a careful analysis of the operation of the H compiler and of the object code it produced, and consist mainly of a series of pragmatic improvements, especially in the area of register allocation.

The optimization at the highest level proceeds in three distinct stages, each requiring passes over the intermediate text. In order, they are text optimization, register optimization and branch optimization; a number of miscellaneous optimizations are also applied, and these are described first.

2. Miscellaneous Optimizations

One of the first procedures performed by the compiler is to generate an internal intermediate text from the source code of the program. This intermediate text is the one which will be used in the subsequent optimizing stages. Already at this stage certain local transformations of the text are possible, regardless of the optimization level chosen. For instance, if the source code contains an exponentiation by an integer constant (*e.g.* A**5), this is substituted by a sequence of multiplications and squaring operations, generated as a function of the bit pattern in the exponent. In this example the substitution is (A*A)*(A*A)*A, where the term in parentheses is calculated only once and re-used. Multiplication of integers by a power of two (*e.g.* I*16) is replaced by a shift operation on the other operand, and a multiplication by 2.0 is replaced by an addition, *i.e.* 2.0*A becomes A + A.

In order to save a complement operation, some expressions containing subtractions are converted to a simpler form: thus $-(A-B)$ would become $(B-A)$.

A final optimization is made where subscript expressions employ constants. In the array reference $A(6,I-6,I+6)$, for example, the origin of the array can be moved such that the resulting references no longer contain any constants, as they can be consolidated into a single constant displacement. This is just as if a slightly irregular EQUIVALENCE statement of the following form had been used:

    REAL A(20,20,20),AA(20,20)
    EQUIVALENCE (A(6, - 6,6),AA(1,1))

allowing the subscript computation to proceed as if the doubly dimensioned AA rather than the triply dimensioned A were to be referenced. This procedure is applied to variably dimensioned arrays as far as is possible.

3. Text Optimization

Before beginning the optimization passes, the compiler analyses the structure of the source text, in order to identify any loops (see Section 3.7). A loop in this context means not only a DO-loop, but also an IF-loop, if it is equivalent in the sense that it is entered at only one point, for example

        I = 0
    1   I = I+1
        :
        :
        IF (I.LT.10) GO TO 1

The nesting level of each loop is noted, and on the assumption that the deepest loops are those most frequently executed, optimization proceeds outwards through the loops, starting with the innermost ones.

The first of the five text optimizations is called *commutation of subscript dimension computations*, one of two optimizations which are applied to subscript calculations in addition to the one already described above. Let us suppose that an array A has been declared as having dimensions D1, D2 and D3. When stepping through the array in the first dimension, the increment each time will be one, in the second dimension D1, and in the third dimension D1*D2. (In fact, the addresses are calculated as byte addresses, and these increments are multiplied by four to take this into account. We shall ignore this fact in the following discussion).

If, in a loop, the array is referenced as A(K1,J,K3), where K1 and K3 are constant expressions, and J depends on the loop control variable, then the address of an element is given by the base address of A added to $K1 + (J-1)*D1 + (K3-1)*D1*D2$. From this expression we see that it is possible to combine the two constant terms into a single expression, which will be moved out of the loop during a later optimization step.

The full address of an array element is composed of several parts. These are:

i) the base address, BASE, which is the address of the storage area containing the array — a COMMON block address or subroutine address, for example;

ii) the displacement, DISP, which is the displacement of the zeroth element with respect to BASE, combined with any possible displacement calculated from constant subscripts;

iii) the constant index, CONST, which is the constant part of the subscript expression inside the current loop;

iv) the variable index, VAR, which is the term depending directly or indirectly on the loop control variable.

In the procedure known as *optimization of subscript component combinations*, these four components are reordered in a fashion which takes advantage of machine instructions which allow components to be added together implicitly, without having to perform an explicit add operation. Thus, the components are combined in the order defined by

$$VAR + (CONST + (DISP + BASE))$$

where the three fixed components are combined outside the loop into one value, which is implicitly added to the variable index inside the loop. This means that no explicit addition, or multiplication, is required for subscript calculations within loops, and this makes the efficiency of the code less dependent on the number of array dimensions. An exception occurs when an intermediate displacement is negative, or greater than 4095 bytes; in this case an explicit addition is required, as these values exceed the capacity of the displacement field of instructions with implicit additions.

```
DO 1 I = 1,N              DO 1 I = 7*1,7*N,7*1
   A(7*I) = 0                A(I) = 0
1 CONTINUE                1 CONTINUE

DO 1 I = 1,N              DO 1 I = 7+1,7+N,+1
   A(7+I) = 0               A(I) = 0
1 CONTINUE                1 CONTINUE

DO 1 I = 1,N              DO 1 I = 7-1,7-N,-1
   A(7-I) = 0               A(I) = 0
1 CONTINUE                1 CONTINUE
```

Example 44

The third text optimization is referred to as *strength reduction of induction variable computations*. An induction variable is a variable which is incremented (or decremented) in one place only by a fixed amount, for each iteration of a loop. The most common induction variable is the loop control variable itself. Subscript computations based on an induction variable can often be reduced to a new induction variable, thereby saving subscript computations inside loops. In the case of subscript expressions, this is an alternative optimization to the one just described, and the compiler will choose that method which minimizes both the number of instructions required, and the number of registers required for subscripting. This might depend on whether, for instance, there are components of subscript expressions which are common to a number of array references. Examples of the equivalent code produced by the compiler for multiplication, addition and subtraction are given in Ex. 44. No explicit arithmetic operations are required and the multiplication by four required to produce a byte address from a word address is also included in this optimization; all additions are performed implicitly by appropriate machine instructions.

This optimization is useful in undoing any possible damage done by attempts to hand-optimize code by the introduction of vectors in the place of arrays, or by performing explicit subscripting. Thus in Ex. 45 the variables I3 and I6 will never appear explicitly inside the loop. The compiler also attempts to use any induction variable as often as possible. In the loop

```
      DO 1 I = 1,N
        I3 = I+3
        I6 = I+6
        A(I3) = A(I6)
    1  CONTINUE
```

Example 45

```
      DO 1 I = 1,N
        A(I+J) = A(I+K) + A(I+L)
    1  CONTINUE
```

a single induction variable based on $I+J$ can be used for all the subscripts, as each subscript is incremented by the same constant (one), in the same statement. For the two array references on the right-hand side of the assignment it will be combined with a constant offset of $-J$ to compensate for the different subscript values required. Here again, all the additions are performed implicitly by the use of appropriate machine instructions.

The fourth text optimization is the *elimination of duplicate computations*. A computation is represented by one of the quadruples into which the source code has been decomposed. For instance, the original source statement

$$A = B+C$$

will appear in the intermediate text as

$$+,A,B,C.$$

In order to scan for common expressions the code is divided into basic blocks, each of which consists of a sequence of statements, in which the first statement is the only one which can be referenced in a branch, and the last is the only one containing a branch. The relationships between the blocks are then established, so that it is known for each block which other blocks are executed before it, the so called dominance relationship (Section 3.7). A scan is made within each block for common expressions, and for the same expressions in preceding blocks, always checking that there is no intermediate store into either of the operands. The operands may appear in reverse order, so C*B is common to B*C, as the operand pairs containing additions and multiplications are stored alphabetically. For the common expressions thus identified the first calculated value can be used in place of all others. Common expressions actually include quadruples which are combinations of smaller expressions, but the types of common expressions most frequently encountered are not those in arithmetic expressions, but those arising from duplicate subscript expressions, for example, the multiple use of B(I,J,K) within a loop. In order to limit the time spent in this scan, it is restricted to the preceding 10 blocks.

The final text optimization consists of the *backward movement of invariant computations*, that is, of any quadruple whose operands do not depend on a loop (as defined in Section 3.7). Once one quadruple is moved backwards it may well be that another is revealed to depend only on the first, and therefore is itself invariant and may be moved. Thus, if for the pair of statements

$$Y = C + D$$
$$X = Y + E$$

the variables C, D and E are not defined within the loop, and X and Y are defined nowhere else in the loop, then Y and X are both invariant, and these computations can be removed from the body of the loop to its initialization.

At the same time as this optimization is carried out, any dead variables, *i.e.* those which appear only once on the left-hand side of a single assignment statement, are identified. Where such variables are subsequently referenced, the reference can be subsumed (replaced directly) by the variable or constant to which the dead variable was itself defined. Thus, in

$$Y = A$$
$$Z = Y + 4.$$
$$X = 2. + Y$$

the second two references to Y can be replaced by references to A, if Y is defined nowhere else.

A concurrent evaluation of some numeric constant calculations is also performed during this step. (The VS compiler performs some constant calculations during the earlier syntax scanning stage.)

4. Register Optimization

It will be recalled that the IBM System/370 architecture defines two sets of registers (see Section 2.5). The first is a set of 16 32-bit general registers, and the second a set of four 64-bit floating-point operand registers. The purpose of the register optimization phase is to ensure the best possible use of this limited number of registers. The optimization proceeds in five steps, three of which are not available under the H compiler, and these new steps were largely responsible for the considerable improvement shown by the Q compiler, both in terms of the speed and of the size of the object code generated. These improvements have been carried over into the VS Fortran compiler.

The first of the five steps is *local register optimization*, for which a subset of registers is made available. Here, the result of the evaluation of each quadruple is kept, if possible, in a register for use when referenced in a subsequent quadruple. Whenever there is no register available for a new result, one of the variables currently kept in a register has to be stored in virtual storage in order to make a register available. This optimization minimizes the number of storage references required during expression evaluation.

The second step is *global register optimization*, in which an attempt is made to keep the most frequently referenced variables and constants in registers reserved for this purpose, together with any registers not used during local register optimization. The decision whether to allocate a quantity to a register is based on a count kept of the number of references, with particular account being taken of register allocation inside inner loops, including the need to balance register allocation between global variables and fast branch instructions which need three registers.

After the two foregoing steps are complete, it may well be that some variables are common to both local and global register allocations, and that instructions for loads between registers have been introduced in order to transfer a global variable into or out of a local code sequence. These unnecessary loads can be eliminated either by performing the local code sequence entirely in the local register, if a calculated result is not required outside the sequence, or alternatively by performing the local code sequence entirely in the global register, if a result is required outside the sequence, or if the operand of a computation is in any case available in a global register. This procedure is called *global register remapping*.

After this step has been performed, there may be some local registers which have become unused inside loops, because the computations involving them have been transferred to global registers. In addition, the registers which by convention are reserved for subroutine linkage may also be unused within a loop. A fourth step, known as *global register scavenging* attempts to use such spare registers for any address constants which should be assigned to global registers, but for which there were previously no free registers available. (This step could make use of these registers for other quantities, but this is not done.)

The last register optimization, *global register purging*, deals with the situation in which global registers are initialized unnecessarily. This can happen when loops are nested, or when an outer loop contains a series of separate inner loops. In the first case the global registers may be initialized for one level of loop, and then re-intialized for the next level without having been used in between. In the second case, an inner loop may restore global registers ready for the outer loop, only for them to be destroyed again immediately by the following inner loop. In this step such unnecessary initializations are removed.

5. Branch Optimization

For subprograms whose total address range does not exceed about 8192 bytes, the exact size depending on the presence of such items as FORMAT statements, it is possible to perform all branches by using machine instructions which form the branch address by adding implicitly a 12-bit displacement to a 24-bit base address kept in a register. These direct branch instructions are faster than indirect branches which require the load of an address from memory followed by a branch to that address. Two address registers are allocated for direct branching.

When a subprogram is too long for the span of the two registers, the part beyond 8192 bytes is divided into sections of 4096 bytes, each of which can be addressed for internal branches using just one register. For branches inside the second and subsequent sections a third register is required for this purpose; this register is then no longer available for optimization purposes. At the beginning of each section, this third register is loaded with the section address to be used for direct branching.

Branching between sections requires the loading of the target section's address followed by a direct branch. This slower branching between sections is, of course, much less often needed than branching within sections.

6. Program Size and Structure

The way in which the intermediate text and the object code of a subprogram are optimized has certain consequences for the manner in which programs and data are structured, and code is written.

These, together with considerations arising from IBM system architecture, form the subject matter of the remaining sections of this chapter, which should be considered in conjunction with Chapters 5 and 7.

(Some of these points are equally valid for other IBM compatible or byte-addressable machines, such as the Amdahl and Fujitsu computers, which have similar instruction sets and Fortran extensions, and use comparable compiling techniques.)

We have seen that the compiler divides the intermediate text into blocks of code. In small subprograms it is advantageous to make these basic blocks as independent of one another as possible. This means especially that temporary variable names, and particularly loop control variables, should not be repeatedly re-used, but rather that a fresh name be introduced for each new independent occurrence of a temporary variable. This breaks any spurious and misleading links between blocks, allowing a higher degree of local optimization, and no waste of global registers for variables which are not truly global, but only seemingly so. The total number of variables and temporaries which can be subject to optimization is limited. However, this limit is larger than that required for even very large subprograms, and should cause no restriction on the choice of names, as it is anyway poor programming practice to write very large subprograms. (Under the H compiler it might have been necessary to re-use temporary names in large program units to avoid exceeding its much lower limit, even at the expense of risking artificial links between blocks). Since optimization is based on blocks, it is advantageous to limit their number by avoiding excessive use of statement labels and branches. The IF...THEN...ELSE control structure helps to achieve this.

As we have seen in the previous section, program units which exceed 8192 bytes in length require the use of a third address register to hold the section address. This register cannot be used for optimization purposes, and therefore some degradation in optimization is caused. This may amount to about 5%. It is then a good practice to keep the length of program units below the limit, both by dividing large routines into several smaller ones and by placing selected large local arrays in a COMMON block created for that purpose. Keeping program units to a reasonable size is in any case an excellent programming practice. The length of each subroutine may be determined by printing a program load-map during the load or link-edit job step.

A further degradation in optimization can result from the use of variables from too large a number of COMMON blocks within a given DO-loop. Each COMMON block reference requires a register to hold its base address, and if there are insufficient registers, those which otherwise would be used for other optimizations will be taken. This difficulty can be avoided by following the good programming practice of grouping variables in COMMON blocks according to their logical affinity. This tends to ensure that at a given place in the program only a few different blocks are being referenced, as all the variables required for the computation in question will be contained in one or a few blocks, and not be distributed in an untidy fashion over a larger number.

Within a given COMMON block some attention needs to be given to the order in which scalars and arrays of different lengths are declared. The address of a variable in a COMMON block is obtained by a reference to the base address of the block, adding it to a 12-bit displacement in a register. Since these 12 bits span only 4096 bytes, a second register is required to reach either scalars which are further than this from the base address, or arrays whose first element is similarly positioned. From this we can see that the optimum order is: scalars followed by small arrays followed by large arrays; thus in

COMMON/DATA/XIN,XOUT,NAME(10),BUFFER(4000)

the scalars and the first element of each array can be reached using a single register. If the large array BUFFER were to appear first in the sequence, the two scalars and the small array could be reached only by using a second register, which then becomes lost to the optimization procedures.

In critical cases a further gain can be obtained by keeping a frequently referenced COMMON variable as a local temporary variable. This eliminates the need to use repeatedly a COMMON block base address register for that variable, but this can be a dangerous practice, especially if the variable's value is changed inside the program unit, or by another program unit called from it.

7. Input/Output Operations

Input/output operations were discussed in a general fashion in Section 5.11, and the practices recommended there are valid for IBM computers. In particular, each I/O operation generates an initial and a final call to the Fortran I/O library, and the output list generates one additional call for each array and scalar referenced. Thus

```
REAL  A(100),B(100)
:
WRITE(NUNIT) A,(B(I),I  =  1,50)
```

generates a total of four calls to the Fortran I/O library subroutines. For an array not referenced either simply by its name, or through an implied DO-loop over contiguous elements of the arrays, the call is in a loop over the number of elements referenced. (The VS compiler does this for all array references.)

There are a number of problems, however, which are particularly troublesome on IBM computers, and which need to be considered when designing I/O lists. One is that it is inconvenient to read a record whose length is unknown, and records should therefore contain explicit length information if the program or programs are not dealing with lists of a permanently fixed length. This then encourages READ statements of the type

```
READ(NUNIT) N,  (A(I),I  =  1,N)
```

or of the type

```
READ(NUNIT) A
```

in the latter fixed length case.

Records of unknown length require recourse to special non-standard I/O packages (see, for instance, Matthews, 1980), or the repeated use of the system error recovery, after a preliminary call to the ERRSET routine to inform the system that this error is to be accepted:

```
CALL  ERRSET(213,256,5,1,1)
```

allows an unsatisfied list error (213) to occur an unlimited number of times (256). The first five occurrences will result in an error message being printed (5), but without traceback information (1), and with the default error recovery option selected (1).

This has the disadvantage of producing an additional overhead for each execution of the READ statement due to the need to perform the error recovery.

No particular problem arises from the use of special data types, which will be discussed further in the following section. To read or write an array which has been defined as INTEGER*2, where each array element is two bytes in length, it is perfectly possible to write code of the type

>   INTEGER*2 LEN,IBUF(100)
>   :
>   READ(NUNIT) LEN,(IBUF(I),I = 1,LEN)

There is a difficulty, however, in processing data which do not conform to the VS or VBS spanned record formats, as the U format itself is inadequately supported by the Fortran I/O library. This problem often arises when reading magnetic tapes written on non-IBM computers. In order to avoid the grossly inefficient method of using a formatted I/O statement with the A edit descriptor, combined with a RECFM = U declaration, it is once again necessary to resort to special purpose routines (Matthews, 1980).

When performing WRITE operations in Fortran, it is possible to keep to an irreducible minimum the amount of time spent in performing the physical output operations by appropriate choices of the logical record and block lengths, defined in the Job Control Language (JCL) by the Data Control Block (DCB) parameter. The savings thus obtained in supervisor overheads are repeated every time the data are read.

In general, the logical record length LRECL for formatted data is determined by the nature of the records being transmitted, for instance 80 bytes for card images. The block size, BLKSIZE, however, should be chosen so as to reduce the number of physical operations performed, by specifying as large a size as possible. This parameter determines the number of logical records which are transmitted in each physical block transfer; the IBM default value is a mere 800 bytes, which would imply the transfer of only 10 logical records if LRECL is defined to be 80 bytes.

For unformatted data the logical record length should be at least as large as the length of the records being transferred, and can be as long as four bytes less than the block size (or longer still for spanned records). When using magnetic tape the block size itself can have a maximum of 32760 bytes, and so here the ideal combination is

$$LRECL = 32756, BLKSIZE = 32760.$$

provided there is sufficient space available for the two buffers of 32760 bytes that this implies. However, to make the most efficient use of direct access peripheral devices, such as the IBM 3330 disc drives, which are used also as spool discs in the IBM 3850 Mass

Storage System, it is necessary to keep the maximum block size down to 13030 bytes in order to fill to the maximum each track on the disc. For the IBM 3350 disc drives a block size of 19069 bytes makes the best use of each track, and for the IBM 3380 the best size is 32760 bytes.

When writing to disc storage, the expected space required must be specified in the SPACE parameter, together with the amount by which the actual space taken may be extended; up to 16 extents are possible. It is advisable to make an over-estimate of the initial space required, in order to reduce or even eliminate the number of inefficient extents which actually occur, and to release any unused space at job completion by specifying RLSE (release) as the final SPACE sub-parameter.

For large scale I/O operations, the choice of the I/O list structure, logical record size, block size and access method, together with the avoidance of formatted operations and non-standard record formats can be crucial factors in the overall efficiency of a program. A final gain can be obtained by using the asynchronous READ/WRITE features mentioned in Section 5.11.

As a last point, it must be mentioned that the direct access I/O of Fortran 77 is considerably slower than the equivalent use of sequential files.

8. Special Data Types

The IBM Fortran compilers allow the use of data types in which the number of bytes per element may be specified. They are

```
LOGICAL    * 1
INTEGER    * 2
LOGICAL    * 4    (equivalent to LOGICAL)
INTEGER    * 4    (equivalent to INTEGER)
REAL       * 4    (equivalent to REAL)
REAL       * 8    (equivalent to DOUBLE PRECISION)
COMPLEX    * 8    (equivalent to COMPLEX)
REAL       * 16
COMPLEX    * 16
COMPLEX    * 32
```

For portability reasons, the use of the five declarations which have ANSI Fortran equivalents should be avoided, and the ANSI form used instead.

The use of double-precision on IBM computers leads to no loss of efficiency, as the floating-point registers are anyway 64 bits long, and all floating-point arithmetic operations are carried out in double-precision. Where double-precision has to be used extensively, it is more efficient to declare all floating-point variables to be double-precision, preferably with an IMPLICIT statement. This avoids intermediate conversions.

The extended precision declarations for complex and real quantities are sometimes required to obtain a sufficient degree of precision, but their use should be limited to those cases where it is really required, as portability is once again adversely affected, and still more storage space for arrays is required. Whereas the use of type COMPLEX involves no particular overhead, COMPLEX*16 and REAL*16 require two of the four floating-point registers for each variable, and this leads to an obvious problem in register allocation, and so to frequent stores and fetches, as only two variables can be stored in registers at any one time. COMPLEX*32 requires all four floating-point registers if both real and imaginary parts are accessed together!

A particular problem is that extended precision division is performed by software invoked after a specially generated system interrupt. The code in Ex. 46, due to Knoble, by which the expression X/Y can be replaced by the reference QDIV(X,Y), is about eight times faster, at the cost of a small loss in precision. The statement functions may equally well be built into an extended precision function.

```
* NEWTON-RAPHSON APPROX. FOR 1/Y
* (CACM 4(1961) 98). AGREEMENT TO 8
* LOW-ORDER BITS OF STANDARD METHOD
      REAL * 16 X,Y,QDIV
      DOUBLE PRECISION QPTODP
      QPTODP(Y) = Y
      QDIV(X,Y) =
   +    X*(1.D0/QPTODP(Y))*(2.Q0 - Y*(1.D0/QPTODP(Y)))
```

Example 46

The reduced precision declarations are often used to save space, but their use can cause considerable losses not only in portability but also in efficiency, and it should be restricted to those occasions when it is required to support data interchange with 8- or 16-bit computers.

The reasons for this loss in efficiency are various. When a

register is loaded with LOGICAL*1 variable, only the appropriate number of low-order bytes in the register are altered. This means that prior to the load the high-order bytes have to be zeroed by clearing the register. This operation requires an extra instruction, an overhead which may be reduced by instead clearing a register and assigning it to the variable throughout a sequence of references. Either way optimization is affected, either by the unnecessary extra instructions or by the loss of a register to a more deserving purpose.

It is also a fact that INTEGER*2 variables are less well optimized than full length integers – no strength reduction of arithmetic operations is performed, which makes their use as loop control variables an especially poor practice, as subscript calculations become slower.

The use of arrays of differing element lengths in DO-loops is another source of hidden overheads, as any apparently identical subscripts will, in fact, have to be evaluated separately for each array; thus in

```
      INTEGER*2 I(10)
      INTEGER J(10)
      :
      DO 1 K = 1,10
        J(K) = I(K)
    1 CONTINUE
```

the subscript expressions K require separate evaluations, but could be calculated just once if the array I were promoted to INTEGER*4.

Another problem occurs when assigning the contents of an INTEGER*2 variable to an INTEGER*4 variable without wishing to have the most significant bit treated as a sign bit, as is normally the case, but rather keeping the bit string intact and transferred directly into the lower two bytes of the longer word. The following cumbersome code sets the unchanged contents of I into the lower half of J, regardless of the sign of I, using the equivalenced array M as a vehicle:

```
      INTEGER * 2 I,M(2)
      EQUIVALENCE (J,M)
      :
      M(1) = 0
      M(2) = I
```

A hidden danger arising from the use of any variables other

than full word integers, logicals or reals occurs when their positioning in COMMON blocks or EQUIVALENCE statements causes either full-word quantities to be mis-aligned across half-word boundaries, or double-word quantities to be mis-aligned across word boundaries (see Section 2.5). Examples are

```
COMMON/DATA/IN,A(1000)
INTEGER*2 IN
```

and

```
COMMON/CALC/B(101),C(101)
COMPLEX C
```

in which each element of A is half in one word and half in the next, and each part of each element of C is in the wrong half of a double-word.

The compiler generates correct object code, but the fetches by the CPU are inefficient on badly aligned data in these instances (but not on the completely byte organized 308X computers). Fortunately the situation is reported by a diagnostic message, and remedial action should be taken wherever it is seen. All that is normally required is a padding variable of the length necessary to restore the correct alignment:

```
COMMON/DATA/IN,IPAD,A(1000)
INTEGER*2 IN,IPAD
```

9. Use of Storage

We have seen in Chapter 2 that IBM computers have four levels of storage of increasing size and decreasing access speed: registers, cache (buffer) storage, main storage and disc. The IBM System/370 virtual storage architecture is supported by the last three levels, and it is impossible for a programmer to know whether, during the execution of the code, a given variable will be in any particular one of the three levels. Only the transfers between registers and virtual storage are under direct object program control, and the actual location of a variable depends not only on the characteristics of a given program but also on all other system activity.

The large IBM mainframes are normally configured in such a way that all levels of storage are sufficiently large to cause no significant overheads for user programs. On smaller machines, and in exceptional but conceivable circumstances on large ones, there are nevertheless a number of considerations which should be borne in mind, and they form the subject matter of this section.

The first is the question of the interleaving of data fetches and stores from main storage. The transfer of data between the main and cache storage takes place in units of double-words of eight bytes. Consecutive double-words in program storage locations are kept physically in separate memory banks, so that when a sequence of double-words is transferred the first pair of words will move to (or from) one bank, the next pair to the next bank and so on, up to the number of banks, which is typically four, eight or sixteen. It is possible for a program to contain inadvertently an addressing pattern such that only one memory bank is addressed, thereby causing a very significant reduction in the transfer rate of data between the cache and main memories. This can happen if an array's first dimension coincides with the bank interleaving factor, and if the array is then referenced row-wise rather than column-wise. Assuming four-way interleaving, the following is such an example:

```
      REAL  A(8,1000)
      DO 1 I  =  1,1000
         A(1,I)  =  FLOAT(I)
    1 CONTINUE
```

Here one bank is continuously referenced, and in addition the second half of the double-word transferred each time, A(2,I), is never used. This situation can be avoided at the cost of some storage by increasing the first dimension of A to 9.

A similar problem can arise with any row-wise manipulation of an array, as in

$$A(I,J) = A(I,J-1)+A(I,J+1)$$

or in back-to-back arrays:

```
      REAL  A(64),B(64)
      DO 1 I  =  1,64
         A(I)  =  B(I)+1.
    1 CONTINUE
```

We have seen in the example above how half of the words transferred were never actually referenced, as the transfer of any word involves the transfer of its neighbour, and stepping row-wise through an array will imply twice as many fetches as are really required. The situation is, in fact, somewhat worse than this, as during the following machine cycles the next three (IBM S/370-168) or seven (IBM 3033) double words will also be fetched, on the assumption that they too will be required. This type of waste can also occur with other addressing patterns if the array is unfortunately positioned. Consider the array A in

COMMON/DATA/I,A(1600)

On the IBM 168 the quadruple double-word block pattern begins with the sequence I to A(7), and continues with A(8) to A(15), then A(16) to A(23) *etc.* If we now step through the array using the following loop

```
      K = 1
      DO 1 I = 7,1591,16
         B(K) = A(I) + A(I + 1)
         K = K + 1
    1 CONTINUE
```

then every word of A will be transferred from virtual storage to cache, as the loop succeeds in addressing one word in each of the stored quadruple double-word blocks. If, on the other hand, the variable I were not in the COMMON block the storage block pattern would be A(1) to A(8) followed by A(9) to A(16) etc., and only every second complete block would be accessed, so that only half the number of transfers would be required, and fewer unnecessary transfers would take place.

The cache memory plays an important role in lessening the interleaving problem described above, as once the data words have been transferred to the cache, they are likely to remain there if frequently referenced, and the interleaving presents no further difficulty. On models prior to the IBM 3081, the interleaving problem still existed for storage operations, as any store instruction caused an immediate update of the data in main memory. If the store was not of a double-word, the double-word to which the data word belonged also had to be fetched and updated first in the cache, unless it was already there.

The size of the installed cache should be known to any programmer making intensive use of all the elements of large arrays, as otherwise a disastrous condition know as *thrashing* can occur in which it is impossible for the operating system to fit the whole of the arrays into the cache, because it is simply too small to accommodate them. This leads to continual flushing and reloading of the cache and is very inefficient. Fortunately this problem is rarely met.

Another way in which poor use of the cache occurs is when using several separate long arrays in the following manner:

```
REAL X(10000), Y(10000), Z(10000), W(10000)
:
DO 1 I = 1,10000
    W(I) = X(I) + Y(I) + Z(I)
1 CONTINUE
```

In this case three separate fetch streams are required for X, Y, and Z. If the arrays were combined into a single array of triplets

$$XYZ(3,10000)$$

then the values required simultaneously would automatically be transferred and be available together.

The last consideration with respect to the use of storage on IBM systems is concerned with the virtual storage architecture and paging. The IBM System/370 software and hardware contain very sophisticated mechanisms for ensuring that for the normal user the transfer of the 4 Kbyte pages between disc and main memory remains unnoticed. Since paging activity is dependent on the state of the whole system rather than on just a single program, it is hardly possible to assess any inefficiencies which can arise in this environment. However, it is possible to state some guidelines which will certainly minimize any paging overheads, whatever their magnitude may be (see also Schneck, 1983).

The first guideline is to maintain *locality of reference*. This implies the need to process sequentially through a given area of both data and code during program execution. In other words, program units treating a certain set of data should be grouped together, and references to the data should not jump around wildly inside the set of data. In this way the program passes steadily through each page of both data and instructions. Large arrays should be dimensioned and referenced in DO-loops in a conventional fashion, as described in Section 7.3.

The second guideline is to reduce the amount of *instantaneous real storage* to a minimum. There will be less paging activity if there are fewer pages being referenced at any point in the program's execution. This once again implies writing code in a modular way and also grouping data logically, so that only a few separate pages of data are referenced at any one time.

The last guideline is to ensure *validity of reference*. This is a means of reducing paging by eliminating unnecessary references to data. For instance, if long searches through data are made, then only a small number of words from a large number of pages may actually be required. This type of unnecessary paging can be reduced by an appropriate selection of data structures, for example using arrays which can be directly addressed, rather than chains which cannot and which have to be searched. Any form of indirect addressing in large data structures is harmful in this respect.

10. Error Recovery

During the execution of a program, it is possible that certain system errors such as floating-point underflow occur. If this happens, the error will be detected by the hardware, and the following sequence of events will take place:

i) the CPU signals the underflow to the operating system;

ii) the operating system determines that control should return to the user program;

iii) the interrupt is analysed;

iv) an error message is prepared;

v) the Fortran error monitor routine is called;

vi) the error monitor prints the error message, or determines that no message is to be printed;

vii) the erroneous result is set to 0 if the standard corrective action is taken;

viii) the interrupt handler restarts the Fortran program.

It is a not uncommon practice to set the allowed number of underflows to an unlimited value by a call to ERRSET:

$$\text{CALL ERRSET}(208,256,-1,1,1)$$

will suppress all error messages and trace back information, and eliminate this part of the overhead even though the interrupt must still be handled. The default corrective action taken, setting the result to zero, is almost certainly what is required, and the results calculated are correct, but at the cost of a hidden overhead if the error is very frequent. The number of occurrences is printed at the end of each job.

There are two ways in which this inefficiency can be eliminated. The first is the obvious one of tracking down the source of the underflow and modifying the code accordingly. The second, if the first course is too difficult, is to modify the Program Status Word (PSW), which is a word held by the system and which contains status bits indicating the way in which the program should be controlled. By calling the following assembly language routine at the beginning of the program execution (CALL ZERO), no interrupt is ever signalled and the result is set to zero directly by the CPU (see IBM, 1980a):

```
ZERO    CSECT
        SR  1,1         Clear general register 1
        SPM 1           Unset exception condition bits
        BR  14          Return to calling routine
        END
```

9 THE CDC FTN COMPILERS

1. Background

With their introduction in 1965 of the CDC 6600 computer, the Control Data Corporation achieved a pre-eminent position in the field of large-scale scientific and engineering computing (see also Section 2.6). The subsequent CDC 7600 and larger CYBER series machines have enabled CDC to maintain this position, although they are now by no means unchallenged in this expanding area of the market. The full potential of the novel architecture of these machines can be exploited only by sophisticated compilers which are not only able to perform the standard optimizations we have met in Chapters 3 and 7, but in addition are capable of issuing the machine instructions in a sequence which ensures that the pipelining and parallel processing features of the multiple functional units are effectively used.

There are two principal CDC Fortran compilers, both of which generate efficient object code, the now obsolete and unsupported FTN compiler corresponding to Fortran 66 with extensions, and the modern FTN 5 compiler (CDC, 1979a) corresponding to Fortran 77 with extensions. The optimization techniques used are largely common to both, and there is a large degree of backwards compatibility built into the new compiler. When program conversion is nevertheless necessary, an automatic tool, F45 (CDC, 1979b) is available to deal with the most common outstanding problems in a convenient way. Guidance to various aspects of Fortran usage in the CYBER environment is given in a user's guide (CDC, 1981). The FTN 5 compiler provides excellent compile-time diagnostics and source cross-reference maps, and incorporates a *post mortem* dump analyser which prints annotated, translated memory dumps in the event of program failure at execution-time. The FTN 5 compiler contains four levels of optimization, designated as OPT = 0, 1, 2 and 3.

As a first step to optimizing programs running under FTN 5, the advice given in Chapters 5 and 7 should be followed, as this is directly applicable and in many instances sufficient. The remainder of this chapter is devoted to a brief description of the optimization carried out by the compiler at its highest optimization levels, and to some of the ensuing implications, as well as to some considerations deriving from the CYBER architecture itself.

2. FTN 5 Optimizations

The highest levels of optimization, OPT = 2 and 3, perform an identical set of operations, with two exceptions which will be indicated below. As a first step, any constant expressions are evaluated by the compiler itself, for example, 2*3.3 would be replaced by 6.6. Next, any unnecessary expressions and instructions within each statement are eliminated, for instance

$$(A + B)/C + D*(A + B)$$

would become, symbolically, with Ri standing for a register,

R1 = A		R5 = R3/R4
R2 = B		R6 = D
R3 = R1 + R2		R7 = R3*R6
R4 = C		R8 = R5 + R7

thus eliminating the common expression. The program is next divided into basic blocks, and a similar operation performed over a range of several statements. Thus, in

```
1   X = Y * Z
    A = X + B
    X = X / R
2   ......
```

the first store of the value of X can be eliminated as it is redefined immediately afterwards in the same basic block. In a similar way dead-code, code which can never be entered, can be removed: in

```
      GOTO 1
      X = Y + Z
   2  A = B ** 2
```

the second statement can never be executed, and is deleted.

The DO- and IF-loops within the program are analysed and certain optimizations performed in loops satisfying the following conditions:

— the loop has no entry other than the normal entry at the beginning;

— the loop has no exit other than the normal exit at the end;

— the loop contains no external references, *i.e.* references to user defined functions or subroutines, to any I/O operation, to any STOP or PAUSE, or to any reference to those intrinsic functions which are referenced *via* an external reference rather than through substitution by in-line code;

— the loop contains no GOTO or IF-statement which branches back to a statement appearing previously in the loop.

In innermost loops which do not fail on any of these counts, any array subscript expressions will be simplified, and the values of simple integer variables will be stored in registers throughout loop execution. Thus in

```
      REAL  A(10), B(10), C(10, 20)
      :
      DO 1  I = 1, N
         A(I) = B (I) * C (4 * I + J, K)
   1  CONTINUE
```

the values of I and N will be maintained in registers, and the base array subscript of C will become

$$10 * K - 6 + J$$

which is then incremented by four on each iteration.

At this stage, the compiler collects information about the whole program unit, in order to perform a number of global optimizations. The first of these is to eliminate redundant storage operations of local variables where values are no longer required within the program. In the sequence

```
X = Y * Z
A = X + B
END
```

where X is a local variable and A a COMMON variable, it is unnecessary to retain the final value of X in memory, and no store instruction to this effect will be issued.

Next, a search is made for invariant code inside loops. Any invariant sub-expressions which are found are moved to the prologue of the loop containing them. Invariant code is not moved from an innermost loop to the outermost of a set of nested loops, as the innermost loop may never be executed if it is, in effect, a zero-trip loop. This slight loss of efficiency can be regained by selecting the $DO = OT$ compiler option, which ensures that each loop is executed at least once, as happened with the old FTN compiler. In addition, this option relieves the compiler of the obligation of making the test for completion before the first iteration of the loop, and so the amount of code generated is considerably less for short nested loops. If programs are compiled without this option, it is more important than ever that the innermost loop is the one which has the largest number of iterations.

Following this, a check is made for any array subscript expression inside a loop which contains an induction variable, that is, an integer whose value is incremented once during each iteration of the loop. Where possible, the strength of any operation involving such a variable is reduced by substituting an addition for a multiplication. The reference to the array B in

```
      K = 4 * N + 3
      DO 1  I = 1, N
        K = K + 1
        A (I) = B (J, K)
    1 CONTINUE
```

contains a subscript expression

$$(K - 1) *(\text{column length of } B) + J$$

for which an initial value of

$[(4*N + 3 - 1)*(\text{column length of } B) + J]$

can be established, and this value can then be incremented by the column length of B at the beginning of each iteration.

To the extent that registers are available, array addresses, the values of central memory scalar variables and subscript expressions are kept in them throughout the execution of each loop. In the case of both loops and complicated sections of straight-line code, the values of array elements and subscripts are also kept in registers.

A final optimization is the pre-fetching of array elements in short loops. In

```
      REAL  A(100, 100)
      :
      DO 1  I = 1, 100, 10
        S = S + A (J, I)
    1 CONTINUE
```

each array element $A(J, I+10)$ is fetched during the Ith iteration of the loop, to be ready for the following iteration. In the case of OPT = 2, a check is made to ensure that it is unlikely that a reference to a location beyond the program's field length will be made, which would then cause an address range error. For OPT = 3, the so-called unsafe optimization level, no such check is made, and the final reference to A (J,101) might produce an execution-time error if A is located at the end of the field length.

One further optimization is provided by OPT = 3, namely the assumption that calling intrinsic functions will leave the contents of certain index registers untouched. This means that in the presence of such function references, the contents of those registers do not have to be saved and restored, as would otherwise be the case. This optimization becomes unsafe only if a non-standard mathematical library is used in conjunction with the compiler.

The final optimization stage of the compiler at all levels other than OPT = 0, is to attempt to ensure that the instructions it generates are issued in an order which makes the fullest possible use of the functional units. This is achieved by performing a critical path analysis of each section of the code, using the known dependencies between the instructions and the time each one will require to execute. A simple example of this has been given in Section 2.6.

3. Program Size and Structure

The compiler decomposes the source code into basic blocks, which are segments of code having a single entry and a single exit point (see also Section 3.7); this enables it to eliminate any unnecessary operations within a block, as shown in the examples at the beginning of the previous section. The compiler should not be allowed to become confused in its basic block analysis by the presence of redundant or unnecessary statement labels. To this end, the use of IF-blocks rather than logical and arithmetic IF's is recommended.

In its basic block analysis, the compiler does not distinguish between program loops defined by DO-loops or by IF-statements, to the extent that an IF-loop resembles a DO-loop. IF-loops should be written in as simple a form as possible, and will then benefit from the same optimization procedures as are applied to DO-loops, particularly the movement of invariant code and the elimination of common sub-expressions.

```
      TEMP = A ** 2
      C = TEMP + B
      Q = X * TEMP
  1   ............
      :
      TEMP = D + 4.0
      Y = TEMP + 3.0
      Z = 9. * TEMP
```

Example 47

The optimization procedures are helped by a straightforward program logic, with a minimum of statement labels and a simple path through the code; the total length of a subprogram is ideally about 100 statements, but should in no case exceed 600. An effort should be made not to link artificially parts of the code which are, in fact, independent. This might happen when temporary variable names are re-used. The two blocks in Ex. 47 are badly written because the common expression elimination is anyway unnecessary, and the use of the name TEMP twice can confuse the compiler into believing that there is some logical connection between the two blocks, leading it to save the value of TEMP at the end of each block. The compiler is able to perform the same optimization using a register in each case.

Similarly, DO-loops should always have different control

variables. In short loops such as

```
    DO 1  I = 1, 10
      A(2, I) = 2. * B
  1 CONTINUE
```

in which I is used as a simple index and is not a COMMON variable, nor required outside the loop, its value will be retained only within a register, and will never be stored in central memory, provided the DO = OT compiler option is used. Such a variable is said not to *materialize.*

The FTN compilers also have the feature that any multiplication used in a subscript calculation is replaced by a shift if all the dimensions but the last of the array specification are powers of two. Thus, it can be advantageous to write an array dimension as, for instance, A(16,5) rather than A(15,5), gaining some extra speed at the cost of a larger memory requirement. This is useful mainly in long sections of straight-line code containing subscripts which do not benefit from the strength reduction optimization applied to subscript calculations inside loops.

CDC CYBER computers provide 14 decimal digits of precision for single-precision floating-point operations. This implies that it is rarely necessary to make use of double-precision arithmetic, and if this should become necessary it might be worth some effort to locate the area of code causing the loss of significance, and to use a more robust algorithm. Double-precision calculations generate nearly 20 operations for an addition or a multiplication, as arithmetic operations are carried out in double-precision by the hardware in a 96-bit mantissa register, but the lower half is accessible only using additional instructions, and so double-precision arithmetic has effectively to be performed by software. Thus, to add two quantities Aa and Bb in double-precision, the following basic operations will be performed (normalizations are ignored):

   i) add lower part of Aa, a, to lower part of Bb, b;
      retain upper part of sum u(ab);

  ii) add upper part of Aa, A, to upper part of Bb, B;
      retain lower part of sum l(AB);

 iii) add A to B; retain upper part of sum u(AB);

  iv) add u(ab) to l(AB); retain upper part of sum u(u(ab)l(AB));

v) add u(u(ab)l(AB)) to u(AB);
   retain lower part of sum l(u(u(ab)l(AB))u(AB));

vi) add u(u(ab)l(AB)) to u(AB);
   retain upper part of sum u(u(u(ab)l(AB))u(AB));

vii) add l(u(u(ab)l(AB))u(AB)) to u(u(u(ab)l(AB))u(AB));
   store lower part of sum;

viii) add l(u(u(ab)l(AB))u(AB)) to u(u(u(ab)l(AB))u(AB));
   store upper part of sum.

This laborious procedure is much slower than single-precision arithmetic, occupies all the operand registers, and is to be avoided unless absolutely necessary.

4. Intrinsic Functions

The intrinsic functions provided by the FTN 5 compiler may be divided into two classes − those which compile as in-line code, and those which generate references to external functions. The first class corresponds to those functions described as basic intrinsic functions in the old FTN manual (Table 8-1 of CDC,1977), and contains some important extensions to the functions described in the ANSI standard.

```
      IF (X.LT.Y) GOTO 1
      IF (Y.LT.Z) GOTO 2
      SMALL = Z
      GOTO 4
   1  IF (X.LT.Z) GOTO 3
      SMALL = Z
      GOTO 4
   2  SMALL = Y
      GOTO 4
   3  SMALL = X
   4  ....
```

Example 48

It is always more efficient to choose from the highly optimized functions of this class than to write the equivalent code in Fortran, but extensive use of the non-standard functions renders a program non-portable, and they should be confined to sections of the code where they are demonstrably necessary. Thus, the code of Ex. 48 should always be replaced by the much more efficient

$$SMALL = MIN (X, Y, Z)$$

in all cases.

On the other hand, in the case of the masking and shifting functions great care is needed to isolate their use to a few parts of a program, in order to make any conversion to a different type of computer easier. Use of the masking operators is highly undesirable in any program which is likely to be run on other computers, and their completely equivalent functions should be used instead:

$$
\begin{array}{lll}
& \text{COMPL (I)} & \text{for} \quad \text{.NOT.I} \\
& \text{AND (I,J,K)} & \text{for} \quad \text{I.AND.J.AND.K} \\
\text{and} & \text{OR (I,J,K)} & \text{for} \quad \text{I.OR.J.OR.K}
\end{array}
$$

To mask, for example, the leftmost 12 bits of a word, the statement

$$I = AND (J, MASK (12))$$

is optimized in terms of both space and memory references, as the mask is generated with a short instruction, obviating the need to use a long instruction to fetch a pre-defined mask from memory, where one location would also be required to store its value. This form should normally be used.

The AND function can be used to replace the far slower MOD function for a modulus which is a power of two and a constant:

$$J = AND (I, 511)$$

is faster than

$$I = MOD (I, 512)$$

For functions which have constants as arguments, and which are referred to many times, it is possible to call them just once at compile-time by placing them in a non-standard PARAMETER statement:

```
BOOLEAN MASK50
PARAMETER (MASK50 = SHIFT (1, 50))
```

5. DO-loop Inspection

If the LO = M parameter is selected on the FTN5 control statement, a DO-loop map will be printed following the source listing. From this map it is possible to see whether any loss of optimization in DO-loops has occurred. Loss of optimization can occur for one of four reasons, denoted by the so-called properties:

XREF   the loop contains some form of external reference;
OPEN   the loop is re-entered from outside its range;
OUTER   the loop contains other loops;
EXIT   the loop refers to statement labels outside its range.

It is always worth considering these messages if they are generated for critical loops, and to attempt to remove any impediment to optimization.

In Section 2.6 the operation of the instruction word stack (IWS) has been described, and the manner in which the instructions of short loops can be maintained in the stack, rather than being fetched repeatedly from memory, has been indicated. By selecting the LO = O option, it is possible to see whether a given loop fits into the IWS, which is the case if it occupies no more than ten instruction words. If a critical loop is marginally too long to fit completely into the IWS, it may be worth trying to find a means to shorten it by the required amount, for instance by checking that it contains no unnecessary calculations or memory references, or that it is not suffering from attempts to hand-optimize it in a clumsy way.

A library of routines for vector operations, written with all loops in the stack, is available (McMahon *et al.*, 1972), but its use renders the source code non-portable as the library is incompatible with any other computer system.

6. Second Level Memory

CDC CYBER systems are normally provided with a central memory backed by a larger second level memory, which, depending on the system, is known as Large Core Memory, Extended Core Store, Large Semi-conductor Store or External Extended Memory. Access to this level of storage from a Fortran program is by one of two methods, designated LEVEL 2 and LEVEL 3; LEVEL 2 refers to second level storage only on the CYBER 170/176, 70/76 and 7600 computers, on all other systems it defaults to central memory. The LEVEL 3 statement refers to second level storage on all systems.

The only quantities which may appear in a LEVEL statement are COMMON block names and dummy argument names; in

```
SUBROUTINE SHOW (X)
COMMON/EXTEND/A (10000), B (10000)
REAL X(*)
LEVEL 3,/EXTEND/, X
```

the arrays A and B are assigned to second level storage, and the compiler is informed that the array X has also been located there by the calling subroutine.

On systems which assign LEVEL 2 quantities to second level storage, there is no restriction on the use of any of those quantities. In particular, any LEVEL 2 variable may appear in an expression. LEVEL 3 quantities may, on the other hand, be referenced only *via* the MOVLEV system routine, which performs block copies of arrays between the two levels of storage, or within one level:

```
COMMON/EXTEND/A (1000)
LEVEL 3,/EXTEND/
REAL B(500)
          :
CALL MOVLEV (A (501), B, 500)
```

The second level storage systems are characterised by long access times and fast transfer rates. Thus, to fetch isolated words or short arrays from second level storage into central memory is inefficient, whereas long block copies are very efficient, and may safely be heavily used to organize large data arrays. A 512 word buffer between the two levels means that efficient access to small, neighbouring areas of storage is also possible. However, in spite of this fast transfer, it is clearly desirable to organize the logic flow of a program in such a way as to minimize the total number of transfers, as this adversely affects the overall performance of the program. Transfers should, in all cases, be of a few long blocks rather than many short ones.

A special routine, MOVLCH, is available for block copies of CHARACTER data between storage levels, or between two character strings in the same level of storage.

7. Input/Output Operations

Efficiency considerations for I/O operations have been described in Section 5.11, and the points mentioned there are applicable to the CYBER systems and the FTN 5 compiler. It is, however, worthwhile mentioning here a few points which are specific to these systems, and which can have an important effect on the efficiency of programs performing relatively large amounts of I/O.

A primary consideration is the use of the buffer which is required for each file. This circular buffer is provided by the system and filled each time a read buffer becomes empty or emptied when a write buffer becomes full. The size of the buffer is of critical importance when performing large amounts of I/O, as a small buffer implies a larger than necessary number of physical I/O operations. The size of a buffer is by default 1024 words, and may be conveniently redefined using the non-standard BUFL parameter of the OPEN statement. The size of a buffer may safely be reduced to a minimum of 65 words for files which are hardly used or have very small units of transfer, for instance for terminal I/O; this is a simple way of saving space. Medium activity files should be larger, and be allocated in multiples of the 64 words of a physical record unit (PRU), which is the unit of size of disc file records. Magnetic tape buffers with high throughput require larger buffers of at least 128 words for formatted data and 512 words for unformatted data. These minimum buffer sizes should be doubled to achieve high performance. I/O buffers are released when a CLOSE statement is executed on a file, and this option should be used on any files which are read just once at the beginning of program execution, in order to release the buffer space.

No I/O buffer at all is required if the BUFFER IN or BUFFER OUT statements are used in place of standard Fortran I/O. In this case data transfers take place directly into or out of a buffer defined in the Fortran program. In

```
REAL BUFFER(1000)
BUFFER IN (1, 1) (BUFFER (1), BUFFER (1000))
IF (UNIT (1).LT.0.) THEN
    LENB = LENGTH (1)
    :
```

the program requests the transfer of 1000 words directly into BUFFER. The UNIT function, if negative, indicates that a successful transfer has taken place, and returns control to the calling program only when the operation is complete. The actual number of words transferred is provided by the LENGTH function.

When reading records from magnetic tape, the read operations are under control of a Peripheral Processor Unit (PPU) rather than of the CPU itself (Section 2.6). A single PPU is able to deal only with records which do not exceed 512 words in length; records in excess of this require double buffering and a second PPU is taken from the system. This implies that heavy use of long records from magnetic tape can result in performance degradations for the whole system, as a PPU removed from the pool of available PPU's for this purpose is unable to accept any other system tasks while the read is in progress.

Another point to consider is the use of direct or random access files. These may be used in a straightforward manner *via* standard Fortran 77 commands, and may be more efficient than sequential files if their use removes the need to perform repeated searches through long files. In most other cases sequential files are probably faster, and in doubtful situations tests should be carried out to compare the two access methods for a particular application.

Lastly, the use of system default record and blocking formats is likely to result in much faster data transfers than is achieved using formats which require additional processing by the I/O routines.

10 FORTRAN PORTABILITY

1. Software Portability

There are certain attributes associated with any piece of software; these might include its robustness, degree of modularity, ease of maintenance, standard of internal and external documentation, storage requirements or run-time efficiency. The circumstances in which the software is used will normally determine which of any possible attributes are of greatest importance – a library routine should be robust and a utility package well documented. In an ideal world all software would combine the highest standards of all these desirable features.

Another attribute which is sometimes of no importance but which can sometimes be an overriding consideration is program portability – the ability to move software from one computer system to another with an insignificant number of changes, and to obtain essentially identical results. In this definition a computer system is the ensemble of the hardware and the operating system, including its compiler, and implies that a change in any of its parts, including the use of a different compiler, creates a different computer system. The definition of portability is often extended to include the statement that a program should be cancelled if it cannot be run correctly on a computer system, rather than be allowed to run and give wrong results.

The nature of portability is linked to the level of the language as well as to the types of mainframes on which a program must run. Operating systems written in low-level languages often need to be portable between computers within the range of a given architecture, but are excluded by the language used from being moved to an incompatible machine. Applications programs written in high-level languages must not only possess this degree of portability, but must additionally often be portable over a range of computers of varying power, memory size and word length. In a world in which the costs of software development are rising steeply compared to the cost of hardware, the question of portability is one which takes on an increasing degree of importance, as there is a general need to reduce the effort involved in program conversion. The topic of general software portability has been treated in Brown (1977), an exhaustive check list of points to consider appears in Tannenbaum *et al.* (1978) and a list of points specifically for Fortran programs is given in Metcalf (1985). In this chapter the discussion will be confined to the problem of the portability of Fortran 77 programs, its background and its consequences.

2. Fortran and Portability

For almost all mathematical and scientific applications Fortran is now the language which has acquired an unrivalled degree of universality. A scientist travelling to a new location will certainly expect to find a computer with a Fortran compiler installed as part of the standard equipment available to him. What he will probably not expect to find is a system which is so similar in all respects to the one with which he is familiar, that he is not obliged to go through the dreaded process of program conversion and testing, necessary to get his programs into a working state in their new environment. The major problems in this respect are those of Fortran dialects, error conditions and recovery, character handling, I/O features and the precision of the computer arithmetic; this assumes that the program source code and its associated input data have themselves been successfully transported and embedded into the new host job control language, which is often itself a non-trivial task.

During the 1970's a number of studies were undertaken on the problems of writing Fortran in such a way as to be compatible with the largest possible number of compilers (see, for example, Larmouth, 1973 (a) and (b), and Day, 1978). The guidelines they describe are still relevant for those writing or dealing with programs written for compilers conforming to the obsolete 1966 Fortran standard. Here the problems were legion, as the deficiencies of the standard were a positive inducement to compiler writers to introduce extensions which were eagerly used by programmers. The purpose of having a standard was only partially achieved, as to adhere to the letter of the standard required a degree of knowledge and discipline which is only rarely found (Muxworthy, 1976). There came into existence a widely used set of common extensions. The new standard has brought some semblance of order to the situation, and has greatly lessened the need to use local syntax extensions and non-standard I/O features. The new CHARACTER variables and direct access I/O features are especially useful, but underline the often serious conflict between portability and efficiency which has been touched upon in Section 4.4, as their definitions are now perfectly standardised but their implementations are often inefficient.

However, just as many Fortran 66 compilers included extensions, so we now see a comparable development in the new Fortran 77 compilers. Those of DEC and Fujitsu, for example, contain control constructs like DO...WHILE or DO...UNTIL which are highly non-portable, and this distinct trend to extend the standard in new ways and in a disorganized fashion can only be regretted.

The fact that some of the present Fortran 77 compilers are relatively new means that they are sometimes likely to contain a significant number of errors, and in particular may not always conform to the standard in every respect. A study of the conformity of early Fortran 77 compilers was conducted by Vallance (1981) and resulted in the publication of a number of small programs which test some of the more tricky areas of compiler conformity, and may be used as an initial test of an unfamiliar compiler, before attempting to convert a large program. It is clearly difficult to transport a program which is written according to the standard if the compiler to be used does not itself conform.

It is now in order to ask what advice can be given to ease the problem of Fortran 77 program portability. The most trivial suggestion is to keep rigidly to the standard, to avoid any extensions which might be offered by a given compiler and to avoid probing too deeply into the areas where the standard sets no precise bounds, such as in defining the maximum possible length of a variable of type CHARACTER. However, this advice by itself is insufficient, as few programmers actually read and are familiar with the standard, and are anyway reluctant to discipline their coding sufficiently strictly. Nor are certain obvious machine dependencies, such as arithmetic precision, in any way treated by the standard. In order to make some rather more helpful suggestions, the following section discusses a number of the more important points of the standard and their implications for portability. Non-standard items will not be dealt with. The inspiration for much of this information comes from a study by Larmouth (1981), and fuller details may be obtained by referring to his comprehensive analysis.

One important aid to portability which can be provided by any serious compiler is a means to warn a programmer that he is using the language in a non-standard way. This may be done in two ways, the first by marking non-standard features in a clear way in the compiler manual, and the second by diagnosing with a warning message non-standard use at compile-time. Manufacturers who do not provide at least one of these two facilities, should have this deficiency brought to their attention by their users' representatives in no uncertain terms, as a major obstacle to producing portable code is simple ignorance of what conforms and what does not conform to the standard.

It is also interesting to consider one positive aspect of portability: it will often be found that installing a large program on a radically different computer will reveal the presence of some previously undetected errors, and converting a new program to run on an another system before its final release can be a useful exercise just for this purpose.

3. Problem Areas in the Language

In this section the hints on achieving portability follow the order of the relevant sections of the standard, and the references in square brackets are to those sections.

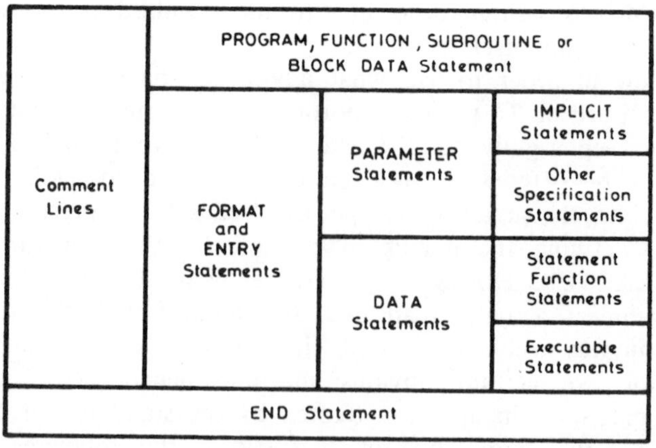

Fig. 22   Order of Statements

The *collating sequence* of the Fortran character set [3.1.5] is only partially defined as being 'A, B, C ..... X, Y, Z' and '0, 1 ..... 8, 9' in two distinct sequences whose order with respect to one another is not defined. The position of the character blank is defined to be less than ʼAʼ and less than ʼ0ʼ, but the collating position of no other special character is defined. We may therefore see that portable code should either not rely on a particular order beyond that just given, or should contain its own user defined sequence, as described by Larmouth (p. 1092 of the reference). For making relational tests on composite character strings, the intrinsic functions LGE *etc.* should be preferred to the relational operators .GE. *etc.,* as the former refer to the ASCII collating sequence rather than the Fortran one, and are therefore processor independent for all characters in the ASCII character set; for example

IF (LGT(STRNG1,STRNG2)) GO TO 1

The standard does not define the *mapping of variables* of type CHARACTER [4.8] onto the word of a computer. The number of characters stored in a word is, therefore, processor-dependent and it follows that character variables may not be mixed in their storage association with variables of other types, as their relative positions would change depending on the computer used. This means that character variables may not appear in a COMMON declaration with variables of other types, nor may an association be made by an EQUIVALENCE statement. The fact that this is allowed by some compilers can result in non-portable code.

The *order of statements* [3.5] is shown graphically in Fig. 22. This order should always be adhered to, in spite of the lax rules of many compilers. IMPLICIT declarations of a given letter and type declarations or DATA definitions of a given variable should appear once only.

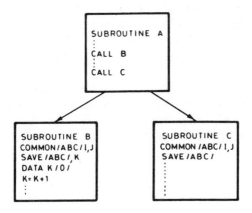

Fig. 23   Use of SAVE for COMMON Blocks

The *SAVE statement* [8.9] is ignored by many compilers, and failure to use it can then lead to code producing wrong results on computers where it is required. All local variables which are modified during the execution of a subprogram, and whose new values are required when the subprogram is next called, should be listed in a SAVE statement. Similarly, COMMON blocks which do not appear in subprograms which reference directly or indirectly a given subprogram, and whose variables are required upon a subsequent call to that subprogram, or in another subprogram which is on a different calling path, should have their names listed between slashes in a SAVE declaration. This is illustrated in Fig. 23 where the block ABC is in a SAVE declaration in order to ensure that its variables are retained for joint use in the subprograms B and C. It could just as well be referenced in subprogram A to achieve the same effect.

The *assigned GOTO statement* [11.3] contains an optional list of statement labels which must include the assigned statement label if it is present. Some non-conforming compilers ignore the list, but it is a good practice to write all assigned GOTO's with the list, as potential errors will be found by any conforming compiler used for the program:

ASSIGN 10 TO I

:

GOTO I, (10, 20, 30)

The *block IF statement* [11.6] and the *DO-loop* [11.10] both have a range which is defined as the section of code between the beginning of the block or loop and its termination with an ENDIF or loop termination, respectively. Transfer into the range of a block or loop is prohibited by the standard but allowed by some compilers; portable code should never contain such branches. Similarly, control may not be transferred into an ELSEIF or ELSE block from outside its range.

Nested DO-loops which share a common terminator should contain no jump from an outer loop to the terminator since this may, under some compilers, cause incorrect results, as the range of the innermost loop may thereby be entered at its termination, causing unpredictable behaviour:

```
DO 1    I = 1, 10
    :
    IF (...)    GO TO 1           < - -    illegal branch
    :
    DO 1 J = 1, 10
        :
1   CONTINUE
```

The extension of DO-loops in the new standard to allow real control variables and loop parameters can cause problems for program portability, as any rounding errors in the calculation of the number of iterations can lead to a difference in the number of iterations (see also Section 5.6). In addition, as the control variable is incremented at each iteration by the value of the third loop parameter, a loop with a large number of iterations can cause the rounding errors in the incrementing to accumulate slowly. This feature of the language should not be used in portable programs, especially as it is likely to be removed from future standards (see Chapter 12).

The area of Fortran *Input/Output* [12] was one which was insufficiently well defined in the old standard. In particular, there was no mention of error handling, and this meant that each implementation provided its own method of dealing with this obvious requirement. The new standard contains important extensions to the I/O facilities, especially for direct access I/O, internal files (replacing the former non-standard ENCODE/DECODE), execution-time format specification, file enquiry and list-directed I/O. This means that a major advance in the definition of the syntax of the I/O statements has been made, rationalizing many different extensions but, nevertheless, the detailed interpretation of the statements is still often processor-dependent, that is, a function of the computer architecture, operating system and compiler. These processor-dependent areas are clearly the ones most likely to cause problems for program portability; their use should be restricted to an absolute minimum and they should be concentrated into a well documented part of the program so that they may be easily modified. These processor-dependent areas are treated individually in the following paragraphs.

The *length of a record* [12.1] is normally determined by the number of characters in a formatted record, but the standard allows the length to depend also on the processor and the external medium. This could mean that, for instance, an output record is padded by the processor to a whole number of computer words, and will thus be longer on input than on output. For unformatted data, both the form of the values in a record and the length of a record are processor-dependent. This implies that for the transfer of unformatted data it is necessary to standardise on an agreed form of number representation, and to provide the corresponding conversion routines. This involves a processing overhead when the data are written and read, but for large quantities of data unformatted records provide a far more compact means of transferring data than formatted ones.

The two related questions of whether a file *exists* [12.2.1 and B 12], and whether a file is *connected* to a program [12.3.1], are ones for which the authors of portable programs need to find an answer. In general, the existence of a file is not to be interpreted in the usual sense that it is known to the system, but in the particular sense that it exists for a given program which has the right to manipulate it. The continued existence of a file after program termination is also system-dependent. Many systems provide a set of pre-connected system files, such as INPUT and OUTPUT, whose existence may be assumed by all programs running on that system. In addition, a restricted set of other file names may be connected by means of OPEN statements; these files may be kept at the termination of the program by an appropriate CLOSE statement, and at any time during the execution of the program an INQUIRE statement should reveal whether the files exist or are connected, or not. Each file which is connected for a program is associated with a unit; the set of allowable units is processor-dependent. A unit is connected to a file because either it is pre-connected by the system or is connected explicitly by an OPEN statement. It is then clear that the range of options can vary from one system to another.

It is probably as well for portable programs to bring all files into existence in the job control language and to connect them definitely to the program by means of OPEN statements with no FILE parameter. These should be checked by INQUIRE's with the EXIST and OPENED parameters. Upon completion, the program should CLOSE all files, at least to ensure that any output buffers are emptied, and possibly to guide the system as to which files ought to be retained, using the KEEP parameter, should this happen to be necessary. In this way the use of system-dependent names can be kept out of the Fortran text which then operates entirely by unit numbers; these in turn should be variables defined in a BLOCK DATA routine or in some similar localized way, in order to be able to take account of the particular set of valid unit numbers available on each processor used. Use of the asterisk to specify a processor defined default unit should be reserved for test input and output; here again, the devices which may be used for printing are processor-dependent, and the execution of a PRINT or WRITE statement does not imply that physical output will actually occur [12.9.5.2.3].

As a general rule, all operations on files should be kept simple and straightforward – tricky programming on one processor is likely to lead to enormous problems on another.

In a similar fashion, the *file access methods* [12.2.4] are processor- and medium-dependent. In particular, the use of direct access files should normally be restricted to those residing on disc, as magnetic tapes are normally reserved for sequential access only.

Fortran 77 provides a means of testing for the successful completion of any I/O operation [12.7] using the parameters IOSTAT = IOS, ERR = *sl* and, for the READ statement, END = *sl* (where IOS is an integer variable or array element, and *sl* a statement label). A portable program should make full use of these facilities by providing an error recovery routine which is called whenever an error condition occurs. As part of the recovery procedure the value of IOS may be tested, but its possible values are processor-dependent, being defined only as negative for an end-of-file condition with no other associated error, and positive for any other error condition; no tests on actual values should be included. Examples of actual read error recovery statements appear in Appendix B.

The use of the OPEN parameter STATUS = 'UNKNOWN' is totally processor-dependent and should be used with care [12.10.1]. The value associated to the parameter RECL = , to define a record length, should remain within reasonable limits as the upper bound is also processor-dependent. The position of a file after an OPEN statement has been executed is indeterminate.

In the well-defined area of *format specifications*, the only item left to the processor to define is whether the leading plus sign should be suppressed by default with I, F, E, D and G editing, or be retained [13.5.6]. For highly portable programs it is better to select SS or SP explicitly, as preferred. This is an aid to the automatic comparison of formatted output files:

100 FORMAT (SS,10F8.3)

The *list-directed output* facility [12.8.1], by which appropriate formats are provided by the system as a function of the output list, is clearly processor-dependent and has no place in a portable program, although it is a useful aid for test output.

Some care is required when coding *function references* [15.2]. An optimizing compiler is allowed to evaluate the function references in a single statement in any order, and this order may vary from compiler to compiler, and can lead to unexpected results if the function modifies any other quantities than its own value. In the statement

$$A = FUNC(X) + FUNC(X)$$

the compiler may generate code equivalent to

```
T = FUNC(X)
A = T + T
```

and this means that any expected effect of the second reference to FUNC will be absent. Similarly, in the conditional statement

$$IF (X.EQ.0.. OR. FUNC(Y).EQ.0.) GO TO 1$$

FUNC(Y) may or may not be evaluated if X is zero, depending on the compiler. Portable code should contain functions which have no side-effects, thus making them independent of the vagaries of compilers. Where side-effects are unavoidable, for instance in random number generators, the function references should be written in a way which forces separate evaluation:

$$A = RANDOM(X) + RANDOM(Y)$$

and

```
T = FUNC(Y)
IF (X.EQ.0.. OR. T.EQ.0.) GO TO 1
```

Some compilers allow recursive functions. These are both non-portable and inefficient, and should not be used.

The use of *external functions* [15.5] is not standardised, except that any name which corresponds to one of the standard intrinsic functions must be treated by the processor in the expected way. This means that for user supplied externals the processor may supply its own functions if there happens to be a name clash, and so portable code should declare all user functions explicitly as EXTERNAL:

```
EXTERNAL MYFUNC
:
Y = MYFUNC(X)
```

or use function names which are very unlikely to appear in other systems:

Y = QPAKF1(X)

4. Processor-dependent Limits

There are certain limits which any processor has to impose upon a program due to the finite size of its store and power of its CPU. At the same time it would be unreasonable for the standard to restrict the language unnecessarily, by setting obligatory limits based on small processors, only to have them ignored anyway on larger ones. Thus, for instance, neither the range nor the precision of floating-point quantities is defined, nor is the range of integer quantities. This section provides a list of these processor-dependent quantities.

The maximum length of a quantity of type CHARACTER is not specified, but must be at least 1316 to accommodate a constant assignment spread over the maximum number of allowed continuation lines (19):

```
CHARACTER * 1316 C
C = '................................................
:
+  ................................................'
```

and 1320 to allow a Fortran compiler or text manipulator to be written conveniently in Fortran (see Appendix B). Any limit lower than this must be regarded as inconsistent with the standard itself (IBM VS Fortran : 500 as default, or 32767 with the CHARLEN compiler option). Character constants may be subject to a different limit (IBM : 255).

The standard imposes no limit on the number of statements or lines in a program unit, nor on the number of possible statement labels (IBM : 2000) and variables (IBM : 1000). As a given processor will have limits for all of these quantities, and as most compilers will be unable to optimize fully very long units, portable code should maintain the good programming practice of keeping program units shorter than six pages or so, in order to steer clear of both difficulties. There may be limits on the total number of different COMMON blocks (CDC : 125).

A processor may impose some limit on the number of arguments passed in a subroutine or function reference. To be consistent with 19 continuation lines, this limit should be set at 447, obtained as the sum of 26 different single-character dummy arguments and 421 double-character dummy arguments in a function call, but in all honesty this does seem to be quite excessive, although CDC does allow up to 500 arguments for some intrinsic function calls. A similar limit applies to the number of arguments in statement functions (IBM : 20) and to the nesting of statement function references (IBM : 50).

The maximum extent of a single dimension of an array and its maximum total size will be subject to processor limits, just as is the total size of a complete program (IBM : 16 Mbytes, or 2 Gbytes under MVS/XA). These restrictions are usually associated with the size of the address field of the machine instructions. Once again, some restraint is required in portable code.

The total number of iterations of a DO-loop may also be limited to less 'DO-loop' than the range of an integer constant, as the iteration counter may be kept in a register or field of shorter length (CDC : 131072). The nesting level of both DO-loops (IBM : 25) and IF-blocks (IBM : 25) will also be subject to a processor limit which may be rather low. As nested IF-blocks seem anyway to become incomprehensible when deeply nested, a fairly low value like four should be taken as a guide to an appropriate limit for most code.

The maximum nesting level of expressions in parentheses is not specified, but presumably most compilers would successfully process statements up to the maximum length allowed by the continuation line limit, (IBM : 150 successive left parentheses).

The STOP and PAUSE statements may both have an optional string of digits or characters as a 'parameter'. This string is intentionally provided for the processor to use in any appropriate way, perhaps to display it on a terminal or to list it in printed output. However, since the use to which it is put is not standardised, it may be used by portable programs only as an optional feature, for instance as a debugging aid.

For formatted I/O there are two unspecified limits, that on the length of a record in general, and that on the length of an output line intended for a particular device, such as a terminal or printer. Here again, it is as well to choose fairly low numbers for portable programs, 80 for terminals and 120 for printers. The use of tabulations which exceed the maximum line length at an intermediate stage of their processing may cause a problem and should be avoided, for example

```
1 FORMAT (TR500, TL499, I10)
```

I/O unit numbers often lie in a limited range (CDC : 1 to 99).

Finally, the number of parenthesis groups in a FORMAT statement is a processor limit (IBM : 50).

5. Computer Arithmetic

This section is not intended to be an introduction to numerical analysis, but merely to serve as a reminder of the need to have some appreciation of the problems inherent in computer arithmetic, and to provide some guidelines on how they might be circumvented in portable programs. For more details the interested reader is referred to chapter 4 of Knuth (1969b) and other specialised works.

We have seen in Section 2.1 that only a limited number of floating-point values can be exactly represented in a computer word, as only a finite number of bits or bytes are available in the mantissa, leading to an inevitable limitation in precision. In addition, the range of values which the exponent may take is also limited, so that only values within a certain range can be represented at all. Attempts to generate values outside this range lead to underflow and overflow execution-time errors. There are only a few computers which present virtually no problems in this regard. The CDC CYBER range has 48 bits of precision for the mantissa and a range of approximately 10^{-300} to 10^{300}; the CRAY-1 has even greater precision and range. On machines of this type it is rare to meet the need to worry about precision and to have to scale or to re-order calculations to keep them within range. This is definitely not the case for many of the widespread 32-bit word architectures, where the fact that normalization is performed on hexadecimal digits rather than bits means that on these machines between zero and three bits are lost from an already insufficient precision. Fortunately, machines built to the IBM S/370 architecture usually perform double-precision calculations at the same speed as single-precision calculations, and only space is adversely affected by the exclusive use, as a prophylactic measure, of double-precision arithmetic.

For portable code, the Fortran 77 standard has brought with it a powerful aid to the writing of programs which may be readily changed from one precision to the other, in the form of the so-called generic functions. These functions assume the type of their argument, and this means that it becomes relatively easy to alter precision globally by use of the IMPLICIT statement, particularly if the Fortran typing defaults are used otherwise. In

IMPLICIT DOUBLE PRECISION (A – H, O – Z)

:

A = SQRT(B)

the correct double-precision function will be supplied by the compiler. On a machine with greater precision, the IMPLICIT statements can be removed or turned into comment lines by a global edit operation. Further aids to flexible code are the use of the D, E, F and G edit descriptors, which accept either precision on input.

One area where care is needed is when double-precision variables are set equal to single-precision constants in a DATA statement, as the effect is not standardised. It is recommended that in such cases the double-precision exponent D0 is appended to each constant; this will remain valid for any change in the type of the variable:

DATA PI/3.141592653D0/

It is, of course, not usually necessary to go to the extreme of using double-precision throughout a whole program, if the sensitive areas can be identified, and even re-coded to reduce their sensitivity to machine precision. A frequent problem is the loss of significance when adding or subtracting numbers which themselves consist of the sum of a large and a small component. An example given by Knoble (1979) is the result -39.0625 instead of 1.0000 obtained for the expression

$$((X+Y)**2 - X**2 - 2*X*Y) / Y**2$$

with $X = 100.$ and $Y = 0.01$, calculated in IBM single-precision. The main problem is that the value for Y is a recurring binary fraction which cannot be exactly represented, and which loses a great part of its significance when right shifted for the addition to X, and again in the multiplication of $X+Y$ by itself. This example gives an obviously wrong result, but small, less easily detectable errors may be made in simpler expressions such as

X + Y

with $X = 0.1$ and $Y = 0.0000001$, where the last decimal digit is simply lost in rounding the result to the available precision. A great danger in precision loss of this kind is the fact that the error in the result varies as a function of the input values, and programs must be carefully tested over the whole range of their expected input data values, especially the extremes, before even being considered ready to be transferred to another computer.

Portable programs need to be kept insensitive to rounding and loss of significance. Tests on equality of floating-point quantities should be made using a small tolerance to allow for possible errors:

IF (ABS(A − B).LT.EPS) GO TO 1

where EPS is a small value commensurate with machine precision and the application.

As previously mentioned, DO-loops with floating-point control variables are to be abjured, as is any loop which progressively adds a value to itself, rather than performing a multiplication.

It is sometimes necessary to use parentheses to ensure that significance losses are kept to a minimum. If, in the assignment

$$A = B + C - D$$

B and D are much greater in magnitude than C, the expression should be reordered as

$$A = B - D + C$$

or

$$A = C + (B - D)$$

taking advantage of Fortran's left-to-right evaluation rule which is, however, not always observed by optimizing compilers. In expressions involving mixed single- and double-precision, the evaluation can be forced to be performed in double-precision throughout, by ensuring that the operands are grouped such that the expresssion begins with a double-precision operand:

$$D = (D + S) + S$$

rather than

$$D = S + S + D$$

where D is double-precision and S single-precision. To force a double-precision multiplication, an intrinsic function is available:

$$D = DPROD(S,S)$$

As a last point about precision, it is important to avoid any confusion by limiting the output fields defined in format specifications to a width which does not exceed the significance of the result, which is about six decimal digits for IBM S/370 architectures and 13 for CDC CYBER. These values are 16 and 28 for double-precision quantities.

The less common but more difficult problem of exceeding the range of the computer representation of floating-point quantities can be tackled in one of three different ways, all of which try to force the magnitude of the variables used in the direction of unity. The first method is to ensure that the units used for the problem are appropriate. Stellar distances should be measured in light-years or parsecs, and not millimetres, and the weights of microscopic quantities in micrograms rather than tonnes.

The second method is applicable when the range of the expected results is too large: if a result x can lie anywhere between 10^{-100} and 10^{100}, it might be more reasonable to deal with $\log x$ rather than with x itself.

The most difficult problem arises when intermediate results overflow in the course of a calculation. This is a recurrent problem in numerical analysis, and solutions may be found in any standard text.

6. Word Alignment

A problem can sometimes arise for programs which contain double-precision or complex variables. Some computers require that such variables be exactly aligned on even word boundaries, and if they are mixed with variables of other types in COMMON blocks, or through EQUIVALENCE statements, unexpected compile-time messages can occur. This difficulty can be avoided by ordering variables in COMMON blocks, beginning with those having the longest unit length, and finishing with the shortest:

```
COMMON/EX/C(100),D(50),A(151)
COMPLEX C
DOUBLE PRECISION D
```

or by using separate blocks for variables of different types. This rule can be extended to the non-standard data types found on many small or byte-oriented computers.

11 VECTOR PROCESSORS

1. A New Opportunity

Until now, all of the computing systems we have considered have been of the type known as scalar or serial computers, that is processors whose functional units carry out operations on at most two scalar operands at a time and which use compilers requiring that each such operation be described explicitly. Thus, to form the element-by-element product of two vectors of equal length requires a DO-loop which generates machine instructions which specify the exact operations to be performed on each element of the arrays, treating each element as a scalar entity at the point at which the operation on it is performed.

This chapter is concerned with a quite different type of computer architecture, capable under certain conditions of performing arithmetic operations at a rate an order of magnitude faster than the most powerful scalar machines − the true 'super-computers'. Computers with this performance are often referred to as array or vector processors, because of their ability to process arrays of operands efficiently. They are produced in a variety of architectures (Infotech, 1979) and, following the classification of Paul (1980), we shall consider only examples of that type referred to as vector instruction processors, that is, computers which have the ability to perform operations on whole vectors with a single instruction.

The introduction of these computers has opened up whole new vistas of computing in scientific fields such as meteorology, plasma physics, weapons research, hydrodynamics and nuclear chemistry (see Kascic, 1979), and there is an active exchange of ideas and experience concerning the new computing techniques which are required (Infotech, 1979b, Rodrigue, 1982 and Chester, 1982).

These powerful machines do not always lend themselves easily to use for general computing tasks, and therefore they often require a so-called front-end computer to act as a job preparation station. This need is reinforced by the large costs of developing general purpose software; this would be difficult to amortize over the few dozen super-computers of any one type which are sold. However, in spite of the relatively small numbers installed, since they can often be accessed through networks, they are now achieving considerable success amongst scientists engaged in large-scale scientific computing. We can certainly expect to see other manufacturers developing yet more powerful models in the course of the decade. This chapter can provide only a glimpse into a highly specialized and rapidly expanding field of computing; extensive details may be found, for example, in Hockney and Jesshope (1981), and an annotated bibliography appears in Jesshope (1979). A short review was given by Levine (1982).

In order to be able to obtain the highest possible degree of performance from these computers, the algorithms have to be selected and presented in a way that fully exploits their vector-processing capability. There are basically four levels at which this can be achieved:

i) the program is written in a conventional way, and its vector nature is recognized automatically by the Fortran compiler, and translated into machine language vector instructions accordingly;

ii) the program code is restructured in an unconventional way, in order to take greater advantage of the automatic translation;

iii) the program is written using vector extensions to the Fortran language, which are translated directly into machine language by the compiler;

iv) the kernel of the program, that part which is used most intensively, is written directly in vector machine language, (which is often simpler than the standard machine language as fewer instructions need to be coded).

Because of the diversity of applications, general statements about the optimal approach to achieving high performance are difficult. Those programs which have to remain highly portable, on scalar machines as well as on vector processors, require a high level of automatic translation, in order to avoid the need to maintain different program versions corresponding to the various types of machine. Other applications may only be conceivable at all on a vector processor, and no effort will be spared to ensure the highest possible performance. For the former class of programs, a vector processor is of interest only if the compiler relieves the programmer of the bulk of the task of vectorizing the code. For the latter class, the processor is that much simpler to use if powerful syntactic extensions to the language are made available by the compiler (and we shall see in Chapter 12 that some extensions of this type may become part of the Fortran language in the future). In the following sections, the way in which this problem has been tackled by three different manufacturers will be briefly examined, and some common features concerning code restructuring without the use of language extensions will be identified. However, first a basic principle of vector architectures, the pipeline, needs to be recalled (a detailed description is given by Ramamoorthy and Li, 1977).

In the description of the CDC CYBER computers in Section 2.6 we met the concept of the pipeline in the context of scalar functional units. The operation performed by a unit is segmented into a number of sections, each lasting one machine cycle, and these sub-operations proceed independently as operands pass through the unit, a new pair of input operands being accepted by the unit at every cycle. In the case of vector processors, it is possible to sustain a very high duty cycle in the functional units, as the operands are presented continuously as whole vectors, and the processing flow is not interrupted by the branches typically present when a Fortran DO-loop controls a vector operation. It is also unnecessary to load and decode the large number of instructions required for scalar operations. This means, in principle, that when correctly programmed, the processor can provide a result every clock-cycle, and this provides a means of calculating the asymptotic performance of the processor — the number of floating-point operations which, theoretically, can be performed per second. This is usually measured in millions of floating-point operations per second, or megaflops, and the asymptotic value for a single functional unit is simply the reciprocal of the cycle-time, *i.e.* from the 12.5 nsec cycle-time of the CRAY-1 we obtain an asymptotic value of 80 megaflops. This figure can be exceeded for the whole CPU because functional units can operate in parallel, but in practice substantially lower average rates are often obtained, as these features cannot easily be fully exploited.

A particular problem, as will be seen below, is the presence of IF-statements in loops. This may be dealt with either by compressing the elements of vectors into shorter vectors containing only those elements which should participate in the calculation, or by performing calculations on all elements and storing only those results which are actually required. Either way an overhead is incurred.

Before describing three particular processors, two basic and common points with respect to programming these machines must be made. The first is the need to ensure that the compiler actually has the opportunity to detect the vectors for which it is supposed to generate vector instructions. This means that loops need to be pushed into subroutines, rather than those subroutines being called inside loops (see Section 5.9).

Secondly, each vector operation requires what is known as a start-up time. This is the time required to fetch and decode an instruction and to prime the registers and functional units with their first operands. Depending on the machine, these operands are stored either in memory or in vector registers. Although the start-up time varies from machine to machine, it does mean that the longer a vector can be, the less significant this time is with respect to the total time required for processing the instruction. The general principle of keeping the innermost loops the longest, in terms of number of iterations (Section 5.6.2), stands particularly for this type of computer.

2. Hitachi Integrated Array Processor

One of the earlier types of vector processors which had been developed and successfully marketed was the attached array processor (see, for example, Harte, 1979). This is a device which is connected using direct memory access (DMA) to a conventional mainframe, and which is supplied with the data on which it performs its specialized operations. It often requires some special programming (Brode, 1981 and Wilson, 1982) and is suitable usually only for processing large data arrays, for example in the field of signal processing. In contrast, Hitachi has developed the concept of the integrated array processor (IAP) for use with its M-200H and M-280H computers. This device is built directly into the CPU and uses the functional units of the scalar processor to perform vector operations;   it is able to supply them with vector operands, as described in the last section, giving a maximum processing rate of 33 megaflops on the M-280H. The results of the operations are available directly in the CPU, and this integrated architecture simplifies the use of such array processors.

The IAP (Fig. 24) consists basically of a vector address control unit, a vector operand control unit and a control store for the

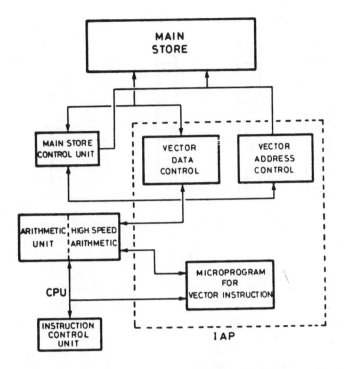

Fig. 24   The hardware organization of the Hitachi IAP

microprogrammed instructions. The instructions control directly the conventional arithmetic unit and the High Speed Arithmetic unit. The address control unit performs the address calculations required for fetching and controlling vectors, whose elements must occupy contiguous words in main memory. The single-precision word length is 32 bits. The operand control unit controls the buffers used for holding operands and results. The IAP for the M-280H features a control vector of one bit per element being processed. This control vector allows processing of selected elements of an array, depending on whether the corresponding bit in the control vector is set or unset. Its operation is depicted in Fig. 25 The control vector is filled by the element-by-element comparison of two vectors, a situation arising when an IF-statement is present in a DO-loop.

The IAP features a vector instruction set for single-, double- and extended-precision variables which allows the operations shown in Table 4 to be performed with a single machine instruction (in the Table, X, Y and Z are vectors, S a scalar, and C a bit or control vector).

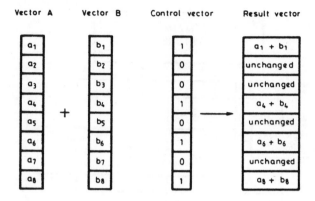

Fig. 25   The operation of a bit control vector

Table 4

The vector instruction set of the Hitachi M-280H IAP

No.	Name	Operation
1	First order iteration	$Z_{i+1} \leftarrow X_i + Y_i {*} Z_i$
2	Scalar multiply and add	$Z_i \leftarrow Z_i + S{*}Y_i$
3	Scalar multiply and subtract	$Z_i \leftarrow Z_i - S{*}Y_i$
4	Vector element sum	$S \leftarrow S + \Sigma\, X_i$
5	Vector element sum with complement	$S \leftarrow S - \Sigma\, X_i$
6	Vector elementwise add	$Z_i \leftarrow X_i + Y_i$
7	Vector elementwise complement	$Z_i \leftarrow -X_i$
8	Vector elementwise divide	$Z_i \leftarrow X_i / Y_i$
9	Vector elementwise multiply	$Z_i \leftarrow X_i {*} Y_i$
10	Vector elementwise subtract	$Z_i \leftarrow X_i - Y_i$
11	Vector inner product	$S \leftarrow S + \Sigma X_i {*} Y_i$
12	Vector inner product with complement	$S \leftarrow S - \Sigma X_i {*} Y_i$
13	Vector move	$Z_i \leftarrow X_i$
14	Convert double to single precision	$Z_i \leftarrow X_i$
15	Convert single to double precision	$Z_i \leftarrow X_i$
16	Vector compare equal	$C_i \leftarrow X_i = Y_i$
17	Vector compare not equal	$C_i \leftarrow X_i \neq Y_i$
18	Vector compare greater or equal	$C_i \leftarrow X_i \geqslant Y_i$
19	Vector compare greater than	$C_i \leftarrow X_i > Y_i$
20	Vector compare less or equal	$C_i \leftarrow X_i \leqslant Y_i$
21	Vector compare less than	$C_i \leftarrow X_i < Y_i$

This instruction set was established after a study of the kernels of a number of Fortran programs, and contains some instructions with three operands, including the interesting first-order iteration instruction which allows an operand to depend on a value calculated in the previous step through the functional unit. With this one exception the operations are executed memory to memory, that is, operands are fetched directly from memory and the results stored there after completion of the operation. Addition and multiplication may proceed in parallel, and the vector inner product

```
        S = 0.
        DO 1 I = 1,N
          S = S + X(I)*Y(I)
     1  CONTINUE
```

which would normally compile into the serial instruction sequence

> load operands X(I) and Y(I)
> multiply operands
> add result to S
> test iteration counter and branch

compiles into the single instruction required to perform the vector inner product. The flow of operands through the functional units is depicted diagrammatically in Fig. 26.

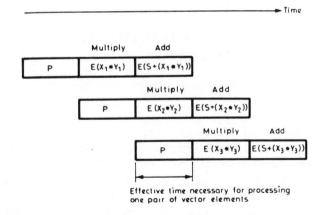

Effective time necessary for processing one pair of vector elements

Addition is performed in parallel with multiplication
E : Execution stage
P : Preparation stage (instruction prefetch, operand prefetch)

Fig. 26   Flow of operands through parallel functional units

The Hitachi Fortran 77 compiler offers no vector extensions to the language, and relies instead on its ability to identify automatically any vectorizable loops. This places on the programmer the onus of structuring the code to make the best possible use of the power of the vector instructions. Some of the basic rules coincide with ones we have met already with scalar code in the discussion on loop nesting (see Section 5.6.2). Since the processing of a vector instruction requires a certain amount of start-up time, the vector should be as long as possible and so the innermost loop should contain the largest number of iterations. At the same time the elements of the arrays must be in contiguous sections in main memory, and so the arrays must be processed in column-major order. Where there is a conflict between both the left-hand side and right-hand side of a statement being processed in this order, it is preferable to have the left-hand side correctly treated.

The conditions under which vectorization of an inner loop will be attempted on the M-280H, always assuming it contains vector operands, are:

i) that it contains only arithmetic assignment statements, and IF-statements and GO TO's referencing labels in the loop;

ii) that no user function is referenced;

iii) that there is no backward sequencing between an assignment and a reference, (see below);

iv) that no variables in EQUIVALENCE statements appear on the left-hand side of an assignment;

v) that the iteration count is greater than nine (this is a hardware characteristic).

An example of backward sequencing is given in Ex. 49, in which the first loop is vectorizable, in spite of the data dependence, as $A(I+1)$ is defined before $A(I)$ references the same element in the next iteration. In the second loop, however, the use of $A(I+1)$ before $A(I)$ has redefined it inhibits vectorization.

In general, the first order iteration instruction enables the vectorization of recursive loops which cannot be vectorized by other systems; an example is

```
DO 1 I = 1,100              DO 1 I = 1,100
  A(I + 1) = B(I) + C(I)      A(I) = B(I) + C(I)
  E(I) = A(I)*D(I)            E(I) = A(I + 1)*D(I)
1 CONTINUE                 1 CONTINUE
```

Example 49

```
DO 1 I = 1,N
  X(I,J) = W(I,J) + B(I,J)*X(I - 1,J)
1  CONTINUE
```

The IAP is a new and interesting addition to the vector processing range, but matches in neither raw processor speed nor compiler extensions the power of the other two processors we shall discuss.

3. The CRAY Range

The CRAY-1S vector processor is an earlier example of a range of the most powerful computers currently in use; its basic hardware block diagram is shown in Fig. 27. An important feature of this machine is the fact that it has sets of vector registers, and that the vector operations are, therefore, able to proceed from register to register, rather than from memory to memory, resulting in a short start-up time, once the registers are loaded.

The CRAY-1S model is a 64-bit word machine with a large, fast, main memory possessing a high band-width, backed up by high-speed disc drives. It is supplied with a small front-end computer for job preparation, but normally is also connected directly to a conventional large main frame *via* a link. It possesses a set of scalar functional units, a set of shared floating-point functional units for either scalar or vector operands, and four units exclusively for vector operands — add, logical, shift and population count (to count the number of set bits in a vector). Divisions are performed by a reciprocal approximation of the divisor followed by a multiplication with the numerator. A 64-bit vector mask, or control vector, which may be created by vector compare instructions, is used to control the flow of vectors between registers. The scalar and address registers are of two types, those directly accessible to the functional units, and another group eight times larger which acts as a buffer between memory and the main registers. The eight vector registers are loaded directly from memory and each may contain vectors up to 64 full words in length. All the functional units are fully segmented pipelines; the floating-point add requires six cycles for a complete single

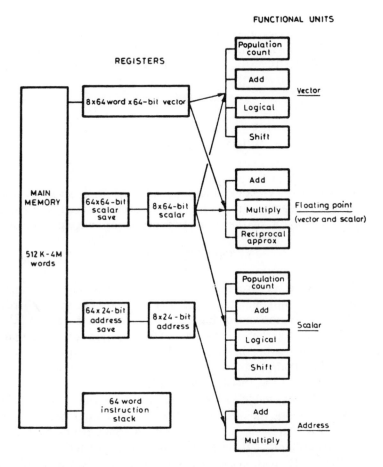

Fig. 27   The hardware organization of the CRAY-1S

operation, the floating-point multiply seven, and the floating-point reciprocal fourteen cycles, but each can then produce one new result every cycle. The units are able to operate in parallel, bringing a further enhancement to the processing speed, which is augmented still further by an additional feature known as chaining. This is a procedure whereby the results of a vector operation may be fed directly from the target register into a second functional unit, without the whole vector operation having first to be completed. For instance, a vector add may proceed in parallel with a dependent vector multiply, as the results from the multiply are available almost immediately to the add unit. Program instructions are kept in a 64-word stack, which eliminates the need to fetch each instruction from memory if loops are shorter than the stack (*cf.* CYBER stack description in Section 2.6). Fuller details of the hardware of this computer appear in Russell (1978) and Dungworth (1979).

In 1982, Cray Research announced the CRAY X-MP, a dual-processor computer with a 9.5 nsec cycle-time; this machine represents an important upward extension of its range of computers, but its basic architectural features are similar to those just described. It benefits from improved chaining, and a much higher memory bandwidth. A buffer memory between the disc store and a main memory (also usable with the CRAY-1S) is an optional part of the configuration. A single program may use both CPU's concurrently. A multi-processor CRAY-2, with a 4 nsec cycle-time and liquid immersion cooling, has been announced for the mid-1980's.

A CRAY computer is essentially a Fortran engine, as the main software tools it offers are a program maintenance system and a compiler for the CFT language, essentially Fortran 77 with some extensions. The compiler versions beyond release 1.10 are able, under certain conditions, to recognize vectorizable loops, and it once again falls to the programmer to structure loops to take the best advantage of this feature. It is possible via a compiler directive to force the compiler to vectorize a loop which it would otherwise consider to be unsafe to vectorize because of some possible data dependence (see below).

The machine vector instructions are only of the simple vector/vector and scalar/vector add, multiply, divide and logic type, and accept only two operands. The fact that the vector registers are 64 words long and that vectors must therefore be broken into 64-word sections is handled by the compiler. Although vectors need not be in contiguous words in memory, the elements must be separated by a constant stride or increment.

For the Fortran programmer this can all imply a completely new way of structuring problems and their coded algorithms, in order to take advantage of the vector facilities and to avoid inadvertently rendering DO-loops non-vectorizable. This may happen particularly in any case where the execution of a vector operation may need as an operand a quantity modified in an earlier step of the same operation, a situation occurring in loops which are apparently or actually recursive, as in

```
     DO 1 I = 2,100
        X(I) = X(I - 1) + 1.
   1  CONTINUE
```

where the value of X(I) depends on a value from the previous step. A loop such as

```
     DO 1 I = 1,99
        X(I) = X(I + 1) + 1.
   1 CONTINUE
```

is, however, not recursive, as the value of X(I + 1) is already available for use in the evaluation of X(I).

To be automatically vectorizable, a loop must contain no GOTO or IF-statement, and no CALL or reference to an external function. In addition, all variables within a loop must fall into one of the following categories:

  i) invariant - any constant, variable, expression or array element which remains unchanged;

 ii) constant increment integer (CII) − this is an induction variable, an integer which at one point only in the loop is incremented by a constant value on each pass through the loop; it may reference a single CII in its definition;

iii) vector array references − the subscripts must all be invariants, except one which may have the general form:

$$[\text{ invariant } *] \quad \text{CII} \quad [\pm \text{ invariant expression}]$$

 iv) scalar temporary − a variable set equal to a vectorizable expression at one point only in the loop;

  v) component of a reduction array operation − appears on both sides of an assignment of a form such as

$$X = X + A(I)$$

Thus the following loop is vectorizable:

```
     DO 10 I = 3,101,2
        K = K − KDELTA
        J = 107 − I
        A(3,I − 2) =
   +       COS(B(J))**C(M − 2*K + L*M/7,L,M/L)*X*D(L,M)
  10 CONTINUE
```

(I,J and K are CII's, A,B, and C are vector array references, KDELTA, X, D, L, and M are invariants, and COS is an intrinsic function which is expanded in-line).

Great attention to the structure of loops is required. In the matrix multiplication

```
      DO 1 I = 1,N
        DO 1 J = 1,M
          A(I,J) = 0.
          DO 1 L = 1,K
            A(I,J) = A(I,J)+B(I,L)*C(L,J)
    1 CONTINUE
```

we see that A(I,J) is independent of the inner DO-loop index, and therefore a recursive variable rendering the loop non-vectorizable. The same sequence, written with the inner loops exchanged and the setting to zero performed then on a row basis, executes six times faster:

```
      DO 1 I = 1,N
        DO 2 J = 1,M
          A(I,J) = 0.
    2     CONTINUE
        DO 1 L = 1,K
          DO 1 J = 1,M
            A(I,J) = A(I,J)+B(I,L)*C(L,J)
    1 CONTINUE
```

Care is needed to avoid interdependencies which can inhibit the vectorization of loops. In the loop

```
      JMINUS1 = J-1
      DO 1 I = 2,100
        A(I,J) = A(I-1,JMINUS1)
    1 CONTINUE
```

the compiler cannot determine whether JMINUS1 is ever equal to J, whereas in

```
      DO 1 I = 2,100
        A(I,J) = A(I-1,J-1)
    1 CONTINUE
```

this is clearly never the case, and automatic vectorization takes place. Vectorization of the first loop can, however, be forced by a compiler directive.

Another problem which can arise is the use of indirect addressing, shown in

```
  DO 1 I = 1,100
      J = INDEX(I)
      X(I) = Y(J)*C+4.
1 CONTINUE
```

where the compiler is unable to assemble the elements of the vector Y for use in a vector instruction, as the values of INDEX are unknown. The loop may be rewritten with the help once again of a temporary vector, as shown in Ex. 50. Where temporary vectors are used extensively, it may be desirable on a small configuration to break the processing into 64-word sections, in order to limit the amount of extra storage space required.

```
  DO 1 I = 1,100
      TEMP(I) = Y(INDEX(I))
1 CONTINUE
  DO 2 I = 1,100
      X(I) = TEMP(I)*C+4.
2 CONTINUE
```

Example 50

The CFT compiler expands many of the Fortran intrinsic functions as in-line code, so that the presence of a SQRT or trigonometric function inside a loop does not inhibit vectorization (*cf.* Section 5.10). However, an IF-statement presents a more difficult problem, and it often needs to be replaced either by a standard Fortran function (Ex. 51), or by one of the conditional functions provided as an extension to the language (Ex. 52).

```
  DO 1 I = 1,100                    DO 1 I = 1,100
      IF(A(I).LT.0.)A(I)=0.             A(I)=AMAX1(A(I),0.)
      B(I)=SQRT(A(I))+1.                B(I)=SQRT(A(I))+1.
1 CONTINUE                         1 CONTINUE
```

Example 51

In Ex. 52, the conditional code in the loop is replaced by a CFT function using the vector mask which assigns to each element of B the result of one of two possible expressions, depending on the value of the relational expression appearing as the third argument.

```
      DO 1 I = 1,100
          IF (A(I).LT.0.) GO TO 2
          B(I) = A(I) + D(I)
          GO TO 1
    2     B(I) = A(I) + C(I)
    1 CONTINUE
```

becomes

```
      DO 1 I = 1,100
          B(I) = CVMGT(A(I) + C(I),A(I) + D(I),A(I).LT.0.)
    1 CONTINUE
```

Example 52

The CRAY range possesses an extensive library of vectorized routines which help the user to make use of the capabilities of the machine, without having to involve himself too deeply in writing highly optimized or assembly language code. They have the advantage of conforming to standard Fortran syntax. A guide to CFT programming has been prepared by Higbie (1979).

This computer system is straightforward to use, and program conversion usually presents no great problem. However, full advantage of its power can only be taken for certain types of code, and considerable effort is sometimes required to obtain really large gains compared to the performance of a serial machine, especially by avoiding recursive or conditional code in inner loops.

4. CDC CYBER 205

Until recently, the CYBER 205 (Fig. 28) was arguably the most powerful vector processor available, with a maximum peak rate of 800 megaflops for vector operations, in its largest configuration. These high vector rates can, however, only be approached asymptotically by an appropriate algorithm operating on long vectors and coded so as to take advantage of the full capabilities of the hardware, and the CRAY X-MP is able to outperform the CYBER 205 for many applications.

The main memory is between one and eight million 64-bit words in size, and is bit addressable; high speed disc units provide the means of supporting a virtual memory environment. The mainfame needs to be interfaced by a front-end computer for job preparation and submission, and to obtain access to magnetic tape storage.

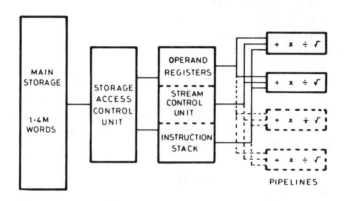

Fig. 28   The hardware organization of the CYBER 205

The vector CPU is organized into four sections which operate in parallel. The storage access control unit controls the system I/O and virtual memory. The stream control unit controls the whole system, performing all the operations necessary to fetch and decode instructions, and to control the flow of operands to the functional units, whose operation it also controls. The unit contains a set of 256 64-bit registers for operands and a stack containing 64 64-bit instructions. The arithmetic functional unit consists of either two or four pipelines, each able to perform add, subtract, multiply, divide and square-root operations. They are governed by micro-code controlled by the stream control unit. The pipelines operate in parallel, but not on separate instructions; instead, each pipeline processes every second (or fourth) operand pair or triplet from the stream required for a single instruction. The pipelines can accept as operands either full 64-bit words, or can operate at double speed on 32-bit half-precision operands. The peak rate for a single pipeline processing these half-precision operands is nearly 200 megaflops when performing a triadic operation of a type such as

$$\text{vector} + \text{scalar} \times \text{vector}$$

or

(vector + scalar) x vector

on vectors which are several thousand elements long, and whose elements are in contiguous virtual memory locations. Machine instructions are available to gather randomly or evenly dispersed elements into a contiguous block, and others to scatter the results. It is not always necessary for a functional unit to wait for the result of a previous operation to be placed in a register and to retrieved from it again; a procedure known as shortstop allows an operand to be intercepted on its way to the target register and to be directed also to the waiting unit, thus saving about three cycles.

A string processing unit performs operations on non-arithmetic data, and in particular controls the control vectors, which in turn control the floating-point operations in the pipelines. The control vectors are vectors of single bits which determine which results will be stored or, in the case of the sparse vector instructions, which operands participate in the operation and which are transmitted (see Paul, 1980).

For the Fortran programmer using the CYBER 205 there are several ways to optimize codes. A prerequisite is, however, that the program kernels are actually handling vectors of some substantial length, as the start-up time for the memory to memory operations is comparatively long, and the processing rate for vectors of length 32 is four to eight times slower than the rate for vectors which are many thousands of words long.

Given that this first requirement is fulfilled the FTN200 compiler, compatible with Fortran 77 and the old FTN compiler, offers three ways of ensuring that the Fortran code generates vector rather than scalar instructions: automatic vectorization, the use of explicit descriptors and the use of implicit descriptors. These last two are a means of writing code using extensions of Fortran, in order to make the vector nature of the problem obvious to the compiler when automatic vectorization fails. This failure might occur for a number of reasons, because to be vectorizable a loop must fulfil the following principal conditions:

i) the loops contains no external reference, other than to a restricted list of functions which generate either vector instructions (*e.g.* IABS) or vector results (*e.g.* SIN)

ii) the loop contains no IF-statement or GO TO statement;

iii) the loop-dependent array subscripts are of the type J, J + N,

$J - N$, $J*N$ or $J*N + N1$ (where J is the loop index and N an integer constant);

iv) the data elements are either contiguous in memory or separated by a constant stride;

v) the loop is not recursive, apart from a small class of recursive assignments which correspond to system vector macro-instructions, such as

$$S = S + X(I)*Y(I)$$

These points are discussed in detail in Mossberg (1981), which contains detailed hints on optimization for this computer.

Where automatic vectorization fails, the use of explicit or implicit descriptors is possible; these Fortran extensions render the code completely non-portable, but this is unlikely to be a primary consideration for programs using such a powerful system. We note also that the library of routines for vector operations mentioned in Section 9.5 has been rewritten for the CYBER 205.

The explicit descriptor provides a convenient method of introducing an array notation into the standard syntax. A vector is referred to by its lower bound and its length separated by a semi-colon: A(1;1000) is a vector whose first element is A(1) and which is of length 1000. It is also possible to force an array to be stored in row-major order by using the ROWWISE declaration instead of a DIMENSION declaration: using

ROWWISE A(1000,2000)

the array reference

A(6,1001;1000)

means the vector $(A(6,I), I = 1001,2000)$.

Using this explicit notation it is now possible to write a loop such as

```
     DO 1 J = 1,1000
       R(J) = S(J) + T(J + K)
   1 CONTINUE
```

in the form

$$R(1;1000) = S(1;1000) + T(1+K;1000)$$

The implicit descriptor, on the other hand, represents a far more powerful syntax, and is defined as a special data type. In Ex. 53, the first N elements of A, B and C are assigned to their respective descriptors AD, BD and CD, and from this point on in the program the descriptors may be used to refer to these parts of the vectors.

```
REAL  A(1000),B(1000),C(1000)
DESCRIPTOR  AD,BD,CD
:
ASSIGN  AD,A(1;N)
ASSIGN  BD,B(1;N)
ASSIGN  CD,C(1;N)
AD  =  BD*CD
```

Example 53

A further aid to vectorization, in the presence of an obstructive IF-statement, is the possibility to use the control vector mechanism directly by the definition of BIT vectors, either combined with the WHERE statement or used in conjunction with one of the conditional functions provided in the Fortran run-time library.

```
DO 1 I = 1,N
   IF  (Y(I).GE.0.) X(I)  =  SQRT(Y(I))
1  CONTINUE
```

```
PARAMETER (N  =  1000)
REAL  X(N),Y(N)
BIT BITS(N),BITSD
DESCRIPTOR BITSD
ASSIGN BITSD,BITS(1;N)
BITSD  =  Y(1;N).GE.0.
WHERE (BITSD) X(1;N)  =  VSQRT(Y(1;N);X(1;N))
```

Example 54

Ex. 54 shows the scalar and vector versions of a simple conditional loop. In the vector example an array BITS of type BIT, whose elements consist of single bits, is assigned to a descriptor BITSD. This descriptor is then used in the WHERE statement in a

manner such that no root of a negative number can be assigned to
X, as an assignment takes place only for those elements of X corresponding to positive values of Y, as described by the descriptor
BITSD (the calculation actually takes place, but the result is
unused). We note that the vector SQRT function, VSQRT, requires
information about the target array as one of its arguments. The
result vector follows a semi-colon. This is the case too for the next
example, using the vector library function Q8VCTRL, which transfers one vector to another, under control of a bit vector. Using declarations which have already appeared in Exs. 53 and 54, we may
write the non-vectorizable loop

```
        DO 1 I = 1,1000
            IF (A(I).GT.0.) B(I) = A(I)
    1   CONTINUE
```

in the vector form

```
        BITSD = A(1;1000).GT.0.
        BD = Q8VCTRL(AD,BITSD;BD)
```

The last example shows how the fast vector gather/scatter functions
allow loops containing arrays referenced via indirect addressing to be
vectorized. The loop

```
        DO 1 I = 1,100
            A(IA(I)) = B(IB(I))*C(I)
    1   CONTINUE
```

may be written as

```
        BTEMP(1;100) =
    +         Q8VGATHR(B(1;100),IB(1;100);BTEMP(1;100))
        DO 1 I = 1,100
            ATEMP(I) = BTEMP(I)*C(I)
    1   CONTINUE
        A(1;100) = Q8VSCTR(ATEMP(1;100),IA(1;100);A(1;100))
```

where BTEMP and ATEMP are temporary arrays into which the
operands are gathered and from where the results are scattered,
respectively; they hold the elements from A and B in contiguous
locations during the vector operation. Periodic gather and scatter
functions are available for vectorizing over outer loops. The recursive
loop

```
        DO 1 J  =  1,1000
          DO 1 I  =  2,100
          X(I,J)  =  C(J)*X(I – 1,J) + D(I)
    1   CONTINUE
```

may be vectorized as shown in Ex. 55, in which a dynamically allocated temporary array TD is used to gather the elements from a row of X ready for the calculation. The temporary array is updated for the next iteration, and is scattered back into the row of X. LEN is the number of words from the beginning of the row of X to the end of the array, inclusive.

```
        REAL  X(100,1000)
        DESCRIPTOR TD
        ASSIGN TD, .DYN.1000
        TD  =  Q8VGATHP(X(1,1;1000),100,1000;TD)
        DO 1 I  =  2,100
            TD  =  TD*C(1;1000) + D(I)
            LEN  =  100001 – I
            X(I,1;LEN)  =  Q8VSCATP(TD,100,1000;X(I,1;LEN))
    1   CONTINUE
```

Example 55

The CYBER 205 is not only a very powerful computer, but provides interesting means of fully exploiting that power by the provision in its compiler of syntactical extensions to Fortran. Like all current vector processors, however, it has only a limited capability for dealing with recursive loops.

5. Summary

This chapter has briefly reviewed the quite different machine architectures of three current vector processors, machines which are able, when appropriately programmed, to achieve very large increases in execution speeds compared with scalar computers. The three computers differ quite fundamentally in their hardware design, in their instruction sets, and in the way in which a Fortran programmer can attempt to gain the highest possible degree of efficiency from the vector processors (the scalar processors have not been discussed).

The simplest approach is provided by the Hitachi IAP, which has, however, a very powerful instruction set, and which can vectorize certain Fortran recursive loops which cannot be executed in vector mode on either of the other two machines. Some of the instructions accept three operands. This type of machine is an attractive alternative for those installations not wishing to commit themselves to a dedicated vector processor.

The CRAY range of computers offers a vector capability which is able to help solve computing problems even where the vectors are relatively short, since the simple register to register instructions imply a short start-up time. Various means are provided, and are usually necessary, to allow changes to be made to Fortran programs to ensure a high degree of vectorization; these changes remain compatible with standard Fortran syntax.

The CYBER 205 is a very powerful computer, but is at its most efficient only when processing vectors of considerable length. Powerful syntactic extensions to Fortran allow the programmer to make the best possible use of the vector CPU. The rich instruction set includes operations on three operands.

It is certain that as more vector processors are designed, built and installed, a whole new branch of scientific computing is developing, and it will be desirable to rationalize the various vector Fortran extensions in order to ensure a high level of program portability, placing on the compiler writer the onus of providing the means by which the source code is translated into the most efficient object code for a given machine. This development will be greatly eased by the anticipated introduction of the next Fortran standard towards the end of the 1980's (see Chapter 12), but we can perhaps expect to see some of the proposed changes creep into vector processor compilers long before then. Indeed, the new super-computer company ETA, founded in 1983, has announced such extensions for its planned GF-10 computer, scheduled for 1987. For the moment, the problems of portability for explicitly vectorized code remain considerable, as may be seen by inspection of the examples given in the preceding sections.

One last problem should be mentioned, namely the importance of the speed of the scalar units in achieving high speeds; tests have shown that this can be critical in the overall improvement with respect to a conventional serial computer, depending on the degree of vectorization attainable.

12 FUTURE FORTRAN

1. Standardisation

A great strength of Fortran is the fact that, from the outset, it was intended to be a language capable of producing efficient object code; the purpose of this book has been to indicate how this strength may be exploited to the full. During the course of nearly three decades, Fortran has twice been subject to a formal standardisation, in 1966 and again in 1978, and each of these two standards remained faithful to the principle of efficiency of implementation.

The Fortran language is standardised formally by a committee known as X3J3, which reports to the X3 committee of the American National Standards Institute (ANSI). At the international level, the International Standards Organization, ISO, bears responsibility for the standard, but this is delegated to X3J3 on the understanding that it makes every reasonable effort to consult foreign opinion on the matter. This it does by having a small number of non-American members, by consulting foreign bodies like the British Computer Society, by presenting draft proposals to foreign experts every year or two, and by taking account of international comments during the period allowed for public comment between the publications of a draft standard and the final document (see also Meek and Hill, 1981).

The first two standards were standards in the true sense, in that they were an attempt to reconcile divergent trends in the development of the language, incorporating mainly ideas and features that were to be found already in individual compilers or popular pre-processors. No real attempt was made to develop the language in line with modern programming language theory, except perhaps for one concession to structured programming in the introduction, at the eleventh hour, of the IF...THEN...ELSE construct into Fortran 77.

After the publication of the current standard, X3J3 re-formed and began to consider its future work. It was decided to undertake a major redesign of the language, and to publish a draft standard by 1982. This target soon became unrealistic, and present plans are to have a draft standard ready by 1985, for implementation before the end of the decade, thus falling into a eleven-year revision cycle. To reflect this time-table, the present working name for the new standard is Fortran 8x.

Progress on the new standard is steady rather than spectacular, as the committee now meets only four rather than five times a year, but always for a full week, as recent U.S. federal budget restrictions have led to an unfortunate slowdown in its activities. The work of the committee, and other Fortran developments, are chronicled by Meissner (1982). At the time of writing (the Summer of 1984) the proposals have been collected into a single working document, known as S7 (X3J3, 1984), and are about to undergo a period of consolidation into a coherent whole.

At the same time the design of a new language, ADA (DoD, 1983), has reached its conclusion and it is due to become available on a similar time-scale; it is widely thought to be a serious challenger to the supremacy of Fortran in some spheres of scientific computing. Similar predictions, with respect to encroachments on Fortran by ALGOL and PASCAL, have been made in the past, but it seems difficult to make accurately any firm prediction of this type (see Muxworthy, 1976), although in this case ADA does have powerful interest groups backing it. Rather, it appears that each new language captures a community of users who appreciate some particular features, and who are reluctant to accept certain limitations or difficulties in other languages. It might be supposed that two popular features of Fortran are its efficiency and ease of use. Many users even live comfortably with its much-derided dangerous features, such as storage association. The success or failure of any new Fortran standard, and the prospects for the long-term viability of the language, will be determined according to how users judge the new standard, and efficiency will certainly be one of the major criteria against which it will be measured (Metcalf, 1984).

2. The Overall Design

The current 1977 Fortran standard defines a single monolithic language. The new standard, known as Fortran 8x, will probably be separated into parts to allow a formalised evolution of the language,

and a recognized way of extending it. This is known as the CORE
+ MODULE concept, and can be expressed diagrammatically as
shown in Fig. 29.

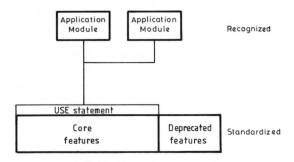

Fig. 29   The proposed structure of the Fortran 8x standard

The *deprecated features* are those features which are candidates
for eventual removal from the language in a future revision cycle.
These features fall into three classes: those connected with storage
association, such as COMMON, those considered to be redundant,
such as the arithmetic IF, and those which are considered bad practice, such as the alternate RETURN. Their presence in the standard
means that the whole of Fortran 77 is included in Fortran 8x. The
contents of the core itself are intended to satisfy each of seven
requirements, given here in no particular order:

> specially suitable for scientific applications
> portable
> safe
> efficient
> concise and consistent
> contemporary
> minimize non-automatable conversion from Fortran 77

The applications modules would be submitted to X3J3 for approval
but not for definition, and are intended to cover such areas as
graphics, data base and real-time needs, but could also be used to
provide, for instance, the functionality of a variable length character
data type. Applications modules must conform with the core.

3. Changing the Flavour of Fortran?

Table 5

The proposed changes to Fortran

Added to the standard	Deprecated features
Free form source	Fortran 77 source form
Larger character set	
Longer names	
Significance of blanks	
Data structures	EQUIVALENCE
MODULES	COMMON and BLOCK DATA
Dynamic storage	DATA
IMPLICIT NONE	DIMENSION
Precision specification	DOUBLE PRECISION
Extended declarations	
BIT data type ·n	
Programmer defined	
data types	
CASE structure	Arithmetic IF
Array processing	Computed GOTO
CHARACTER extension	ASSIGN, and assigned GOTO
Loop structure	Fortran 77 DO
Exception handling	Alternate RETURN
Recursion	Statement functions
Enhanced CALL	Specific names for intrinsic
Internal procedures	functions
Environmental enquiry	ENTRY
I/O extensions	
	Assumed size arrays
	Passing a scalar to a dummy
	array
	PAUSE

The current revision is likely to transform Fortran from a language which gives a real 'feel' for the underlying object code into which it is compiled, into a language which much more resembles those which contain modern constructs and avoid such traps as storage association and a heavy reliance on statement labels. Table 5 summarises those features which will probably be introduced into the standard, and those which will be regarded as deprecated features for eventual exclusion.

4. The New Features

The contents of this section reflect the current state of the revision of the standard. It must be stressed that X3J3 may modify or even delete entirely any of the features listed below, and might add features which are not mentioned here, particularly in the area of event (or error) handling. The recently agreed BIT data type is not included.

Source form

The rigid form based on the punched card will be abandoned, and replaced by a free form source with in-line comments. An input record of 72 characters per line will still be accepted. The names of variables may include underscores and may be up to 31 characters in length. The larger ASCII character set includes lower case, which is interpreted as upper case if used in Fortran syntax, but not in character constants or Hollerith edit descriptors. In-line comments following an exclamation mark are allowed, and a continuation line is indicated by an ampersand on the previous line. Several statements may appear on one line, if separated by a semi-colon. An example input from a terminal (CR stands for carriage return), could be

```
SUBROUTINE CROSS_PRODUCT(X,Y,Z)! Z = X x Y CR
REAL  X(3),Y(3),Z(3)CR
    z1 = x(2)*y(3)-x(3)*y(2) ; z2= x(3)*y(1)-    &CR
x(1)*y(3) !  Save 2 termsCR
    z(3)= x(1)*y(2)-x(2)*y(1) ; z(1)= z1 ; z(2)=    &CR
z2                      ! Fill Z and returnCR
endCR
```

One hopes that the untidy input that this free form allows will not be copied by compilers to the list output, as one could reasonably expect them to reformat the input into a more readable style.

Extended declarations

It will be possible to declare the attributes of data entities using a list of entities preceded by their common attributes:

REAL,ARRAY(1000),INITIAL(1000*0.) :: A,B,C

declares A, B, and C to be real arrays of length 1000, each of which is initialized to zero by the INITIAL attribute, (replacing the DATA statement). The exact form of this type of declaration is currently under review.

Data structures and derived data types

A data structure is defined as a named collection of heterogeneous data. Within a data structure are elements called fields, which may be variables, arrays, or data structures. Fields are normally of fixed length.

A data structure form, or pattern, is described and named by a TYPE declaration, which also supplies the identifiers and attributes (types, length or precision, size, dimension or structure) of the constituent fields. A collection of field declarations is called a type block, terminated by an END TYPE statement, *e.g.*

```
TYPE ID
   CHARACTER * 20 NAME
   LOGICAL SEX
END TYPE
```

describes a TYPE comprising a character variable of length 20 plus a logical variable. An instance, or an actual occurrence, of a data structure is declared by reference to a form in a data structure declaration:

TYPE(ID),ARRAY(100) :: PEOPLE

makes available a data structure containing 100 elements of the form described by ID. We can now refer to all the attributes of a person, as in

IF (PEOPLE(I).EQ.PEOPLE(J)) THEN

or to just the name of a person by using a field reference with the qualification symbol % (which is likely to change)

IF (PEOPLE(I)%NAME.EQ.'SMITH') THEN

The possibility of defining data structures within data structures allows such constructs as that shown in Ex. 56.

```
TYPE CROWD               ! Describe a type
   TYPE(ID),ARRAY(50) :: PEOPLE ! Use previously
                             ! described form ID
   CHARACTER * 20  :: TOWN,COUNTRY
END TYPE                 ! End of description of form
:
CROWD,ARRAY(50) :: LIST  ! TYPE CROWD
                         ! declares data structure
TYPE(ID) :: PERSON       ! TYPE(ID) again declares data
                         ! structure
:
PERSON%NAME = 'SMITH'
PERSON%SEX  = .TRUE.
:
IF (LIST(I)%TOWN.EQ.'GENEVA'.AND.    &
    LIST(I)%PEOPLE(J).EQ.PERSON) THEN
:
:
```

Example 56

There are, of course, rules associated with references to field names, sub-structures and structures, which need not be enumerated in this summary.

More advanced proposals associated with data structures will allow users to define *derived data types,* and to *overload* (redefine) operators to perform user defined operations on those data types. This mechanism will permit such user defined types as STRING (variable length CHARACTERs), as well as allowing high-precision and rational arithmetic to be written in application modules. In addition, a pointer data type is under discussion.

Array processing

There is a clear requirement in a scientific an engineering programming language to provide a simple means of manipulating vectors and arrays; this requirement will grow with the increasing use of vector processors, and is valuable too for the increased functionality it provides even programming scalar machines. The discussions on which facilities to provide have been based on existing experience with the vector processors described in Chapter 11, and on previous vector extensions to Fortran such as VECTRAN (Paul, 1982). The introduction of these facilities has important consequences for program efficiency, as the responsibility for generating efficient code moves squarely to the compiler writers, who are best able to ensure that the particular features of a given processor are well exploited.

Basic array processing

The operations, assignments and intrinsic functions are extended to apply to whole arrays on an element-by-element basis, producing a result of the same shape (dimensionality and dimension sizes) as the operand(s). For operations involving two operands, the operand arrays must be conformable (of the same shape), but a scalar is defined as being conformable to all arrays, and is distributed as necessary. A combined example is thus:

```
ARRAY(20,10) :: A,B,C        ! an entity oriented declaration
:
:
C = 3.*A*SQRT(B)             ! an array valued expression
```

The WHERE statement and WHERE block allow testing on an element-by-element basis:

```
WHERE (B.NE.0)
  C = A/B
ELSEWHERE
  C = A
END WHERE
```

and the FORALL statement allows element-by-element processing over a specified set of index ranges, where no array element ordering is implied.

In order to permit the addressing of array sections, the section subscript symbol : is used. It permits, for example, the columns and rows of a two-dimensional array to be selected in the following manner:

using   ARRAY(−4:0,7) :: A

then   A(−3, :)   selects the second row of A
          A(: ,3)   selects the third column of A.

A triplet notation similar to that used for DO-loop parameters, but using colons as delimiters, will permit references to non-contiguous elements of an array:

$$A(0:-4:-2,1:7:2)$$

selects in reverse order every second element of every second column.

Since an array received by a subprogram as an argument may not necessarily consist of a contiguous sequence of data words, but rather of an array section, array elements passed in an argument list will be subject to certain restrictions, in order to allow compatibility between existing and new programs.

Array constructors are introduced, and specified, for instance, by a list of constants enclosed in either square brackets or slashes and parentheses:

        (/1,2,3,6,12/)

The RESHAPE function may be used to reshape those or any other array objects into an array of specified dimensions.

Dynamic storage

It has been agreed that storage for arrays should be ALLOCATEd and FREEd dynamically using a heap storage implementation.

It will be possible also to define assumed-shape dummy arrays, those with a defined rank but without defined extents, which may be received as arguments without passing their extents:

        REAL A(: , : , :)

The extents can be determined if necessary in the called subprogram by the UBOUND intrinsic function (see below).

Extended array processing

This topic is too vast to develop here; the following lists of proposed functions should just serve to give a feeling for the present ideas.

i) Intrinsic functions return scalar values from arithmetic arrays:

SUM, PRODUCT, MAXVAL, MINVAL and DOTPRODUCT,

and from logical arrays:

COUNT, ANY and ALL.

The first four arithmetic functions may operate under a mask, selecting elements according to the values of corresponding elements of a conformable logical array. These four functions, and the three operating on logical arrays, may also operate only along specified dimensions of arrays to produce array valued results. The three operating on logical arrays count the number of .TRUE. values in an array, or return the value .TRUE. if any or all elements are .TRUE., respectively.

ii) Informative functions return the:

RANK, SHAPE, SIZE, LBOUND and UBOUND

of an array.

iii) In the case of arrays, generative operators may be used to

SPREAD values into an array of higher dimensionality
REPLICATE them within an array dimension
MERGE two arrays according to the logical values of a third array
DIAGONALize *i.e.* produce a diagonal matrix.
PROJECT along an axis

iv) Shift operators can perform

EOSHIFT (end-off) and
CSHIFT (circular) shifts.

v) The matrix operations MATMUL and TRANSPOSE are proposed.

vi) The PACK and UNPACK functions allow an array to be strung out into a vector, and *vice versa,* and the IDENTIFY statement allows dynamic equivalencing of arrays or array sections to a 'virtual' array name which exists for the purpose of simplifying array section refences, *(cf.* implicit descriptors in Section 11.4). and permitting skew sections, *e.g.* matrix diagonals. Elements of the virtual array may be specified in an expression:

REAL X(10,10)
:
IDENTIFY/1:4/XUPPER(I) = X(I,I + 1)
:
A(1:4) = XUPPER(1:4) + B(1:4)

assigns four elements of X, specified by the values of I, to XUPPER which may be referenced in the usual fashion in the program from this point on.

vii) The FIRSTLOC and LASTLOC functions locate the first and last .TRUE. values in logical arrays, respectively.

Internal procedures

Internal procedures are a generalization of statement functions which they are intended to replace. They are placed at the end of the subroutine, and may be invoked by a CALL as well as by a function reference. They may USE variables from the routine in which they appear.

MODULE definition

It will no longer be possible to write confused and confusing storage declarations, as the COMMON declaration and BLOCK DATA give way to the MODULE declarations, which may also contain procedure definitions. MODULEs are written once for a whole program as a means of making unique global specifications:

```
MODULE SPEC
REAL X,Y,Z(10)
END
```

The MODULEs are referenced by the USE statement:

```
USE/SPEC/        ! Import attributes of global variables
```

Within a MODULE, values may be defined using the PARAMETER and the new INITIAL statements.

MODULES may also be used to store internal procedure definitions, which may then be imported in identical forms into procedures, enabling one to construct procedure libraries.

They may also be used to define derived data types, and operators on those data types, providing a mechanism for data abstraction. The operators thus defined may be infix operators.

New looping construct

The proposed new looping construct consists of a DO-block, with optional use of an EXIT statement to leave the loop and of a CYCLE statement to begin the next iteration immediately. An example is

```
DO                        ! repeat endlessly
   val = random()
   IF (VAL.GT.TOL) EXIT    ! now have required value
REPEAT
```

Alternatively, the loop control may be written with the present form of the loop parameters, but with an integer control variable only, or as

```
DO (exp TIMES)            ! exp is an integer expression
```

DO-blocks may be named, with an alphanumeric label, to help with EXITing from nested loops, and to specify which loop's next CYCLE should be initiated.

CASE construct

```
SELECT CASE (expression)
CASE (case-selector-list)
    statements
CASE (case-selector-list)
    statements
:
[CASE DEFAULT
    statements]
END SELECT
```

Example 57

The CASE construct is intended to allow execution of a block of code selected from a sequence of blocks depending on the value of an integer, logical or character expression. It has the general form of Ex. 57. The case selector-lists consist of lists and/or ranges of values, as shown, for instance, in Ex. 58. CASE structures may be named.

```
SELECT CASE (3*I + J)    ! Calculate expression
CASE (0)                 ! If = 0
    Y = SQRT(X)
CASE (1:3, 10:)          ! If 1, 2, or 3, or ⩾10
    Z = X + Y
CASE DEFAULT             ! For all other values
    Z = X
END SELECT
```

Example 58

Precision specification

The ability to specify the precision required for a set of calculations is a need which is acutely felt by numerical analysts. At present, the only possible distinction is between REAL and DOUBLE PRECISION, neither of which has a defined precision or range. One of the proposed forms is

```
REAL(10,99) :: VAR ! VAR needs at least 10 significant
                   ! decimal digits and a base 10 exponent
                   ! range of at least 99.
```

A compiler selects that data type of the host computer which most closely, but completely, satisfies the specification.

Enhanced CALL

The form of the enhanced CALL will include these features: keyword arguments, optional arguments, positional independence, default actions and user defined generic functions (functions which assume the type of their argument). One might have a procedure specification

```
SUBROUTINE PQR(X,Y,RESULT)
```

with procedure calls

```
CALL PQR(A,B,C)                !standard form
CALL PQR(X, RESULT = C,  Y = B)  !position independence
CALL PQR(X = A, RESULT = C)    !optional argument Y
                               !default action to be taken
```

Information about the arguments, for instance that they are optional or whether they may be redefined, may be specified.

Environmental enquiry

A comprehensive set of functions is provided which allows numerical analysts to test the environment in which their code is running. The 'constant' functions provide information on the number base, precision, and range of the host computer, and also return such values as a very large positive number, a very small positive number, and a positive number that is almost negligible compared to 1:

```
chi2 = HUGE(X)                 ! Set value at start of fit
```

Other 'non-constant' functions provide information about the nearest representable number to a given value, the spacing of numbers in the vicinity of a given value, and so on:

IF (ABS(A – B).LE.absspace(A)) .. ! Test for near equality

Extensions to type CHARACTER

A number of character oriented proposals, including zero-length strings, have been adopted, and some additional type CHARACTER intrinsic functions added. In addition, overlap is allowed between the left- and right-hand sides of an assignment:

$$A(:4) = A(2:5)$$

IMPLICIT NONE

This statement requires that all variables in a subprogram appear in an explicit type specification.

Significance of blanks

It has been decided that the blank should become a special character which can later be used as a separator, allowing simpler parsing of source code. Thus, for instance, constants, symbolic names, statement labels, and keywords must be separated by special characters or blanks, and blanks may not appear within the basic syntactic elements of Fortran. This means that

    RE WINDNU NIT0

must become

    REWIND NUNIT0

The keywords GO TO, END IF, ELSE IF and END FILE may appear with or without one blank separating their two parts. For reasons of backward compatibility, the blank will not be imposed as a separator until another revision cycle has passed.

The underscore may be used as a spacer inside constants:

    A = 0.123_456_789_012

Recursion

The decision to introduce the possibility of recursion is of great significance when discussing optimization. It is useful in Fortran programs for purposes such as multi-dimensional integration and list processing, but one fears for the efficiency of the implementations:

```
RECURSIVE FUNCTION FACTORIAL(X)
IF (X.GT.1.) THEN
    FACTORIAL  =  X*FACTORIAL(X – 1.)
ELSE
    RETURN
ENDIF
END
```

Extensions to I/O functions

Extensions are proposed concerning the POSITIONing of a file when it is OPENed, and the type of ACTIONs which may be performed on it (*e.g.* read-only or write-only).

Name directed I/O, similar to existing NAMELIST facilities, but referencing names not lists, is also proposed.

Date and Time

There are proposals to provide intrinsic procedures which return the local date and time (down to milliseconds), and the difference between local time and a reference time (GMT).

Questions

1. Is anyone at your installation responsible for keeping language developments under review, and for channeling information between the users and the standardisation bodies?

2. Which three of the proposals described above do you like the most, and which three the least? State your reasons.

3. Which additional features would you like to see in a future standard?

4. What, in your opinion, is the long-term future of Fortran?

APPENDIX A: FORTRAN 77

This summary is adapted from that of Wagener (1980). See also Metcalf (1985).
Items in *italics* were part of Fortran 66 in substantially the same form.

Fortran statements are contained in columns 7-72 of the lines comprising a program.
The Fortran character set consists of: the upper case letters, A-Z; the numerals,
0-9; the special characters, = + − * / ( ) ' . $, : and the character blank.
An * or C in column 1 indicates a comment line.
A non-blank, non-zero character in col. 6 indicates that a line is a continuation line.
A labelled statement has the <label> in columns 1-5.
<....> indicates a programmer-supplied entry.
[....]   indicates an optional part of statement.
{....}   indicates a sequence of zero or more elements.
A <list> is a sequence of elements separated by commas.

STATEMENT	EXAMPLE

Form of a Fortran Program

PROGRAM <program-name>	PROGRAM MAIN
{ <specification-statement> }	CALL PROC
{ <executable-statement> }	END
END	

Specification Statements

INTEGER <integer-declaration-list>	INTEGER I(40)
REAL <real-declaration-list>	REAL A(10)
CHARACTER[*<length>]	CHARACTER*72 LINE(20)
<character-declaration-list>	

LOGICAL < *logical-declaration-list* >   LOGICAL WRONG
DOUBLE PRECISION   DOUBLE PRECISION Q(9)
    < *double-precision-declaration-list* >
COMPLEX < *complex-declaration-list* >   COMPLEX CURRNT(10)

IMPLICIT < implicit-declaration-list >   IMPLICIT LOGICAL (A-Z)
PARAMETER (< constant-definition-list >)   PARAMETER (PI = 22./7.)
DIMENSION < *array-declaration-list* >
EQUIVALENCE < *equivalence-list* >
EXTERNAL < *procedure-name-list* >
INTRINSIC < intrinsic-function-name-list >   INTRINSIC DSQRT
DATA < *variable-name-list* > /   DATA I,J,K/1,2,3/,A/0./
    < *constant-value-list* > /
    { *[,]* < *variable-name-list* > /
    < *constant-value-list* > / }

Executable Statements

< *variable-name* > = < *expression* >   A = B*SQRT(C)+4.

PRINT *
PRINT *, < output-expression-list >   PRINT *, I,A
READ *, < input-variable-name-list >   READ *, LIST
PRINT < *format* >, < output-expression-list >   PRINT 100,I+J
READ < *format* >, < input-variable-name-list > READ 100,A,B,C
IF   (< logical-expression >) THEN   IF (I.EQ.0) THEN
           { < executable-statement > }   A = A+1.
     {ELSEIF (< logical-expression >) THEN} ELSEIF (I.EQ.1) THEN
     {   { < executable-statement > } }   A = A−4.
     [ELSE   ]   ELSE
     {   { < executable-statement > }]]   A = 0.
ENDIF   ENDIF

        DO < *label* > *[,]* < *indexed-range* >   DO 1 I = J*4,ABS(A), −1
         { < *executable-statement* > }   A(I) = B(I)−1.
< *label* >   *CONTINUE*   1 CONTINUE

CALL < *subroutine-name* >   CALL PROC(A,SQRT,4,*15)
       [(< *actual-argument-list* > *)]*
GOTO < *label* >   GOTO 6
IF (< logical-expression >) GOTO < label >   IF (I.EQ.0) GO TO 10
< *label* >   *CONTINUE*

SIGN <label> TO <variable-name>	ASSIGN 100 TO JUMP
TO <variable-name>	GO TO JUMP
TO (<label-list>)[,] <integer-expression>	GO TO (1,2,3), I+J
(<arithmetic-expression>)	IF (A) 1,2,3
<label>,<label>,<label>	
(<logical-expression>)	IF (I.EQ.0) J = 2
<executable-statement>	

tran Procedures

BROUTINE <subroutine-name>	SUBROUTINE PRC(B,F,K,*)
[(<dummy-argument-list>)]	REAL B(*)
{ *<specification-statement>* }	B(1) = F(K)
{ *<executable-statement>* }	IF (B(1).LT.0.) RETURN 1
D	END

type>] FUNCTION <function-name>
[(<dummy-argument-list>)]
{ *<specification-statement>* }
{ *<executable-statement>* }
D

TRY <entry-name>	ENTRY OTHER (X,Y,Z)
<dummy-argument-list>)]	
VE [<local-variable-list>]	SAVE /NAME/,VAR

e I/O Operations

RITE (<control-list>)	WRITE(4,1)Y,(Z(I),I=9,1,-2)
<output-expression-list>	
AD (<control-list>)	READ (NU,'(A)') NAME
<input-variable-name-list>	
PEN (<unit>,<open-list>)	OPEN (2,FILE='DATA')
LOSE (<unit>,<close-list>)	CLOSE (NUNIT)
QUIRE (<unit>,<inquire-list>)	INQUIRE (2,EXIST=LVAR)
QUIRE (<file>,<inquire-list>)	INQUIRE(NM,OPENED=L)
ACKSPACE <unit>	BACKSPACE 4
EWIND <unit>	REWIND NUNIT
NDFILE <unit>	ENDFILE 2

Global Data Facilities

COMMON [/<common-block-name>/]   COMMON /NAME/ X,A(50)
    <common-variable-list>

BLOCKDATA [<block-data-name>]   BLOCK DATA DEFIN
    { <specification-statement> }   COMMON /D/ I,J,K
END   DATA I,J,K /1,2,3/
                                                      END

Miscellaneous Statements

FORMAT(<format-specification-list>)
PAUSE [....]
RETURN [<integer-expression>]
STOP

Miscellaneous Constructs

<list>	<item> {,<item>}
<name>	1-6 letters and decimal digits, the first of which must be a letter
<label>	sequence of 1-5 decimal digits
<expression>	specification of a data value
<integer-expression>	an expression involving only integer operands and arithmetic operators
<arithmetic-expression>	an expression involving numeric operands and arithmetic operators
arithmetic operators:	+ addition − subtraction (and unary negation) * multiplication / division ** exponentiation
character operator:	// concatenation
substring:	<character-variable-name>(<integer-expression>:

< integer-expression >)

onal operators	*.EQ.*	equal to
	.NE.	not equal to
	.LT.	less than
	.GT.	greater than
	.LE.	less than or equal to
	.GE.	greater than or equal to
al operators:	*.NOT.*	complement
	.AND.	true if both operands true
	.OR.	true if either (or both) operands true
	.EQV.	true if operands have the same value
	.NEQV.	true if operands have different values
al constants:	.TRUE.	
	.FALSE.	
eric constants:	integer constant	
	real constant	
	double precision constant	
	complex constant	
g constant:	' < sequence-of-characters > '	
erith constant:	< integer > H < sequence-of-characters >	
	(integer is character sequence length)	
ray-declaration>	< array-name > (< dimension-bound-list >)	
imension-bound>	< lower-bound > : < upper-bound > or < integer >	
ray-element>	< array-name > (< subscript-list >)	
nplicit-declaration>	< type > (< letter-range-list >)	
onstant-definition>	< constant-name > = < constant-value >	
idexed-range>	< integer-variable-name > = < integer-expression > ,	
	< integer-expression >	
	[, < integer-expression >]	
nplied-do-list>	(< expression-list > , < index-range >)	
quivalence-declaration>	(< variable-name-list >)	

I/O Control

) < control-list > options: [UNIT =] < integer-expression >

[FMT =] < character-expression >
or [FMT =] < FORMAT-statement-label >
REC = < integer-expression >
END = < label >
ERR = < label >
IOSTAT =   < integer-variable-name >

< open-list > options:

[UNIT =] < integer-expression >
FILE = < character-expression >
ACCESS = < character-expression >
STATUS = < character-expression >
FORM = < character-expression >
RECL = < integer-expression >
BLANK = < character-expression >
ERR = < label >
IOSTAT = < integer-variable-name >

< close-list > options:

[UNIT =] < integer-expression >
STATUS = < character-expression >
ERR = < label >
IOSTAT = < integer-variable-name >

< inquire-list > options:

[UNIT =] < integer-expression]
FILE = < character-expression >
EXIST = < logical-variable-name >
OPENED = < logical-variable-name >
NUMBER = < integer-variable-name >
NAMED = < logical-variable-name >
NAME = < character-variable-name >
ACCESS = < character-variable-name >
SEQUENTIAL = < logical-variable-name >
DIRECT = < logical-variable-name >
FORM = < character-variable-name >
FORMATTED = < logical-variable-name >
UNFORMATTED = < logical-variable name >
RECL = < integer-variable-name >
NEXTREC = < integer-variable-name >
BLANK = < character-variable-name >
ERR = < label >
IOSTAT = < integer-variable-name >

< format-specification-list >
repeatable

options:
I< width >   4I10

I < width > . < digits >	I10.3
A	
A < width >	A9
L < width >	L2
F < width > . < digits >	F6.2
E < width > . < digits > [E < digits >]	E10.4
D < width > . < digits >	D10.4
G < width > . < digits > [E < digits >]	G10.4

repeatable

< scale-factor > P	4PE10.4
< string-constant >	'STRING'
< Hollerith-constant >	6HSTRING
T < column-number >	T7
TL < number-of-positions >	TL4
TR < number-of-positions >	TR9
< number-of-positions > X	4X
S	
SP	
SS	
BN	
BZ	
/	
:	

APPENDIX B: LAYOUT PROGRAM

```
      PROGRAM INDENT
*
* * * * * * * * * * * * * * * * * * * * * * * * * * * * * * * * * * * * * * *
*                                                                           *
*                                                                           *
* A PROGRAM TO REFORMAT FORTRAN PROGRAM UNITS BY INDENTING THE              *
* BODY OF ALL DO−LOOPS AND IF−BLOCKS BY ISHIFT COLUMNS. THIS PERMITS A       *
* RAPID VISUAL INSPECTION FOR THE MOST DEEPLY NESTED PARTS OF A             *
* PROGRAM, AS WELL AS BEING A MEANS OF IMPROVING ITS LAYOUT.                *
*                                                                           *
* USAGE: THE PROGRAM READS ONE DATA RECORD IN FREE FORMAT FROM THE          *
*     DEFAULT INPUT UNIT. THIS CONTAINS:                                    *
*                 INDENTATION DEPTH                                         *
*                 MAXIMUM INDENTATION LEVEL                                 *
*                 THE UNIT NO. OF THE INPUT SOURCE STREAM                   *
*                 THE UNIT NO. OF THE OUTPUT STREAM                         *
*     THE DEFAULT VALUES IN THE ABSENCE OF THIS RECORD ARE 3 10 5 6         *
*                                                                           *
* RESTRICTIONS: THE PROGRAM DOES NOT INDENT FORMAT STATEMENTS OR            *
*         ANY STATEMENT CONTAINING A CHARACTER STRING WITH AN               *
*         EMBEDDED MULTIPLE BLANK.                                          *
*         THE ORDER OF COMMENT LINES AND FORTRAN STATEMENTS                 *
*         IS SLIGHTLY MODIFIED IF THERE ARE SEQUENCES OF                    *
*         MORE THAN KKLIM (=200) COMMENT LINES.                             *
*                                                                           *
* REMEMBER − THE FIRST COLUMN OF THE OUTPUT FILE WILL BE TAKEN AS           *
* CARRIAGE CONTROL INFORMATION IF THE OUTPUT UNIT IS A PRINTER              *
*                                                                           *
*           VERSION OF 04/01/84                                            *
*                                                                           *
* * * * * * * * * * * * * * * * * * * * * * * * * * * * * * * * * * * * * * *
*
* INITIALIZE
      CALL START
*
* PROCESS THE LINES OF PROGRAM UNITS
      CALL PUNITS
*
```

```
*     PRINT SOME STATISTICS
      CALL TERMIN
      END
      SUBROUTINE PUNITS
*
* * * * * * * * * * * * * * * * * * * * * * * * * * * * * * * * * * * * *
*     THE PRINCIPAL SUBROUTINE OF INDENT PROCESSES THE              *
*     INPUT STREAM, WHICH IS ASSUMED TO CONTAIN SYNTACTICALLY CORRECT *
*     FORTRAN PROGRAM UNITS. TO PROTECT ITSELF FROM BAD DATA, FAILURE *
*     TO PASS A PRIMITIVE SYNTAX CHECK WILL CAUSE THE PROGRAM TO COPY *
*     THE INPUT STREAM TO THE OUTPUT UNIT UNCHANGED, UNTIL AN END LINE IS *
*     ENCOUNTERED.                                                  *
* * * * * * * * * * * * * * * * * * * * * * * * * * * * * * * * * * * * *
*
      COMMON/DATA/ISHIFT , MXDPTH , NIN , NOUT
*
      COMMON/STATS/MXDO , MXIF , KARD , KNTPU , SYNTAX
*
      SAVE /DATA/ , /STATS/
*
* * * * * * * * * * * * * * * * * * * * * * * * * * * * * * * * * * * * *
*     DEFINE MAXIMUM LEVEL OF DO-LOOP NESTING, AND MAXIMUM LENGTH OF *
*     A FORTRAN STATEMENT. LEN MAY BE REDUCED FOR                   *
*     COMPILERS ACCEPTING A MAXIMUM CHARACTER                       *
*     LENGTH BELOW 1320 AND THIS WILL CAUSE ANY EXCESS              *
*     CONTINUATION LINES AND ALL FOLLOWING LINES TO BE COPIED UNCHANGED. *
*     NEST AND LEN APPEAR IN S/R IDENT AND REFORM ALSO.             *
*     KKLIM DEFINES THE LENGTH OF THE COMMENT LINE BUFFER. IF THIS   *
*     LENGTH IS EXCEEDED, THE STATEMENT PRECEDING THE COMMENTS WILL  *
*     APPEAR AFTER THEM.                                            *
* * * * * * * * * * * * * * * * * * * * * * * * * * * * * * * * * * * * *
*
      PARAMETER (NEST = 32 , LEN = 1320 , KKLIM = 200)
      PARAMETER (KLEN = 72*KKLIM)
*
      COMMON/S1/KNTDO , KNTIF , KNTCOM , LABEL , LENST , SYNERR , LABLNO
     + , LABLDO(NEST)
*
      COMMON/S2/STAMNT , CBUF
*
* * * * * * * * * * * * * * * * * * * * * * * * * * * * * * * * * * * * *
*     USER IS A CHARACTER WHICH MAY BE DEFINED TO IDENTIFY LINES     *
*     IN THE INPUT STREAM WHICH ARE TO BE TREATED AS                *
*     COMMENT LINES ( + IN THIS EXAMPLE).                           *
* * * * * * * * * * * * * * * * * * * * * * * * * * * * * * * * * * * * *
*
      CHARACTER CONTIN , USER , FIN*3 , FIELD*66 , LINE*72 ,
     +        STAMNT*(LEN) , CBUF*(KLEN)
*
      LOGICAL SYNERR , NEWDO , NEWIF , SYNTAX , FORM , STAT , ELSEBL
*
      DATA FIN/'END'/ , USER/'+'/ , STAT/.FALSE./
*
*     START PROCESSING PROGRAM UNITS
      MXDO = 0
      MXIF = 0
      KARD = 0
```

```
      KNTPU = 0
      SYNTAX = .FALSE.
      SYNERR = .FALSE.
      KNTDO = 0
      KNTIF = 0
      KNTCOM = 0
*
*  SET CONTINUATION LINE COUNTER
    1 KNTCON = 0
*
*  SET STATEMENT LENGTH COUNTER
      LENST = 0
*
*  READ ONE LINE INTO AN INTERNAL FILE
*  COLUMNS 73-80 OF ALL LINES ARE IGNORED.
    2 READ (NIN , '(A)' , END = 100 , ERR = 100) LINE
      KARD = KARD+1
*
*  CHECK WHETHER A COMMENT LINE AND IF SO COPY TO BUFFER.
      IF (LINE(:1) .EQ. 'C' .OR. LINE(:1) .EQ. '*' .OR. LINE(:1) .EQ.
     +USER .OR. LINE .EQ. ' ') THEN
        IF (KNTCOM .EQ. KKLIM) THEN
          WRITE (NOUT , '(A72)') (CBUF(72*L5-71:72*L5) , L5 = 1 ,
     +      KNTCOM) , LINE
          KNTCOM = 0
        ELSEIF (SYNERR .OR. .NOT.STAT) THEN
          WRITE (NOUT , '(A72)') LINE
        ELSE
          KNTCOM = KNTCOM+1
          CBUF(72*KNTCOM-71:72*KNTCOM) = LINE
        ENDIF
        GO TO 2
      ENDIF
*
*  LINE IS SOME FORM OF STATEMENT. RE-READ.
      READ (LINE , '(BN , I5 , A1 , A66)') LAB , CONTIN , FIELD
      STAT = .TRUE.
*
*  CHECK ON SYNTAX AND COPY TO STATEMENT BUFFER
    3 IF (CONTIN .NE. ' ') THEN
        IF (SYNERR) THEN
          GO TO 6
        ELSEIF (LENST .EQ. 0 .OR. LENST+66 .GT. LEN .OR. LAB .NE. 0)
     +  THEN
          SYNERR = .TRUE.
          IF (LENST .GT. 0) THEN
            IF (LABEL .NE. 0) THEN
              WRITE (NOUT , '(I5 , 1X , A66:/(5X ,"+", A66))')
     +        LABEL , (STAMNT(66*L9-65:66*L9) , L9 = 1 , (LENST+65)
     +        /66)
            ELSE
              WRITE (NOUT , '(6X , A66:/(5X ,"+", A66))')
     +        (STAMNT(66*L9-65:66*L9) , L9 = 1 , (LENST+65)/66)
            ENDIF
          ENDIF
          IF (LAB .NE. 0) THEN
            WRITE (NOUT , 1000) LAB , CONTIN , FIELD
```

```
        ELSE
          WRITE (NOUT , 1006) CONTIN , FIELD
        ENDIF
        GO TO 1
      ELSE
        KNTCON = KNTCON+1
        STAMNT(LENST+1:LENST+66) = FIELD
        LENST = LENST+66
        GO TO 2
      ENDIF
    ELSEIF (KNTCON .EQ. 0) THEN
      IF (LENST .NE. 0) GO TO 4
      STAMNT(1:66) = FIELD
      LENST = 66
      LABEL = LAB
      IF (SYNERR) GO TO 4
      GO TO 2
    ENDIF
    IF (KNTCON .GT. 0) GO TO 6
*
* HAVE A COMPLETE STATEMENT READY FOR PROCESSING ( THE LAST LINE
* READ IS STILL WAITING IN LINE). THE STATEMENT NOW NEEDS TO BE
* IDENTIFIED.
* THE END STATEMENT IS A SPECIAL CASE — IF FOUND IT WILL BE COPIED
* AND THE NEXT PROGRAM UNIT PROCESSED.
    4 K1 = 1
      DO 5 L1 = 1 , LENST
        IF (STAMNT(L1:L1) .EQ. ' ') GO TO 5
        IF (STAMNT(L1:L1) .NE. FIN(K1:K1)) THEN
          GO TO 6
        ELSE
          K1 = K1+1
          IF (K1 .GT. 3 .AND. (L1 .GE. LENST .OR. STAMNT(L1+1:LENST)
     +      .EQ. ' ')) THEN
            IF (.NOT.SYNERR) THEN
              KNTPU=KNTPU+1
              IF (LABEL .EQ. 0) THEN
                WRITE (NOUT , 1001) FIN
              ELSE
                WRITE (NOUT , 1002) LABEL , FIN
              ENDIF
            ENDIF
*
* SET COUNTERS FOR NEW PROGRAM UNIT
            SYNTAX = SYNTAX .OR. SYNERR
            KNTDO = 0
            KNTIF = 0
            SYNERR = .FALSE.
            KNTCON = 0
            LENST = 0
            IF (KNTCOM .NE. 0) WRITE (NOUT , '(A72)') (CBUF(72*L5-71:
     +        72*L5) , L5 = 1 , KNTCOM)
            KNTCOM = 0
            GO TO 3
          ELSE
            IF (K1 .GT. 3) GO TO 6
          ENDIF
```

```
        ENDIF
     5 CONTINUE
*
*  IF SYNTAX ERROR FLAG SET, COPY AND TAKE NEXT STATEMENT
     6 IF (SYNERR) THEN
        IF (LAB .NE. 0) THEN
          WRITE (NOUT , 1000) LAB , CONTIN , FIELD
        ELSE
          WRITE (NOUT , 1006) CONTIN , FIELD
        ENDIF
        LENST = 0
        GO TO 2
     ENDIF
*
*  HAVE A VALID STATEMENT WHICH IS NOT AN END LINE
*  IDENTIFY STATEMENT AS    DO
*                   IF ( ) THEN
*                   DO TERMINATOR
*                   ENDIF
*                   FORMAT
*                   ELSE OR ELSEIF
*                   NONE OF THESE.
        NEWDO = .FALSE.
        NEWIF = .FALSE.
        FORM  = .FALSE.
        ELSEBL = .FALSE.
        CALL IDENT(*7 , *8 , *10 , *11 , *12 , *13)
        GO TO 14
*
*  NEW DO-LOOP
     7 IF (KNTDO .EQ. NEST) GO TO 14
        NEWDO = .TRUE.
        LABLDO(KNTDO+1) = LABLNO
        GO TO 14
*
*  END OF DO-LOOP(S)
     8 DO 9 L5 = KNTDO , 1 , -1
        IF (LABLDO(L5) .NE. LABEL) GO TO 14
        KNTDO = KNTDO-1
     9 CONTINUE
        GO TO 14
*
*  BEGINNING OF IF-BLOCK
    10 NEWIF = .TRUE.
        GO TO 14
*
*  END OF IF-BLOCK
    11 KNTIF = KNTIF-1
        IF (KNTIF .LT. 0) THEN
          SYNERR = .TRUE.
          KNTIF = 0
        ENDIF
        GO TO 14
*
*  FORMAT STATEMENT
    12 FORM = .TRUE.
        GO TO 14
```

```
*
*  BEGINNING OF ELSE-BLOCK
 13 ELSEBL = .TRUE.
*
*  REFORMAT STATEMENTS AND WRITE
 14 CALL REFORM (FORM , ELSEBL)
*
*  SET VARIABLES FOR NEXT STATEMENT
    IF (NEWDO) KNTDO = KNTDO+1
    IF (NEWIF) KNTIF = KNTIF+1
    KNTCON = 0
    LENST = 0
    MXDO = MAX(MXDO , KNTDO)
    MXIF = MAX(MXIF , KNTIF)
    GO TO 3
*
*  END OF DATA. LAST LINE MUST BE AN END.
 100 IF (LABEL .EQ. 0) WRITE (NOUT , 1001) FIN
    IF (LABEL .NE. 0) WRITE (NOUT , 1002) LABEL , FIN
    KNTPU=KNTPU+1
*
1000 FORMAT(I5 , A1 , A)
1001 FORMAT(6X , A3 , 63X , '**IF**DO')
1002 FORMAT(I5 , 1X , A3 , 63X , '**IF**DO')
1006 FORMAT(5X , A1 , A66)
*
    END
    SUBROUTINE REFORM (FORM , ELSEBL)
*
*  PERFORMS REFORMATTING AND OUTPUT OF ACCEPTED STATEMENTS
*
    PARAMETER (NEST = 32 , LEN = 1320 , KKLIM = 200)
    PARAMETER (KLEN = 72*KKLIM)
*
    COMMON/DATA/ISHIFT , MXDPTH , NIN , NOUT
*
    COMMON/S1/KNTDO , KNTIF , KNTCOM , LABEL , LENST , SYNERR , LABLNO
   + , LABLDO(NEST)
*
    COMMON/S2/STAMNT , CBUF
*
    CHARACTER STAMNT*(LEN) , OUT*(LEN) , CBUF*(KLEN)
*
    LOGICAL FORM , SYNERR , ELSEBL
*
*  IF FORMAT STATEMENT, DO NOT INDENT
    IF (FORM) GO TO 9
*
*  REFORMAT INDENTED STATEMENT AND WRITE. IF REFORMATTING CAUSES IT
*  TO EXCEED LEN CHARACTERS, IT WILL BE COPIED UNCHANGED.
    IDEPTH = MIN(KNTDO+KNTIF , MXDPTH)
    IF (IDEPTH .EQ. 0) GO TO 9
    IF (ELSEBL) IDEPTH = IDEPTH-1
    IPNT = 1
    JPNT = 1
  1 IF (MOD(IPNT , 66) .EQ. 1) THEN
        IF (IPNT+65 .GT. LEN) GO TO 9
```

```
      OUT(IPNT:IPNT+65) = ' '
      IPNT = IPNT+IDEPTH*ISHIFT
   ENDIF
*
*  FIND FIRST NON-BLANK CHARACTER
   DO 2 L2 = JPNT , LENST
      IF (STAMNT(L2:L2) .NE. ' ') GO TO 3
 2 CONTINUE
   IF (JPNT .EQ. 1) THEN
      SYNERR = .TRUE.
      GO TO 9
   ELSE
      GO TO 10
   ENDIF
*
*  FIND FIRST MULTIPLE BLANK (BUT NOT IN A CHARACTER STRING)
 3 KNTAP = 0
   DO 4 L3 = L2+1 , LENST-1
      IF (STAMNT(L3:L3) .EQ. '''') KNTAP = 1-KNTAP
      IF (STAMNT(L3:L3+1) .EQ. ' ') THEN
         IF (KNTAP .EQ. 0) GO TO 5
         GO TO 9
      ENDIF
 4 CONTINUE
   L3 = LENST
*
*  HAVE SECTION WITH NO MULTIPLE BLANKS. THIS CAN BE COPIED TO OUT
*  IF THERE IS ROOM ON THE CURRENT LINE. OTHERWISE CUT THE
*  SECTION AFTER THE NON-ALPHANUMERIC CHARACTER NEAREST TO THE END OF
*  THE LINE, IF ONE EXISTS.
*  AN APOSTROPHE IS CONSIDERED TO BE AN ALPHANUMERIC CHARACTER, IN
*  ORDER TO HOLD CHARACTER STRINGS TOGETHER.
 5 KADD = 0
   IF (L3-L2 .LE. 66-MOD(IPNT , 66)) GO TO 8
   DO 6 L4 = 66+L2-MOD(IPNT , 66) , L2 , -1
      IF (STAMNT(L4:L4) .EQ. '''') GO TO 6
      IF (LGE(STAMNT(L4:L4) , 'A') .AND. LLE(STAMNT(L4:L4) , 'Z'))
 +       GO TO 6
      IF (LLT(STAMNT(L4:L4) , '0') .OR. LGT(STAMNT(L4:L4) , '9'))
 +       GO TO 7
 6 CONTINUE
   L4 = 66-MOD(IPNT , 66)+L2
 7 L3 = L4
   KADD = 1
 8 LOUT = IPNT+L3-L2
   IF (LOUT .GT. LEN) GO TO 9
   OUT(IPNT:LOUT) = STAMNT(L2:L3)
   IF (L3 .EQ. LENST) GO TO 10
*
*  SET POINTERS FOR NEXT SECTION OF STATEMENT
   IPNT = LOUT+1
   IF (KADD .EQ. 1 .AND. MOD(IPNT , 66) .NE. 1 .OR. MOD(IPNT , 66)
 +    .GE. 60) IPNT = ((IPNT+65)/66)*66+1
   IF (MOD(IPNT , 66) .EQ. 0) IPNT = IPNT+1
   JPNT = L3+1
   IF (KADD .EQ. 0) JPNT = JPNT+1
   GO TO 1
```

```
*
*  COPIED STATEMENT
   9 IF (LABEL .NE. 0) THEN
        WRITE (NOUT , 1003) LABEL , STAMNT(:66)
     ELSE
        WRITE (NOUT , 1004) STAMNT(:66)
     ENDIF
     IF (LENST .GT. 66) WRITE (NOUT , 1005)
    +(STAMNT(66*L6-65:66*L6) , L6 = 2 , (LENST+65)/66)
        GO TO 11
*
*  WRITE OUT, KNTIF AND KNTDO TO OUTPUT UNIT
   10 IF (LABEL .NE. 0) THEN
        WRITE (NOUT , 1003) LABEL , OUT(:66) , KNTIF , KNTDO
     ELSE
        WRITE (NOUT , 1004) OUT(:66) , KNTIF , KNTDO
     ENDIF
     IF (LOUT .GT. 66) WRITE (NOUT , 1005)
    + (OUT(66*L5-65:66*L5) , L5 = 2 , (LOUT+65)/66)
*
*  WRITE ANY COMMENTS FOLLOWING STATEMENT
   11 IF (KNTCOM .NE. 0) THEN
        WRITE (NOUT , '(A72)') (CBUF(72*L5-71:72*L5) , L5 = 1 , KNTCOM)
        KNTCOM = 0
     ENDIF
*
 1003 FORMAT(I5 , 1X , A66 , 2I4)
 1004 FORMAT(6X , A66 , 2I4)
 1005 FORMAT(5X , '+' , A66)
*
     END
     SUBROUTINE IDENT (*,*,*,*,*,*)
*
* * * * * * * * * * * * * * * * * * * * * * * * * * * * * * * * * * * * * *
*  TO IDENTIFY STATEMENT AS BEGINNING OR END OF DO-LOOP OR            *
*  IF-BLOCK, OR AS PROBABLE FORMAT.                                   *
*  ATTEMPT TO SCAN AS FEW OF THE INPUT CHARACTERS AS POSSIBLE.        *
* * * * * * * * * * * * * * * * * * * * * * * * * * * * * * * * * * * * * *
*
     PARAMETER (NEST = 32 , LEN = 1320 , KKLIM = 200)
     PARAMETER (KLEN = 72*KKLIM)
*
     COMMON/S1/KNTDO , KNTIF , KNTCOM , LABEL , LENST , SYNERR , LABLNO
    + , LABLDO(NEST)
*
     COMMON/S2/STAMNT , CBUF
     CHARACTER *(LEN) STAMNT  , CBUF*(KLEN)
*
     CHARACTER *5 INTFIL , ENDIF , BIF*3 , THEN , DO*2 , FORMAT*7 ,
    +        ELSE*4
*
     LOGICAL SYNERR
*
     DATA ENDIF/'ENDIF'/ , BIF/'IF('/ , THEN/'NEHT)'/ , DO/'DO'/ ,
    +FORMAT/'FORMAT('/ , ELSE/'ELSE'/
*
*  CHECK WHETHER END OF DO-LOOP
```

```
        IF (KNTDO .NE. 0) THEN
          IF (LABEL .EQ. LABLDO(KNTDO)) RETURN 2
        ENDIF
*
*   CHECK WHETHER ANY OF REMAINING POSSIBILITIES
        DO 1 L7 = 1 , LENST
          IF (STAMNT(L7:L7) .EQ. ' ') GO TO 1
          IF (STAMNT(L7:L7) .EQ. 'E') THEN
            DO 2 L11 = L7+1 , LENST
              IF (STAMNT(L11:L11) .EQ. ' ') GO TO 2
              IF (STAMNT(L11:L11) .EQ. ENDIF(2:2)) GO TO 6
              IF (STAMNT(L11:L11) .EQ. ELSE(2:2)) GO TO 3
              GO TO 99
    2       CONTINUE
          ENDIF
          IF (STAMNT(L7:L7) .EQ. BIF(:1)) GO TO 9
          IF (STAMNT(L7:L7) .EQ. DO(:1)) GO TO 15
          IF (STAMNT(L7:L7) .EQ. FORMAT(:1)) GO TO 31
          GO TO 99
    1   CONTINUE
        GO TO 99
*
*   CHECK WHETHER ELSE OR ELSEIF
    3   K8 = 3
        DO 4 L12 = L11+1 , LENST
          IF (STAMNT(L12:L12) .EQ. ' ') GO TO 4
          IF (STAMNT(L12:L12) .NE. ELSE(K8:K8)) GO TO 99
          IF (K8 .EQ. 4) GO TO 5
          K8 = K8+1
    4   CONTINUE
        GO TO 99
    5   IF (L12 .GE. LENST) RETURN 6
        IF (STAMNT(L12+1:LENST) .EQ. ' ') RETURN 6
        K2 = 1
        IRET = 6
        L7 = L12
        GO TO 10
*
*   CHECK WHETHER END OF IF−BLOCK
    6   K1 = 3
        DO 7 L1 = L11+1,LENST
          IF (STAMNT(L1:L1) .EQ. ' ') GO TO 7
          IF (STAMNT(L1:L1) .NE. ENDIF (K1:K1)) GO TO 99
          IF (K1 .EQ. 5) GO TO 8
          K1 = K1+1
    7   CONTINUE
    8   IF (L1 .GE. LENST) RETURN 4
        IF (STAMNT(L1+1:LENST) .EQ. ' ') RETURN 4
        GO TO 99
*
*   CHECK WHETHER BEGINNING OF IF−BLOCK
    9   K2 = 2
        IRET = 3
   10   DO 11 L2 = L7+1 , LENST
          IF (STAMNT(L2:L2) .EQ. ' ') GO TO 11
          IF (STAMNT(L2:L2) .NE. BIF (K2:K2)) GO TO 99
          IF (K2 .EQ. 3) GO TO 12
```

```
      K2 = K2+1
   11 CONTINUE
      GO TO 99
*
*  BACKWARD SEARCH FOR )THEN AT END OF IF STATEMENT (TO SAVE
*  SCANNING THE CONDITION)
*  AVOID PLACING RETURN STATEMENT INSIDE THE LOOP
   12 K3 = 1
      DO 13 L3 = LENST , L2+1 , −1
         IF (STAMNT(L3:L3) .EQ. ' ') GO TO 13
         IF (STAMNT(L3:L3) .NE. THEN(K3:K3)) GO TO 99
         IF (K3 .EQ. 5) GO TO 14
         K3 = K3+1
   13 CONTINUE
      GO TO 99
   14 RETURN IRET
*
*  CHECK WHETHER BEGINNING OF DO−LOOP
   15 DO 16 L4 = L7+1 , LENST
         IF (STAMNT(L4:L4) .EQ. ' ') GO TO 16
         IF (STAMNT(L4:L4) .EQ. DO(2:2)) GO TO 17
         GO TO 99
   16 CONTINUE
      GO TO 99
*
*  HAVE DO − CHECK LABEL
   17 K5 = 0
      INTFIL = ' '
      DO 18 L5 = L4+1 , LENST
         IF (STAMNT(L5:L5) .EQ. ' ') GO TO 18
         IF (LLT(STAMNT(L5:L5) , '0') .OR. LGT(STAMNT(L5:L5) , '9'))
     +      GO TO 19
         K5 = K5+1
         IF (K5 .GT. 5) GO TO 20
         INTFIL(K5:K5) = STAMNT(L5:L5)
   18 CONTINUE
   19 IF (K5 .EQ. 0) GO TO 99
   20 READ (INTFIL , '(BN , I5)') LABLNO
      IF (LABLNO .EQ. 0) GO TO 99
*
*  HAVE LABEL − CHECK COMMA
      DO 21 L8 = L5 , LENST
         IF (STAMNT(L8:L8) .EQ. ' ') GO TO 21
         IF (STAMNT(L8:L8) .EQ. ',') GO TO 22
         GO TO 23
   21 CONTINUE
   22 RETURN 1
*
*  HAVE A DO AND LABEL WITH NO COMMA.
*  CHECK FOR VARIABLE WHOSE FIRST OF MAXIMUM OF SIX
*  CHARACTERS IS ALPHABETIC, FOLLOWED BY AN EQUALS SIGN,
*  FOLLOWED BY A CHARACTER STRING CONTAINING A COMMA WHICH IS
*  NOT ENCLOSED IN PARENTHESES.
   23 K6 = 0
      DO 24 L9 = L8 , LENST
         IF (STAMNT(L9:L9) .EQ. ' ') GO TO 24
         IF (K6 .EQ. 0) THEN
```

```
         IF (LLT(STAMNT(L9:L9) , 'A') .OR. LGT(STAMNT(L9:L9) , 'Z'))
    +       GO TO 99
         K6 = 1
       ELSEIF (LGE(STAMNT(L9:L9) , 'A') .AND. LLE(STAMNT(L9:L9) , 'Z')
    +    .OR. LGE(STAMNT(L9:L9) , '0') .AND. LLE(STAMNT(L9:L9) , '9'))
    +    THEN
         K6 = K6+1
         IF (K6 .EQ. 6) GO TO 26
       ELSE
         IF (K6 .EQ. 0) GO TO 99
         GO TO 25
       ENDIF
 24 CONTINUE
     GO TO 99
*
*   EXPECT AN EQUALS SIGN
 25 L9=L9-1
 26 DO 27 L10 = L9+1 , LENST
       IF (STAMNT(L10:L10) .EQ. ' ') GO TO 27
       IF (STAMNT(L10:L10) .EQ. '=') GO TO 28
       GO TO 99
 27 CONTINUE
     GO TO 99
*
*   SEARCH FOR BARE COMMA
 28 LPAREN = 0
     KNTCH = 0
     DO 29 L6 = L10+1 , LENST
       IF (STAMNT(L6:L6) .EQ. ' ') GO TO 29
       IF (STAMNT(L6:L6) .EQ. ',') THEN
         IF (KNTCH .NE. 0) THEN
           IF (LPAREN .EQ. 0) GO TO 30
           GO TO 29
         ELSE
           GO TO 99
         ENDIF
       ELSEIF (STAMNT(L6:L6) .EQ. '(') THEN
         LPAREN = LPAREN+1
       ELSEIF (STAMNT(L6:L6) .EQ. ')') THEN
         LPAREN = LPAREN-1
       ENDIF
       KNTCH = 1
 29 CONTINUE
     GO TO 99
 30 RETURN 1
*
*   IDENTIFY FORMAT STATEMENT
 31 IF (LABEL .EQ. 0) GO TO 99
     K7 = 2
     DO 32 L11 = L7+1 , LENST
       IF (STAMNT(L11:L11) .EQ. ' ') GO TO 32
       IF (STAMNT(L11:L11) .NE. FORMAT(K7:K7)) GO TO 99
       IF (K7 .EQ. 7) GO TO 33
       K7 = K7+1
 32 CONTINUE
     GO TO 99
 33 RETURN 5
```

```
*
  99 END
     SUBROUTINE START
*
*  TO PREPARE FOR PUNITS
*
     COMMON/DATA/ISHIFT , MXDPTH , NIN , NOUT
     SAVE /DATA/
*
*  PROMPT FOR INTERACTIVE USE
     WRITE (*,'("1PLEASE TYPE SHIFT, MAX. INDENT LEVEL, INPUT UNIT NO.
    +, OUTPUT UNIT NO.")')
*
*  DOES STANDARD INPUT UNIT CONTAIN AN INPUT RECORD
     READ (* ,* , END = 1 , ERR = 1) ISHIFT , MXDPTH , NIN , NOUT
*
*  IF RECORD PRESENT, CHECK INPUT VALUES ARE REASONABLE
     ISHIFT = MIN(MAX(ISHIFT , 1) , 10)
     MXDPTH = MIN(MAX(MXDPTH , 1) , 36/ISHIFT)
     IF (NIN .LE. 0 .OR. NIN .GT. 99) NIN = 5
     IF (NOUT .LE. 0 .OR. NOUT .EQ. NIN .OR. NOUT .GT. 99) NOUT = 6
     GO TO 2
*
*  SET DEFAULT VALUES
   1 ISHIFT = 3
     MXDPTH = 10
     NIN = 5
     NOUT = 6
*
*  PRINT VALUES TO BE USED
   2 WRITE (*,'("0LOOP BODIES WILL BE INDENTED BY",I3/
    +      " MAXIMUM INDENTING LEVEL IS    ",I3/
    +      " INPUT UNIT EXPECTED IS       ",I3/
    +      " OUTPUT UNIT EXPECTED IS      ",I3)')
    +      ISHIFT , MXDPTH , NIN , NOUT
*
     END
     SUBROUTINE TERMIN
*
*  TO PRINT THE FINAL SUMMARY
*
     COMMON/STATS/MXDO , MXIF , KARD , KNTPU , SYNTAX
     LOGICAL SYNTAX
*
     SAVE /STATS/
*
     WRITE (*,'("0MAXIMUM DEPTH OF DO−LOOP NESTING ",I3/
    +      " MAXIMUM DEPTH OF IF−BLOCK NESTING",I3/
    +" NO. OF LINES READ ",I17/" NO. OF PROGRAM UNITS READ   ",I8/
    +      " GLOBAL SYNTAX ERROR FLAG",L12)')
    +      MXDO , MXIF , KARD , KNTPU , SYNTAX
*
     END
```

BIBLIOGRAPHY

Abel N.E. and Bell J.R. (1972). "Global Optimization in Compilers: A unified Approach." Proc. 1st. USA-Japan Comp. Conf., Tokio.

Aho A.V., Hopcroft J. and Ullman J.D. (1974). "The design and analysis of computer algorithms." Addison-Wesley, Reading, Mass.

Aho A.V. and Ullman J.D. (1972, 1973). "The Theory of Parsing Translation and Compiling." Vols. I and II, Prentice-Hall, Englewood Cliffs, N.J.

Aho A.V. and Ullman J.D. (1977). "Principles of Compiler Design." Addison-Wesley, Reading, Mass.

Allen F.E., Cocke J. and Kennedy K. (1974). "Reduction of Operator Strength." Technical Report 476-093-6, Rice Univ., Houston, Texas.

Allen F.E. (1975). "Bibliography on Program Optimization." RC 5767 IBM T.J. Watson Research Center, Yorktown Heights, N.Y.

ANSI (1978). Programming Language FORTRAN, X3.9-1978, ANSI, New York.

Backus J. et al. (1957). In "Programming Systems and Languages." (S. Rosen, ed.), pp. 29-47. McGraw Hill, New York. (1967)

Beretvas T. (1978). "Performance Timing in OS/VS2 MVS." IBM Sys. J 17, 290-313.

Brode B. (1981). "Precompilation of FORTRAN Programs to Facilitate Array Processing." Computer, Sept. 1981, 46-51.

Brown P.J. (ed.) (1977). "Software Portability." Cambridge University Press, Cambridge.

Brun R. et al. (1982). "GEM - A dynamic memory manager." Internal note, CERN, Geneva, Switzerland.

Busam V.A. and England D.E. (1969). "Optimization of expressions in FORTRAN." *CACM* 12, 666-674.

CDC (1977). FORTRAN Extended Version 4 Reference Manual, 604 97 800, CDC, Sunnyvale, CA.

CDC (1979a). FORTRAN Version 5 Reference Manual, 604 81 300, CDC, Sunnyvale, CA.

CDC (1979b). F45 Reference Manual, 604 83 000, CDC, Sunnyvale, CA.

CDC (1981). FORTRAN Version 5 User's Guide, 604 84 000, CDC, Sunnyvale, CA.

Chester (1982). Proc. Conf. on vector and parallel processors, *Comp. Phys. Comm.,* **26**, 3 & 4.

Conners W.D., Florkowski J.H. and Patton S.K. (1979). "The IBM 3033: an inside look." Datamation, May 1979, 198-218.

Day A.C. (1972) "FORTRAN Techniques." Cambridge University Press, Cambridge.

Day A.C. (1978) "Compatible FORTRAN." Cambridge University Press, Cambridge.

DEC (1982). "Engineering Systems and Software Referal Catalog." Digital Equipment Corp., Marlborough, MA.

DoD (1983).Reference Manual for the Ada Programming Language, U.S. Department of Defense, Washington, D.C.

Dongarra J.J. and Hinds A.R. (1979). "Unrolling Loops in FORTRAN." *Software-Practice and Experience,* 9, 219-226.

Dungworth M. (1979). "The CRAY-1 Computer System." *In* Infotech (1979b), pp. 61-76.

Ford B., Bently J., du Croz J.J. and Hague S.J. (1979). "The NAG Library Machine." *Software-Practice and Experience,* 9, 65-72.

Fosdick L.D. (1974). "BRNANL, A FORTRAN Program to Identify Basic Blocks in FORTRAN Programs." Report CU-CS-040-74, University of Colorado, Boulder, Colorado.

Gentelman W.M. and Munro J.I. (1977). "Designing Overlay Structures." *Software-Practice and Experience,* 7, 493-500.

Goodman S.E. and Hedetniemi (1977). "Introduction to the design and analysis of algorithms." McGraw Hill, New York.

Hamlet R.G. and Haralick R.M. (1980). "Transportable Package Software." *Software-Practice and Experience,* 7, 1009-1027.

Harte J. (1979). "The FPS AP-120B Array Processor." *In* Infotech (1979b).

Hansche B., Hudson S. and Huey B. (1982). "Index to Periodical Literature", *SIGPLAN Notices,* **17**, 8, 74-83.

Hawson D.R. (1983). "Simple Code Optimizations." *Software-Practice and Experience,* **13**, 745-763.

Howden W.E. (1982). "Validation of Scientific Programs." *Computing Surveys,* **14,** 2, 193-227.

Hockney R.W. and Jesshope C.R. (1981). "Parallel Computers." Adam Hilger, Bristol.

Higbie L. (1979). "Vectorization and Conversion of FORTRAN programs for the CRAY-1 (CFT) Compiler." Cray Research publication 2240207, Mendota Heights, MN.

Hitachi, (1982). Integrated Array Processor Reference Manual, HO 5560(S-8), Kanagawa, Japan.

Hoare C.A.R. (1962). "Quicksort." *Comp. J.* **5,** 10-15.

IBM (1980a). IBM System/370 Principles of Operation, GA22-7000-6, IBM, White Plains, N.Y.

IBM (1980b). IBM 3081 Functional Characteristics, GA22-7076-0, IBM, White Plains, N.Y.

IBM (1981a). VS FORTRAN, GC26-3986-0, IBM, White Plains, N.Y.

IBM (1981b). "Engineering and Scientific Applications Programs available from non-IBM sources." IBM, White Plains, N.Y.

IBM (1981c). VS FORTRAN Application Programming: Guide, IBM, White Plains, N.Y.

IBM (1981d). VS FORTRAN Application Programming: Library Reference, IBM, White Plains, N.Y.

IMSL (1979). Library Reference Manual, IMSL, Houston, Texas.

Infotech (1979a). "Supercomputers", Vol. I., Infotech, Maidenhead.

Infotech (1979b). "Supercomputers", Vol. II., Infotech, Maidenhead.

Ingalls D.H.H. (1971). "FETE, A FORTRAN execution time estimator." Stanford Univ. Report 71-204, Stanford, CA.

Jesshope C.R. (1979). "An Annotated Bibliography of Supercomputers." *In* Infotech (1979a).

Johnson R. and Johnston T. (1976). PROGLOOK User's Guide, SLAC, Menlo Park, CA.

Kascic M.J. (1979). "Vector Processing, Problem or Opportunity?" *Proc. COMPCOM '80,* IEEE.

Kilburn T., Payne R.B. and Howarth D.J. (1962). *In* "Programming Systems and Languages." (S. Rosen, ed.). pp 561-682 McGraw Hill, New York (1967).

Knoble H.D. (1979). "A practical look at computer arithmetic." Pennsylvania State Univ., PA.

Knuth D.E. (1969a). "Fundamental Algorithms, The Art of Computer Programming." Vol. I, Addison-Wesley. Reading, Mass.

Knuth D.E. (1969b). "Seminumerical Algorithms, The Art of Computer Programming." Vol. II, Addison-Wesley. Reading, Mass.

Knuth D.E. (1971). "An empirical study of FORTRAN programs."

Software-Practice and Experience, **1**, 105-133.

Knuth D.E. (1973). "Sorting and Searching, The Art of Computer Programming." Vol. III, Addison-Wesley. Reading, Mass.

Larmouth (1973a). "Serious FORTRAN." *Software-Practice and Experience,* **3**, 87-108.

Larmouth (1973b). "Serious FORTRAN-Part 2." *Software-Practice and Experience*, **3**, 197-226.

Larmouth J. (1981). "FORTRAN 77 Portability." *Software-Practice and Experience,* **11**, 1071-1117.

Levine R. (1982). "Supercomputers." *In* Scientific American, Jan. 1982, 112-125.

Lowry E. and Medlock C.W. (1969). "Object code optimization." *CACM,* **12**, 13-22. [+]

Lyon G. and Stillman R.B. (1975). "Simple Transforms for instrumenting FORTRAN decks." *Software-Practice and Experience,* **5**, 347-358.

Matthews R. (1982). "IOPACK User Guide." Z300, CERN, Geneva, Switzerland.

McMahon F.H., Sloan L.J. and Long G.A. (1972). "STACKLIBE - A vector function library of optimum stack-loops for the CDC 7600." Report UCID-30083, Lawrence Livermore Laboratory, CA.

McKeeman W.M. (1965). "Peephole Optimization." *CACM* **8**, 443-444.

Metcalf M. (1984). "Has Fortran a Future?" CERN/DD/84/7, CERN, Geneva, Switzerland.

Metcalf M. (1985). "Effective FORTRAN 77" Oxford University Press, Oxford.

Meek B. and Hill I. (1981). "Program Language Standardisation." Ellis Horwood, Chichester.

Meissner L. (ed.) (1982). FORTEC Forum, ACM, N.Y.

Moler C. and Morrison D. (1981). "Replacing square roots by Pythagorean sums." Dept. of Computer Science, Univ. of New Mexico, Albuquerque, NM.

Mossberg B. (1981). "An informal approach to number crunching on the CYBER 203/205." CDC publication 84002390, Roseville, MN.

Muxworthy D.T. (1976). "A Review of Program Portability and FORTRAN Conventions." European Program Institute, Ispra, Italy.

Paul G. (1980). *In* "Advances in Digital Image Processing." (Stucki P., ed.), pp. 277-300. Plenum Publishing Corp., N.Y.

[+] The fact that Fig. 5 of this paper is printed upside down can lead to momentary confusion.

Paul G. (1982). "VECTRAN and the Proposed Vector/Array Extensions to ANSI FORTRAN for Scientific and Engineering Computation." RC 9223, IBM T.J. Watson Research Center, Yorktown Heights, N.Y.

Pollack B.W. (ed.) (1972). "Compiler Techniques." Auerbach, Princeton, N.J.

Prime (1980). "Engineering." Prime Computer, Natrick, MA.

Ramamoorthy C.V. and Li H.F. (1977). "Pipeline Architecture." *ACM Computing Surveys* **9**, 1, 61-102.

Rodrigue G. (ed.) (1982). "Parallel Computations." Academic Press, New York.

Russel R.M. (1978). "The CRAY-1 Computer System." *CACM,* **21**, 63-72.

Rymarczyk J.W. (1981). "Coding Guidelines for Pipelined Processors." TR 00.3107, IBM, Poughkeepsie, N.Y.

Samet P.A. (1975). "Detailed analysis of a program – an instructive horror story." *Software-Practice and Experience,* **5**, 211-217.

Scarborough R. and Kolsky H. (1980). "Improved Optimization of FORTRAN Object Programs." *IBM J. Res. Develop.,* **24**, 6, 660-676.

Schneck P.B. (1983). "The Myth of Virtual Memory." *Software-Practice and Experience,* **13**, 537-543.

Schneck P.B. and Angel E. (1973). "A FORTRAN to FORTRAN optimizing compiler." *Comp. J.,* **16**, 322-330.

Smith D.M., Dobyns A.H. and Marsh H.M. (1977). "Optimization Guide for Programs compiled under IBM FORTRAN H (OPT = 2)." NASA-TM-X-71307, Goddard Space Flight Center, Greenbelt, MD.

Tannenbaum A.S., Klint P. and Bohm W. (1978). "Guideliness for Software Portability." *Software-Practice and Experience,* **8**, 681-698.

Vallance D.M. (1981). "Some FORTRAN 77 Problem Programs." Internal Report 81/1, Univ. of Salford, Salford.

Wagener J. (1980). "FORTRAN 77 Principles of Programming." Wiley, N.Y.

Waldbaum G. (1978). "Tuning computer users' programs." RJ 2409, IBM T.J. Watson Research Center, Yorktown Heights, N.Y.

Wheeler D.J. (1950). "Programme organization and initial orders for the EDSAC." *Proc. Roy. Soc.,* **A202**, 573-589.

Wilkes M.V. (1951). "The best way to design an automatic calculating machine." Machester Univ. Inaugural Conf., 16-21.

Williams J.W.J. (1964). Algorithm 232: Heapsort, *CACM,* **7**, 347-348.

Wilson K.G. (1982). "Experiences with a Floating Point Systems Array Processor." *In* Rodrigue (1982).

X3J3 (1984). "Proposals approved for FORTRAN 8x." CBEMA, Washington, DC.

SUBJECT INDEX

A.P.I.C. Studies in Data Processing
General Editors: Fraser Duncan and M. J. R. Shave

*Out of print.